Why Do Latinos Have Two Last Names

In Spain, every newborn bears both the father's last name and the mother's maiden name. Thus if Maria's father's surname is Pérez and her mother's maiden name is López, Maria's name is Maria Pérez López. However, when Maria becomes a mother, it is her father's name (Pérez) that she passes on to her offspring.

Was Desi Arnaz Responsible for Bringing Latin Rhythm to the United States

"I Love Lucy's" Desi Arnaz, a Cuban-born actor and musician, was certainly responsible for introducing mainstream television-watching America to the sounds of African-Cuban drums with his famous song "Babaloo." But even before Desi, Xavier Cugat, a Spanish orchestra leader who lived in Cuba and Mexico, had introduced African-Cuban music to Hollywood in the 1930s.

What Is Santería?

Santería is a religion that emerged from the fusion of ancient African religions brought to the Caribbean by West African slaves with Roman Catholic beliefs brought by the Spanish. It became very popular in Cuba, where not only slaves and the descendants of slaves practiced it, but even non-African Cubans believed in it and still do, both in Cuba and the United States. It is also very popular in Puerto Rico and the Dominican Republic.

HIMILCE NOVAS was born in Cuba. She left Cuba with her parents in 1960 and settled in New York City, where she still lives. A former contributing editor/writer for such publications as *Connoisseur,* the *New York Times,* and th̶ lectures on Latino history and cu̶ ̶ ̶ ̶ ̶ ̶ ̶ ̶ ̶ ̶ ̶ ̶ ̶ ̶ at work on several forthcoming b̶ ̶ ̶ ̶ ̶ ̶ ̶ ̶

D1041319

HIMILCE NOVAS

EVERYTHING YOU NEED TO KNOW ABOUT LATINO HISTORY

A PLUME BOOK

PLUME

Published by the Penguin Group
Penguin Books USA Inc., 375 Hudson Street, New York, New York 10014, U.S.A.
Penguin Books Ltd, 27 Wrights Lane, London W8 5TZ, England
Penguin Books Australia Ltd, Ringwood, Victoria, Australia
Penguin Books Canada Ltd, 10 Alcorn Avenue, Toronto, Ontario, Canada M4V 3B2
Penguin Books (N.Z.) Ltd, 182–190 Wairau Road, Auckland 10, New Zealand

Penguin Books Ltd, Registered Offices:
Harmondsworth, Middlesex, England

First published by Plume,
an imprint of Dutton Signet,
a division of Penguin Books USA Inc.

First Printing, October, 1994
3 5 7 9 10 8 6 4

Excerpt from How the García Girls Lost Their Accents © 1991 by Julia
Alvarez. Published by Plume, an imprint of Dutton Signet, a division of Penguin
USA Inc. Published in hardcover by Algonquin Books. Reprinted by permission of
Susan Bergholz Literary Services, New York.

 REGISTERED TRADEMARK—MARCA REGISTRADA

LIBRARY OF CONGRESS CATALOGING IN PUBLICATION DATA:
Novas, Himilce.
Everything you need to know about Latino history / Himilce Novas.
p. cm.
Includes bibliographical references.
ISBN 0-452-27100-2
1. Hispanic Americans—History.   I. Title.
E184.S75N69 1994
973'.0468—dc20   94–18225
                                                                          CIP

Printed in the United States of America
Set in New Baskerville and Pabst

Designed by Steven N. Stathakis

For my mother and father, Herminia del Portal and Lino Novas Calvo, who had the courage to seek a new world and bring me to a new America, and for Rosemary Silva, whose help with this book made the journey joyous.

Acknowledgments

I wish to express my gratitude to the staff and the librarians of the Library of Congress, the New York Public Library, and the Library of the Hispanic Society for their generous assistance in my research. I am indebted in particular to Erminio D'Onofrio, documents librarian at the New York Public Library, for his advice in locating materials and for his computer wizardry. I also wish to thank the Museo del Barrio in New York City and the Spanish History Museum in Albuquerque for their commitment to chronicling the history of the Spanish influence in America and preserving Hispanic culture and arts of the past and present. For her wit and brains, and for her faith in me, I owe special thanks to my agent, Susan Herner. I also wish to express my gratitude to Deb Brody, my editor, for her harmony, wisdom, and art. For her enlightening commitment to unearthing Latino voices for a new generation of Americans, I owe special thanks to Lorraine Elena Roses, professor of Spanish and director of Latin American studies at Wellesley College.

Finally, friends and supporters deserve special acknowledgment. I am indebted to Theresa Mantenfel for countless years of warm friendship and emotional quarterbacking. Special thanks go to Lan Cao for years of loyal friendship and for reminding me that a writer writes. My heartfelt thanks also go to Janet Trubenbach for her leadership, high moral ground, and years of love and support.

Contents

Introduction

When I was a boy who spoke Spanish, I saw America whole. I realized there was a culture here because I lived apart from it. I didn't like America. Then I entered the culture. I entered the culture as you did, by going to school. I became Americanized. I ended up believing in choices as much as any of you do.

From Days of Obligation: An Argument with My Mexican Father, *by* RICHARD RODRIGUEZ

By the year 2000, Latinos, also known as Hispanics, will comprise the largest single minority in the United States.

U.S. corporations in the *Fortune* 500 have identified 30 million Latino consumers with a purchasing power of $300 billion by the end of the decade.

With growth in numbers has come political and economic clout. During the 1992 presidential election, individual Latinos and Hispanic organizations made roughly 30,000 political contributions, totaling more than $20 million. In recent years, the number of Latino-owned businesses in the United States has tripled. And the number of Latinos at the top of major American corporations—from Roberto C. Goizueta, CEO of the Coca-Cola company, to the family-owned and -operated Bacardi International Limited—is on the rise.

Latinos have achieved leading positions in every profession—the arts, science and technology, politics, finance, sports. In the post–*I Love Lucy* decades (after long years when Desi Arnaz and maybe Charo and Xavier Cugat were among the few truly recognizable "Latins" around), Latinos have become household names: Antonia Novello, U.S. surgeon general under President Bush; Henry Cisneros, ex-mayor of San Antonio and HUD secretary under President Clinton; Texas congressman Henry Gonzalez, chair of the Banking Committee; Ricardo Mestres, president of Hollywood Pictures; Trent Dimas, 1992 Olympic gold medalist in gymnastics; Gloria Estefan and Mariah Carey, singer-songwriters; Rosemary Berkett, chief justice of the Florida Supreme Court; Mary Joe Fernandez, tennis player; Miriam Santas, treasurer of the City of Chicago; actors Andy Garcia, Martin Sheen (né Estevez), and countless others.

Still, in spite of enormous social and demographic changes, most Americans know very little about their Latino neighbors, their culture, their history, and how they influence our nation's everyday life.

The history of Latinos goes back as far as American history itself. In fact, you could say that without Latinos there would be no United States of America as we know it today.

Ever since Columbus sailed with his Spanish crew under Queen Isabella's flag, men and women of Spanish ancestry have been coming to American shores in pursuit of their dreams. Hernando de Soto, who discovered the Mississippi River, thought he could find hidden caves of gold in Florida. Francisco Vásquez de Coronado, who explored the West, thought he had found a brave new world destined for Spanish conquest. After the formation of the original thirteen colonies, Spanish and Spanish-Americans from Mexico, Cuba, Puerto Rico, and Colombia and other South American nations began coming north to make their home along the Eastern Seaboard of the United States, right next to their *Mayflower* neighbors.

Since then, thanks to the War of 1812; the Mexican War and the annexation of Texas; the Spanish-American War; the Cuban revolution and the Cuban Missile Crisis; the civil wars in Nicaragua, Guatemala, and El Salvador; and hundreds of other political upheavals from Tijuana to the Argentine pampas, Latinos have settled in the United States by the millions, and in the process have slowly changed the face of America.

Latino influence on the American mainstream has been particularly strong since World War II, when immigration from Puerto Rico and Mexico increased exponentially and words like *enchiladas, fajitas, empanadas,* and *un big Mac* were heard simultaneously from the shores of New England to Monterey Bay.

In spite of my own Latino roots, the Spanish education I received at home, and my very early years spent in Cuba, I began this project cherishing some of the same misinformation and stereotypes subscribed to by many with no Hispanic background whatsoever. After all, I, too, moved through the American school system at a time when the "Anglo" perspective on history was the only valid viewpoint, and when the word "bilingual" was mostly used when referring to an especially gifted secretary.

My exposure to Latino history was virtually nonexistent in school, and my introduction to Latino culture came almost exclusively through the observations of American writers viewing Latinos rather than Latinos viewing themselves.

My reading assignments in the New York City public schools included Stephen Crane's "A Man and Some Others," which offers a simplistic portrayal of Latinos; John Steinbeck's *Tortilla Flat*, which while attempting to honor Mexican-American life paints a picture of Mexican-Americans as lazy drunkards; and the works of Ernest Hemingway, Katherine Ann Porter, Jack Kerouac, and countless others who wrote passionately about Latinos but often missed the key thread and represented Latinos with naive, stereotyped images.

Regrettably, the literature of Hispanic writers, such as Piri Thomas's *Down These Mean Streets*, Antonio Villareal's *Pocho*, and the poetry of Cherríe Moraga, among hundreds of others, were nowhere to be found in school libraries until recently—and even now, their work is often restricted to libraries in urban areas with large Latino populations.

I have learned much in the process of unearthing my own roots during the past twenty years of study. In some cases, I have been as surprised by what I have found as Columbus must have been when he first tasted a habanero chili.

My purpose in answering some basic questions about Latino history has been more an act of *abrir la puerta* (opening the door) to this enduring and rich culture than an effort to cover a vast and complex history in one fell swoop. This has also been an attempt to present historical facts and events fairly, from the perspective of those whose history they represent.

How to Read This Book

I have organized this book for what I call interactive reading, encapsulating the information in a question-and-answer format that allows the reader to pick and choose specific aspects of Latino history and culture that she or he may be wondering about. If you choose to read the book from cover to cover, the result should be greater than the sum of its parts, and the fascinating puzzle of these great American peoples will emerge as a complete picture.

Since the classification "Latino," or "Hispanic," covers a multitude of peoples with very different histories and cultural traditions, I have devoted one chapter to each Latino group in order of population density and seniority in U.S. history. For instance, the chapter on Mexican-Americans, the group with the longest history and largest population, comes earlier and is allocated more space than the chapter on Dominicans and Central Americans, whose history is more recent than that of the Chicanos. Besides the chapters on individual Latino groups, there are also three chapters that present background and cultural information on Latinos as a whole.

This history is meant not to be a dry compilation of dates and details, but to provide a fresh look at one of the richest and most fascinating cultures of all time. Along the way, I have shattered some myths and taken a poke at some stereotypes in an effort to shine the proper light on some remarkable peoples who are changing the ways of America.

Finally, I intend this book above all as a celebration. I had fun writing it and hope to share my joy and excitement with all those who are drawn to its pages.

HIMILCE NOVAS
Nueva York, 1993

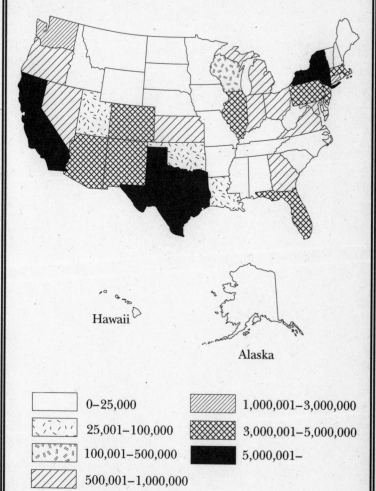

1990 Hispanic Population, by State

Hawaii

Alaska

0–25,000	1,000,001–3,000,000
25,001–100,000	3,000,001–5,000,000
100,001–500,000	5,000,001–
500,001–1,000,000	

Source: 1990 U.S. Census

© Claudia Carlson

UNO

Hispanic:
Sí y No

What's in a name?

Are Brazilian-Americans Hispanic?

What makes Latinos so difficult to count?

Mexicans: As many as the stars in the universe?

Puerto Ricans: Why aren't they considered
immigrants?

Cubans: What makes them different?

Spanish, Dominicans, South Americans, and Central Americans: Americans all?

What's in a Name?

When it comes to the term "Hispanic," you can say a great deal. "Hispanic" comes from *España,* Spain, the country that led the conquest (as in *conquistadors*) of the New World. The many different native peoples, known generally as Amerindians, whom the Spanish discovered, eventually adopted or incorporated the Spanish language, culture, and religion and, to a large extent, intermarried or interbred with their conquerors. Add to that all the African peoples brought as slaves to the Americas by the end of the fifteenth century, who later also intermarried or interbred with the Spanish settlers and *conquistadors,* as well as with the native Amerindians, and you get the whole enchilada defined in the United States as "Hispanic."

Perhaps no other ethnic group in the United States is as diverse in its culture, physical appearance, and traditions as the Hispanics. The reason is that whereas all other ethnic groups have been categorized by their country of origin—the Irish from Ireland, the Germans from Germany, and so on—Hispanics are classified by their own or their ancestors' mother tongue, Spanish, and not by their specific culture, racial makeup, or even geographic background—which encompasses no fewer than twenty-one separate republics, each with its own distinct culture and history, including indigenous languages, religions, foods, and individual philosophies!

In Latin America, the homeland of most of the people known in the United States as Hispanics, no one defines himself or herself as Hispanic. The Mexicans call themselves Mejicanos, the Puerto Ricans Puertorriqueños, the Cubans

Cubanos, the Colombians Colombianos, the Dominicans Dominicanos, and so on.

For Latin Americans, who like North Americans fought hard to win their independence from European rule, identity is derived from their native lands and from the heterogeneous cultures that thrive within their borders. Each Latin American country views itself as the curator of multiethnic, diverse cultures that cannot be totally embraced by the term "Hispanic." In fact, many peoples of Latin America speak ancient native languages and use Spanish merely as their official language.

To the recent immigrant, the realization that she or he is no longer Nicaraguan, Mexican, or Colombian, but now belongs to a new, homogenized group called "Hispanic," often serves as the bridge toward assimilation into a new country. It is, ironically, the first American word that applies to her or him.

In the United States, many Hispanics consider the word "Hispanic" merely a bureaucratic government census term, and call themselves "Latinos" or else use the terms "Mexican-American," "Dominican-American," and so on. Many Latinos, particularly writers and artists, strongly object to "Hispanic" and prefer to be called "Latinos" or "Latinas" (depending on gender).

Novelist **Sandra Cisneros,** author of *Woman Hollering Creek and Other Stories,* goes as far as refusing to let her work appear in anthologies that use the word "Hispanic" because, she says, it smacks of colonization. "It's a repulsive slave name," she declared in an interview for *The New York Times.* **John Leguizamo,** the part-Colombian, part–Puerto Rican writer and actor, creator of the one-man show *Spic-O-Rama,* says he simply used to call himself "Spanish" (the term used for Puerto Ricans in New York until recently), but that he now prefers "Latino," although he does not consider "Hispanic" offensive. "Now 'wetback, greasy spic,' that's derogatory," he told an interviewer.

Many others have embraced the term "Hispanic" as a means to bolster solidarity among the various groups and gain political power. **Raul Yzaguire,** president of the National Council of La Raza, and former congressman **Herman Badillo** both believe that "Hispanic" is a name that promotes unity. **Enrique Fernández,** editor of *Más,* a Spanish-language entertainment magazine, believes that he speaks for many when he says that "Hispanic" is preferable to "Latino," since "Latino," taken back to its roots, refers to an even older empire—the one that took over Spain.

In recent elections, Latinos, united under that single "Hispanic" banner, have demonstrated unprecedented influence and have been responsible for much landmark legislation.

Are Brazilian-Americans Hispanic?

No. Brazilian-Americans speak Portuguese and are of Portuguese, not Spanish, descent.

On April 22, 1500, a Portuguese navigator named **Pedro Alvares Cabral** landed at Porto Seguro, Brazil. Spanish navigators had also seen Brazil's coast for the first time that year. But Portugal had won the rights to Brazil from the Pope in 1494, under the Treaty of Tordesillas with Spain, and thereafter ruled Brazil for more than three hundred years.

There are approximately 1,153,154 Americans of Portuguese descent in the United States. Most live in Rhode Island and Massachusetts and elsewhere along the Northeast Corridor. According to the 1990 census, 94,023 Brazilian-born and 218,525 Portuguese-born Americans reside in the United States.

What Makes Latinos So Difficult to Count?

Hispanics are defined as residents of the United States who belong to Spanish-speaking ethnic groups. Most are U.S. citizens, but others are legal resident aliens with green cards.

Still others are undocumented—mostly workers who entered the country illegally in search of a better life for themselves and their families.

The Immigration Reform and Control Act of 1986 granted amnesty and the opportunity to obtain American citizenship to thousands of undocumented workers. However, because of stiff penalties imposed on U.S. employers who knowingly hired undocumented workers, many Hispanics who would have qualified for amnesty and legal status were unable to do so, since the new law required them to show proof that they had been living and working in the United States before January 1, 1982. In many instances, their employers were reluctant to come forward on their behalf for fear of government reprisal. It was one of those damned-if-you-do and damned-if-you-don't cases that creep up in our history from time to time.

According to U.S. government estimates, Americans of Hispanic origin numbered 22,354,059 (or 9 percent of the population) in 1990. That count was up from 16,940,000 in 1985. This sharp increase in population, combined with the fact that the median age of Hispanics in 1988 was below thirty, makes Latinos the most rapidly growing ethnic minority in the United States.

FACTS AND FIGURES

1. By the year 2040, Latinos will comprise 51 percent of the population of California.

2. In 1993, 90 percent of Latinos lived in urban areas.

3. In 1993, 9 percent of the U.S. population was Latino, while 13 percent of President Clinton's cabinet was Latino.

4. In 1993, 60 percent of Mexicans and 64 percent of Puerto Ricans were Democrats, while 64 percent of Cubans were Republicans.

5. In 1993, 33.7 percent of Puerto Rican households were headed by women, while 15.6 percent of Mexican-American and 15.3 percent of Cuban-American households were headed by women.

6. In March 1993, Latinos comprised 7.7 percent of the Marines, 6.5 percent of the Navy, 4.5 percent of the Army and Coast Guard, and 3.4 percent of the Air Force.

7. According to the 1990 census, 72 percent of Latinos identify themselves as Roman Catholic, while 23 percent identify themselves as Protestant. However, among those who identify themselves as Roman Catholic, a minority also practices *santería*, an African-American religion with roots in the Yoruba religion.

8. In 1990, 34.5 percent of Latino women were registered to vote, as opposed to 30 percent of Latino men.

9. In 1993, there were 650,000 Latino-owned businesses in the United States.

10. The Latino community grew 53 percent between 1980 and 1990, almost five times more than the rest of the population of the United States.

11. By the year 2010, nearly one out of every six Americans between the ages of eighteen and twenty-one will be Latino.

12. In 1993, there were 5.4 million Latino public school students in the United States.

13. As of March 1991, Central and South Americans represented 15.8 percent of the total Latino population in the United States.

14. As of 1991, Central and South Americans enjoyed the highest rate of employment of all Latinos in the United States.

15. As of 1991, 70 percent of all Latino small businesses in New York City were owned by Dominicans.

Mexicans: As Many as the Stars in the Universe?

The largest number of Hispanic-Americans—12,110,000, according to the latest census bureau reports—are of Mexican birth or ancestry. Mexican-Americans, or Chicanos, are mostly *mestizo*, or of mixed Native American (Maya, Aztec, Hopi) and Caucasian descent. They live mostly in the Southwest, particularly Texas, New Mexico, Arizona, Colorado, and California. At last official count, there were 7.68 million Mexican-Americans living in California and 4.33 million in Texas.

However, these figures do not take into account the population known as Hispanos, the direct descendants of residents of the region of Mexico annexed by the United States in the Treaty of Guadalupe Hidalgo after the Mexican War (1846–48). Although Hispanos, who have been here longer than the Anglo descendants of the *Mayflower* pilgrims, live mostly in New Mexico, many have been largely assimilated into the non-Hispanic population of the United States. Many Hispanos are Caucasian, since they are direct descendants of the Spanish *conquistadors*, and many are also *mestizo*.

It is virtually impossible to ascertain how many Hispanics of Mexican origin make their homes in the United States

because of the Hispano assimilation and the scores of undocumented workers and *mojados* ("wetbacks") in the underground. The difficulty is compounded by the fact that before
the Chinese Exclusion Act of 1882 there was no such thing
as an illegal alien, since permission was not required to enter
the country, and that as recently as forty years ago Mexican-
Americans were counted as "whites."

Puerto Ricans: Why Aren't They Considered Immigrants?

Because they aren't—not on their island and not on the isle
of Manhattan, either.

Puerto Ricans comprise the second largest Hispanic
group in the United States. But since Puerto Ricans are American citizens by birth, thanks to the Spanish-American War
(1898), the annexation of Puerto Rico, and its subsequent status as a U.S. Commonwealth (Estado Libre Asociado), their
movement to and from Puerto Rico is considered part of the
internal migration of Americans, and not "immigration" per
se, as is the case for Mexicans, Cubans, Salvadorans, and all
other Hispanic peoples.

According to the 1990 census, Puerto Ricans number
2,471,000 on the U.S. mainland alone. They are concentrated in the Northeast, particularly New York City. In some
years, as many as 5 million Puerto Ricans travel between the
island of Puerto Rico and the continental United States.
Lately, the heavy concentration of Puerto Ricans in New
York City has begun to diminish; many have opted for
kinder, gentler sections of the nation, particularly New England and the Middle Atlantic States.

Puerto Ricans make up the youngest group of Hispanics, with almost half under the age of twenty-one. They also
have the lowest incomes in the nation. In 1985, their unemployment rate was 14 percent, and only 46.3 percent had fin-

ished high school. However, when the second generation of Puerto Ricans on the mainland was considered separately, their educational level approached the national level and their occupational status was seen as advancing at a steady pace.

Cubans: What Makes Them Different?

Cuban-Americans number more than one million, according to the 1990 census. They are mainly concentrated in southern Florida, particularly Miami, where they have transformed the city's culture with their distinct Latin rhythms and their love of enterprise. Cuban-Americans have long identified themselves with other European refugees who came to our shores fleeing communism and other totalitarian regimes, and, like those refugees of old, Cubans have actively pursued the American dream.

Most Cuban-born citizens came to the United States as refugees from the communist revolution led by **Fidel Castro,** who seized power in 1959. In the mid-1970s, a new group of Cubans, known as the Marielitos because they departed from the city of Mariel, entered the country as part of a seven-week airborne and seaborne mass evacuation from Cuba. Their flight to the United States and subsequent resettlement were aided by the U.S. government.

The Cuban-Americans who came by the hundreds of thousands as early as 1960 are largely middle-class. Many are professionals, educators, and entrepreneurs. Their assimilation into the American mainstream has been more rapid than that of other Latinos whose main reason for immigrating was not political but economic, and whose racial makeup included fewer Caucasians than the Cubans'.

However, before the Spanish-American War and the turn of the century, Cubans came to American shores in pursuit of both political and economic freedom. Large numbers settled in Tampa and Key West, opening tobacco factories and shops and helping to make Cuban cigars famous.

Since Castro's revolution forced Cubans to flee to American shores, three generations of Cuban-Americans have made lives for themselves in the United States. Some members of the older generation still profess the desire and determination to return someday to their homeland. But those who have been raised in the United States, such as singer and songwriter **Gloria Estefan,** merely say they hope to be able to visit.

Spanish, Dominicans, South Americans, and Central Americans: Americans All?

Spanish, Dominicans, Central Americans, and South Americans together comprise the third largest group of Latinos in the United States. The Spanish (or Iberians, meaning they come from the Iberian Peninsula), Dominicans, South Americans, and Central Americans are generally scattered among the dominant Hispanic populations in the Northeast, such as those in New York and Washington, D.C., as well as in Texas and Southern California. They number more than 2,200,000 and vary as greatly in their racial makeup, professions, and incomes as the general U.S. population. Most are here as a result of recent revolutions and political upheavals in their native countries. No single group is politically or socially organized the way Mexicans, Puerto Ricans, and Cubans are. In some respects, many of these newer Americans are part of the geopolitical experiments of the past twenty years.

DOS

Roots

If Columbus was Italian, why do Latinos celebrate
Columbus Day?

Did Columbus really discover America?

What was Columbus really looking for?

What was the first thing Columbus saw when he came
to America?

What was Columbus's most amazing feat?

*So who lived in the Americas
before Columbus got there?*

*The Arawak: Who were they and are there any of them
in the United States?*

THE MESOAMERICAN PEOPLES:
THE MAYA, THE AZTEC, THE INCA

*Why is it said the Maya were conquered but never
defeated?*

What are the halls of Montezuma, anyway?

*Besides the halls, what else did the Aztec have to brag
about?*

How did Mexico get its name?

Why did they call them the heart-eating Aztec?

Are there any Aztec left today?

*What was so great about the Inca and what did they do
with all that gold?*

Are Irish potatoes a gift from the Inca?

Why were the Inca not really Inca at all?

How did the Inca get so big?

How did the Inca lose the war and where are they now?

Why is there a Cadillac named El Dorado?

Why do Latinos have two last names?

THE "SPANISH" IN "HISPANIC"

*If "Hispanic" Comes from "Spain," Where Did the
Spanish People Come From?*

*How did Boise, Idaho, become home to many
Americans of Basque descent?*

*Are Latinos in the United States descendants of people
all over Spain?*

*What is the Spanish "lisp" and where did it
really come from?*

Why do Spaniards say "Olé"?

Were there any Jews in Spain?

Who were the Marranos and who were the Sephardim?

How did Queen Isabella and King Ferdinand
become the most powerful rulers of Europe and
the New World combined?

How bad was the Spanish Inquisition?

What happened to the Moors and the Jews in Spain?

What else happened in 1492?

THE AFRICAN PEOPLE

Why are there more people of African descent in some Latino groups than among the Anglo population?

If Columbus Was Italian, Why Do Latinos Celebrate Columbus Day?

Columbus Day is known among Latinos as *El Día de la Raza.* It means "the day of the races," or the day when the two races or ethnic groups—the Spanish and the Amerindians— came together. It is an official holiday throughout Latin America, and Hispanic-Americans celebrate the day with much fanfare. In Spanish, the name for Christopher Columbus is **Cristobal Colón,** and hardly anyone thinks of him as other than Spanish. *La Raza,* particularly among Mexican-Americans, has also come to mean "the people," that is, the Chicano people.

Given the murders, rapes, pilferage, and other atrocities committed by Spanish men against the native peoples—and, in turn, by Amerindian men in self-defense against the Spanish—it may seem puzzling that the day the Spanish and the Amerindians came together is celebrated. But today's Latinos are a product of both cultures, and as such they celebrate the union. They also celebrate the Spanish side of their ancestry, since they are themselves either part Spanish or direct descendants of the Spanish *conquistadors* and later Iberian immigrants to the Americas. Their Columbus Day floats and fiestas often proudly reenact the bravery and daring of the Spanish explorers who sailed perilous and unknown seas and who were, after all, the first to "discover" and conquer the New World.

Columbus may have come originally from Genoa, Italy, but his voyage was commissioned by **King Ferdinand** and **Queen Isabella** of Spain, and he sailed under the Spanish flag. What's more, two famous Spanish brothers, **Martín Alonso Pinzón** and **Vicente Yáñez Pinzón,** were responsible for recruiting the mostly Spanish crew for the first voyage to the New World. Martín received command of the *Pinta,* and Vincente commanded the *Nina.* Columbus sailed in the *Santa Maria.* Later, it was Spanish settlers, missionaries, and *conquistadors,* such as **Hernando Cortés, Álvar Núñez Cabeza de Vaca, Antonio de Espejo, Francisco Vásquez de Coronado, Friar Bartolomé de las Casas,** and countless others who actually opened the way for Spain's final conquest and settlement of the New World. If it hadn't been for Spain, there might not be an America at all—certainly not as it exists today.

Did Columbus Really Discover America?

Christopher Columbus, of course, is credited with discovering America. And the America he discovered was not the landmass we know today as the United States, but rather the Caribbean islands and other regions of Latin America—that is, the homeland of Latinos.

But since you cannot really discover a land that's already populated with advanced ancient civilizations, Columbus could more accurately be said to have discovered a route from Europe and Northern Africa to the Americas. It was all an accident, as we know, since Columbus thought he was sailing to Asia—and, by the way, died thinking he *had* discovered Asia.

It is also certain now that Columbus was not the first European to cross the Atlantic. The Vikings reached the

New World around A.D. 1000, and there is some circumstantial evidence that both the English and the Portuguese may have landed in Newfoundland and Labrador during the fourteenth century.

What Was Columbus Really Looking For?

Columbus was ostensibly looking for two things. The first was gold, gold, and more gold so that he could satisfy **Ferdinand** and **Isabella**'s insatiable desire to make Spain the greatest and most powerful country in the world (which, incidentally, he did). The second was to meet the Grand Khan, or Emperor of China, about whom Columbus's hero, **Marco Polo,** had written extensively.

This second motive, to meet the Chinese emperor, embodied what Columbus truly believed was his entire reason for casting himself headlong into a perilous voyage and, quite possibly, into the abyss. In his *Lettera Rarissima* of July 7, 1503, written to the Spanish king and queen, Columbus quoted Marco Polo as having said that "the emperor of Cathay some time since sent for wise men to teach him one religion of Christ." It was Columbus's wish to be that wise man who could teach the religion of Christ to the "heathen" Chinese emperor.

IMPORTANT DATES

A.D. 415–711	The Visigoths rule Spain.
October 12, 1492	Columbus makes landfall on an island in the Bahamas, and so begins his discovery of the Americas.

May 29, 1506	Columbus dies in Valladolid, Spain.
1554–58	A young Quiché nobleman writes the *Popol Vuh,* the most significant surviving work of Maya literature in the Latin alphabet.
November 8, 1519	Hernando Cortés reaches Tenochtitlán (present-day Mexico City).

But Columbus's grand aspirations did not stop there. His real motive in sailing, as he thought, to Asia was to procure enough gold and enough political clout so that he could organize a crusade to liberate Jerusalem from the Arabs and turn it into a Christian city. Just before he set sail, Columbus made Queen Isabella promise him that, should he be successful in finding a westward route to the East, she would fulfill this desire. The queen agreed but later changed her mind, since she believed she had quite enough on her plate—namely, a whole New World to contend with.

What Was the First Thing Columbus Saw When He Came to America?

All in all, **Columbus** made four voyages to the New World. On his first trip, he landed on October 12, 1492, on an island in the Bahamas, which the native peoples called Guanahani, but which Columbus named San Salvador. It was the first of thousands of Spanish names that were to claim the New World landscape for all time, from Amarillo, Texas, to San Francisco, California.

In San Salvador, Columbus was met by the Arawak residents, whom he named Indians. Some days later, he sailed to Cuba, and delegations from his ship went ashore to seek the court of the Emperor of China and demand gold. In December, Columbus sailed east to Hispaniola (present-day Haiti and the Dominican Republic). Columbus sent his men ashore and left thirty-nine of them on the island while he sailed back to Spain to tell the queen of his remarkable discovery.

By the time he returned a second time to Hispaniola, his men had been killed for looting the native settlements and raping the women. This event marked the start of a mutual and perilous "discovery" between the Spanish and the Native American peoples scattered across the Caribbean, South America, Central America, and parts of North America, a discovery that would last for centuries.

What Was Columbus's Most Amazing Feat?

In the end, **Columbus** proved to be a poor administrator and as a result was returned to Spain a prisoner in shackles. He died in Valladolid, Spain, on May 20, 1506, while pressing his claims at court. He was out of favor with **Queen Isabella** for his inept handling of the Spanish settlements in the West Indies.

Many contemporary historians measure Columbus's greatness not so much by the fact that his "discovery" led to the incorporation of the New World into Europe, but by the fact that, despite major errors in his navigational computations, he was able to find his way back to Europe and to return to the West Indies again and again.

So Who Lived in the Americas Before Columbus Got There?

Aside from the Arawak who first greeted Columbus and his alien-looking crew when they landed in the Bahamas, three other highly developed Native American cultures were thriv-

ing in the Americas at the time of the Spanish "invasion."
These were the Aztec of central Mexico; the Maya, who still
live in their birthplace regions of Yucatán in southern Mexico, and in Guatemala; and the Inca of the Andean highlands and coastal Peru.

In addition, the Spanish eventually had a great deal of
intercourse with the Seminole Indians of Florida and the
Pueblo (Spanish for "town"), the village-dwelling Indians of
the southwestern United States, descendants of the prehistoric Anasazi peoples, including the Hopi of northeastern
Arizona and the Zuni of western New Mexico and the Rio
Grande pueblos.

The Arawak: Who Were They and Are There Any of Them in the United States?

The Arawak comprise various Native American peoples who
inhabit the tropical forests of South America, extending
from the Andean foothills to the Antilles. Although they are
linguistically related, these groups are culturally diverse.

Before **Columbus** and his crew rolled in and, in 1540,
officially conquered the Greater Antilles, the Taino and
Siboney, the Arawakan groups living in the Greater Antilles,
had enjoyed a highly developed social and economic system,
based on farming and fishing. They were peaceful and disci-
plined. They carried out elaborate harvest ceremonies and
held naturalistic beliefs in bush spirits that foretold the coming of messiahs. It is uncertain how many Taino and Siboney
lived in the Caribbean at the time of Columbus's landing,
but judging from the records of **Friar Bartolomé de las
Casas,** the first ordained priest to travel to the New World, it
is estimated that there were between thirty thousand and
fifty thousand Taino around 1492.

Only a short time before the Spanish settled the islands
of the Caribbean, the Carib, a fierce warrior group, had

forced the Arawak off the Lesser Antilles. But with the Spanish occupation, the Antillean Arawak and the Carib were both quickly absorbed into Spanish society and forced to convert to Catholicism. Hundreds were killed by the hard labor imposed on them by the Spanish and by European diseases for which they had no immunological defenses.

The mainland Arawak who survived the Spanish *conquista* lived in the tropical forests of South America, in communities of between one hundred and two hundred persons who occupied a single multifamily dwelling.

The Taino, the Siboney, and the Carib are the ancient ancestors of the people of Cuba, Puerto Rico, and the Dominican Republic. However, because they were either exterminated or assimilated into the Spanish population, the culture and traditions of the Arawak are not as clearly present in the everyday life of these Caribbean nations as, for example, the Maya culture is in Mexico today. However, the gentle Siboney and Taino spirit and, undoubtedly, some of their genes are still part of the Caribbean people, many of whom are Latinos walking the streets of New York and other major U.S. cities.

THE MESOAMERICAN PEOPLES:
THE MAYA, THE AZTEC, THE INCA

The two main cultures that dominated Mexico and Central America before the Spanish *conquista* were the Aztec and the Maya. Their civilizations are known as Mesoamerican, or Middle American. The Olmec culture of the southern Veracruz gulf coast of Mexico is believed to lie at the heart of the Mesoamerican civilization; from the Olmec the extraordinary scientific and artistic accomplishments of the region emerged and evolved.

Why Is It Said the Maya Were Conquered but Never Defeated?

The Maya were descendants of the Olmec. The Maya lived in southern Mexico, particularly in today's states of Chiapas, Tabasco, Campeche, Yucatán, and Quintana Roo, and in Belize, Guatemala, and Honduras. Their ancestors are believed to have crossed the Bering Land Bridge from Asia more than twenty thousand years ago, during the last ice age.

The Maya were the first people of the New World to keep historical records. Their written history begins in 50 B.C., when Spain and the rest of the European countries did not yet exist as national, cultural entities. The Maya wrote their history not on parchment, but on pots, stone monuments, human bones, jade, and the walls of their impressive palaces. Their inscriptions tell the story of great Maya queens and kings right up to the sixteenth century, when the Spanish changed the course of their history forever.

The Maya culture, which dates from around 1200 B.C., is known for monumental architecture, including pyramids that tourists from around the world climb to this day. The Maya carved splendid stelae (stone slabs) from A.D. 300 to 900. On many of their monuments, the Maya lords, who ruled as divine kings, are depicted wearing the masks of the gods. Much of Maya religious practice centered on ancestor worship, and their temples were pantheons filled with gods and goddesses who ruled over their subjects jealously.

By 900 B.C., the Maya had developed extensive and sophisticated skills in water management and agriculture. They were also traders and, over the years, engaged in wars with neighboring peoples. At their peak, approximately 2 million people may have dwelt in the vast Maya empire, with about a hundred thousand alone living in Tikal, their largest center.

The Maya were responsible for astonishing intellectual

achievements, including not only a system of writing but an accurate and complicated calendar based on a high level of mathematical erudition. Their civilization is divided into the Preclassic, Classic, and Postclassic periods much as European history is divided into the Middle Ages, the Renaissance, the modern age, and so on.

Based on the inscriptions the Classic Maya left, linguists believe they spoke a language related to Chol, Yucatec, and Chortu. The Maya had a rich culture: they were artists, architects, astronomers, and poets. In 1502, only a few years after **Columbus** and his son **Ferdinand** had moored their ships off the coast of Honduras, a young nobleman from Quiché wrote the *Popol Vuh*, the most important surviving work of Maya literature in the Latin alphabet. For a people who claimed to have superior intellectual powers, the Spanish were seldom able to learn the languages of those they conquered. However, "primitive" Native Americans learned Spanish rather easily.

By the time the *conquistadors* landed, the dominant Maya civilization was already in decline, racked by war and famine, and by violent divisions among its own city-states. The Spanish took advantage of the internal strife among the Maya and, in 1542, established their own capital at Mérida in Yucatán, on the site of a Maya city called Tiho.

The modern Maya live in the same regions today, and although a great deal of interbreeding took place between them and the Spanish, the Maya people have survived as a whole on the shores of the Apasión-Usumacinta river system in Central America, in the highland plains encircled by volcanoes, and in the lowland tropical forests of that magical area. Many still speak a version of the language of their ancestors and continue to worship their gods. It is said that their roots went so deep and their bond to their earth mother was so great that although the Maya were seemingly conquered, in the end they were never truly defeated.

The faces of the Maya are reflected in the faces of millions of people in present-day Mexico and the United States, and their pyramids and artworks continue to loom tall, a constant reminder of their noble ancestry.

What Are the Halls of Montezuma, Anyway?

Montezuma II, also known as **Moctezuma II,** who reigned from 1502 to 1520, was the Aztec emperor who ruled over what is now present-day Mexico City (Tenochtitlán) and the valley of central Mexico when **Hernando Cortés** (1485–1547) first arrived on November 8, 1519. And Montezuma had halls, all right.

Tenochtitlán was a magical city situated on an island in the middle of a lake. Three wide causeways led to huge white palaces and elaborate pyramids and temples. Montezuma lived in a lavishly ornamented palace, surrounded by obsequious nobles and thousands of slaves who spent much of their day catering to his whims and scrubbing the dazzling white walls. Montezuma II came from a royal lineage, believed to be directly descended from the gods, and as such his subjects owed him endless homage.

All around Montezuma's temple, skillfully constructed bridges carried the streets over the myriad canals in the city. An aqueduct brought drinking water from nearby Chapultepec. The place was neat as a pin and ran as efficiently as a Swiss watch. Order and harmony were divine requirements and every effort was made to keep the emperor happy.

On the other side of town, though, life was quite different for the rest of the drones. Floating island farms called *chinampas,* made of mud dredged up by slaves from the lake bottom, surrounded the city. Farmers lived in wattle-and-daub huts and looked on the halls of Montezuma from afar with wonder and reverence. They led simple lives and worked hard.

But unlike previous Aztec rulers, who had been great warriors and leaders, this Montezuma was more interested in wizardry and the good life than in preserving his great empire or saving his people from certain domination. At first, he was unsure whether the Spanish were gods or men. But after consulting soothsayers and uncovering what he believed were definite omens, he concluded that the *conquistadors* were, categorically, white gods, and that his reign was up.

Rather than fight off the Spaniards, Montezuma tried everything else—from gifts of gold chests and jeweled boxes to sorcery. When none of his strategems worked and he was unable either to buy the Spanish off or to make them magically disappear, Montezuma invited Cortés to enter the island capital of Tenochtitlán and was instantly taken prisoner without resistance. The Aztec emperor's actions enraged the people, who fought the Spanish with enormous daring. They managed several successful ambushes that kept the white men at bay for a while, but eventually the Spanish and their weapons prevailed, and today's Mexico City fell under Spanish domination. Montezuma died under mysterious circumstances, presumably killed by his own people in reprisal for his unspeakable betrayal.

As for his halls, the Spaniards, who were horrified by the Aztec religious rites involving human sacrifice, ruthlessly destroyed Montezuma II's temples. Later, the missionaries who came to the New World to convert the Native Americans to Catholicism completed the desecration of the Aztec temples by burning their records and smashing their idols.

Besides the Halls, What Else Did the Aztec Have to Brag About?

When the *conquistadors* landed, the Aztec had achieved the most advanced civilization in North America. However, the Aztec could be said to have been brilliant imitators rather than privileged originators.

They were great warriors (in fact, one of their biggest pyramids was dedicated to Tezcatlipoca, the god of war). Wherever they traveled, they assimilated the culture of earlier, more advanced peoples, including the Maya, Toltec, and Zapotec.

The Aztec used hieroglyphics and numeric symbols to record events. They learned from the Maya how to determine the solar year. They learned architecture and engineering from other Toltec tribes and then built magnificent temples, as well as the remarkable city of Tenochtitlán, which left **Hernando Cortés** thunderstruck.

All over the territory that now constitutes Mexico, the Aztec were admired for their art, ingenuity, and great technological and agricultural advancements. Their chief produce, which they bartered using cacao beans as change, included pears, tomatoes, tobacco, corn, beans, peppers, squash, cotton, and turkeys—all of which they grew or raised with a high degree of uniformity harvest after harvest.

How Did Mexico Get Its Name?

The Aztec came from the north of what is now Mexico, and spoke the Nahuan or Nahuatl language, which is related to the languages of the Pima and Shoshone tribes of the western United States. The Aztec referred to themselves as the Mexica people—thus, the whole of Mexico is really named after them. They were originally nomadic farmers. In the twelfth century, they began wandering the great expanse known as Mesoamerica, and by the thirteenth century finally settled in the valley of central Mexico, founding Tenochtitlán around 1342. They were also great warriors, and made martial training compulsory for boys. Theirs was a male-dominated society, although girls were allowed to study for the priesthood in their own schools.

When the Spanish arrived, the Aztec ruled from the Gulf of Mexico to the central Cordilleras and southward into what is now Guatemala. The Aztec tribes were divided into families and clans. Each clan had its own elected officials and sent representatives to the council of the tribe. It was a democracy in principle, but the chiefs were always selected from a handful of ruling families. Strict laws protected common citizens and slaves from unfair practices, and any type of crime, particularly stealing, was punished by enslavement or execution.

SOME SITES WHERE YOU CAN RELIVE LATINO HISTORY

1. **The Alamo** San Antonio, Texas

Called the shrine or cradle of Texas liberty, this is the state's biggest tourist attraction. The chapel and barracks are all that remain of the original mission and fort.

2. **Spanish History Museum** Albuquerque, New Mexico

The Spanish History Museum preserves and interprets the history of Spanish influence in America through lectures, exhibits, and tours. The museum also examines the Spanish influence on contemporary American culture.

3. **Columbia State Historic Park** Columbia, California

Columbia was one of the hundreds of towns that sprang up during the California Gold Rush. In its heyday, the town yielded $87 million in gold. By 1860, however, the gold easiest to mine was depleted, and Columbia's population quickly dipped from ten thousand to five hundred inhabitants. In 1945, Columbia was made into a historic park, where you can tour replicas of a miner's cabin, a livery stable, a firehouse, and a church.

4. **Fiesta San Antonio** San Antonio, Texas

The Fiesta San Antonio, held since 1892, honors veterans of the Texas war for independence and celebrates San Antonio's rich cultural heritage. More than 3 million people take part in the celebration each year, which runs for ten days in April and encompasses more than 150 events.

5. **Aztec Theater** San Antonio, Texas

The architect who created the Aztec Theater in the 1920s based it on his study of Maya and Aztec ruins in Mexico. The result is a portrayal of Aztec gods, pre-Columbian sacrificial temples, and the meeting of Montezuma and Cortés.

6. **Museo del Barrio** New York City

This is the only museum in the country dedicated to the arts and culture of South and Central America, the Caribbean, Mexico, and Puerto Rico. It is a vibrant cultural institution where artists, writers, and filmmakers submit their work and Latin American concerts, festivals, competitions, and lectures are held regularly.

7. **Cabrillo National Monument** San Diego, California

This monument commemorates the discovery of the bay at what is now San Diego by the explorer Juan Rodríguez Cabrillo. On September 28, 1542, Cabrillo and his Spanish crew sailed into the bay and claimed all the land surrounding it for the Spanish throne.

8. **Eighteenth-Century Franciscan Missions** California

The Franciscan missions are in and near San Diego, San Juan Capistrano, Santa Barbara, San Luis Obispo, and Carmel, among other places. A guiding principle of the missions was that all natives who accepted the Catholic faith or were learning its teachings had to live near the mission church and contribute to a self-supporting community.

9. **Castillo de San Marcos National Monument** St. Augustine, Florida

On this site stands a massive fort built of shell rock, which the Spanish began to build in 1672 to protect St. Augustine from invasion. It was strategically situated at the entrance to St. Augustine harbor.

10. **De Soto National Memorial Park** Near Bradenton, Florida

This small park commemorates the landing in 1539 of the Spanish explorer Hernando de Soto. U.S. park rangers dressed as Spanish soldiers of the period re-create history by showing young visitors the fine points of the crossbow and letting them try on pieces of Spanish armor.

Why Did They Call Them the Heart-Eating Aztec?

The Aztec religion included hundreds of gods who ruled not only over certain days, but even over certain hours of the day. The Aztec gods personified the forces of nature, and many of the Aztec religious ceremonies were centered around appeasing the gods by performing rites that often included human sacrifice.

At the dedication of the great pyramid temple of Tenochtitlán, twenty thousand captives were killed and offered to the gods. The captives were led up the steps of the high pyramid, where priests slit open their bodies and tore out their hearts. The Aztec frequently ate the flesh of their human sacrifices, in an act they believed would imbue them with the virtues of their victims.

Are There Any Aztec Left Today?

The Native Americans and *mestizos* living in Mexico City today, as well as those Hispanic-Americans who came from the
valley of central Mexico and other areas where the Aztec
traveled and conquered, are the descendants of the proud
Aztec people. Neither **Juan de Grijalba,** the Spaniard who
first sighted Mexico in 1581, nor **Diego Velázquez,** who was
in charge of the Mexican expedition, nor **Hernando Cortés,**
who actually got there and managed to dethrone the most
powerful emperor of all, was able to destroy the Aztec. Aside
from their obvious genetic legacy, the Aztec left a wealth of
wisdom, artistry, and folklore that lives on in the hearts and
minds of their heirs.

What Was So Great About the Inca and What Did They Do with All That Gold?

Francisco Pizarro reached Peru in 1532 and immediately
succumbed to gold fever. He saw hundreds of productive
gold fields, which the people of the Cuzco valley mined
daily. But to the Spaniard's amazement, the citizens of the
Incan empire, which stretched from the Pacific coast across
the Andes to the Atlantic, and from Ecuador three thousand
miles southward to central Chile, did not consider gold
money or any type of commodity at all. Unlike the Europeans, whose economy was based on the gold standard, the
Inca used a system of barter.

The state religion of the Inca revolved around the worship of the sun. The Incan emperors were considered divine
beings directly descended from the sun god. And gold was
the symbol of the sun. Consequently, gold was used exclusively by the rulers and the elite for decorative and ritual
purposes. They had knives, brooches, buckles, plates, head-
dresses, and entire walls made of gold. Although for them

gold was not money, it was just as sacred as it was for the Spaniards.

Gold, however, was not all these extraordinary people were famous for. They irrigated thousands of miles of valleys and had a highly organized political system that kept the vast area prosperous no matter what the sun or rain gods decided to do in any particular season. For instance, if crops failed in one locality, the government records would show where produce was more abundant, and the shortage would be made good immediately by drawing on public warehouses in those districts.

Are Irish Potatoes a Gift from the Inca?

The Inca were the first people in the world to grow potatoes. Some of the potatoes that later found their way to Europe, and especially to Ireland, were first cousins of those cultivated by the Inca. They also grew corn, sweet potatoes, and cassava (known among Latinos as *yuca*, not to be confused with the desert plant yucca). The Inca didn't have horses like the Spanish, but they had llamas, which did just fine as mounts and beasts of burden (and drank less water). And when it came to arts and crafts, few cultures on earth have approached Incan accomplishments. The Inca were great architects. They practiced every style of handweaving known today. They also kept records, not by writing, but by a complex system of knotted cords (called *quipus*), which was used as a basis of taxation and kept track of crops. Their jewelry, much of which is exhibited in museums around the world, was simply dazzling.

Why Were the Inca Not Really Inca at All?

These people have come to be known as Inca, but originally the term "Inca" referred to the ruler of the people, the divine emperor, as well as to the few people who lived in the valley of Cuzco. After the Spanish landed, they used "Inca" to refer to all the peoples in the Tawantinsuyu region, which encompassed dozens of local kingdoms whose people had entirely different identities but were politically and economically subject to the Inca. Quechua was the official language of the empire, but at least twenty other languages were spoken.

Today, Latinos from Ecuador, Peru, and Bolivia who have settled in areas as diverse as Miami, Los Angeles, and the New York City borough of Queens, still pepper their Spanish with many Quechua words. Quechua is still spoken fluently by many of the indigenous people of South America. "Tawantinsuyu," the name the Inca called their land, means "four parts" in Quechua; it was, literally, a land divided into quarters according to the very diverse terrain and climate— from the long coastal desert strip to the high peaks and deep fertile valleys of the Andes, to the mountainous edges of the tropical forests of the east.

How Did the Inca Get So Big?

The Inca were big as in powerful, though they were short people by contemporary U.S. standards: four feet was the average height of an Inca man. For that matter, most of the Spanish *conquistadors* were pretty short themselves. (Check out the Spanish armor at the Metropolitan Museum of Art in New York.)

The beginnings of the Incan empire are shrouded in mystery, because Incan mythology and history are closely intertwined. The Spanish recorded Incan history just as the Inca conveyed it to them, but they may have been writing more fiction than fact. The Incan empire started out as a series of small kingdoms, just like many others that thrived in the Andes around the fourteenth century. **Manco Capac** was listed as the founding ruler, although he may have been fictional.

The Inca were powerful fighters and, apparently, were able to conquer and then rapidly develop their enormous territory by great military might, as well as sophisticated political strategies of "divide and conquer."

How Did the Inca Lose the War and Where Are They Now?

When the *conquistadors* landed, the legendary **Atahualpa** was emperor. Unlike **Montezuma II** of Mexico, Atahualpa was someone to be reckoned with. He was not about to hand over his treasures and his people to the greedy *conquistadors* without a valiant struggle. In the end, though, the Spanish decided that Atahualpa had to be captured and killed to show the people that their emperor was, in fact, a man of flesh and blood who had feet not of gold but of clay.

Atahualpa's treacherous half brother, **Manco Inca Yupanqui,** collaborated with the Spanish and became a puppet ruler. He was mistreated and scoffed at by the Europeans. In 1536, Manco Inca fled Cuzco for Vitcos, a city on the edge of the jungle, and set up an inaccessible fortress from which to begin reconquering his land. Eventually, though, he negotiated a surrender in exchange for his life. After him, other Incan nobles continued their guerrilla efforts against the Spanish. They won an impressive number of skirmishes and left a trail of decapitated Spaniards along the Andean hills, but they lost the war when the last Incan leader, **Tupac Amarú,** was captured and executed in 1572.

The Incan regional capitals were immediately transformed into Spanish towns bearing Spanish names, and most of the people were forced into slavery—principally as gold miners and workers who filled the Spanish galleons and the king's coffers to the brim.

As with most of the indigenous populations conquered by the Europeans, the Inca and their culture could never be entirely erased. Incan arts and crafts, traditions, recipes, language, religious beliefs, and even philosophy and world-view live on among their descendants, including those who now live in Lima, Peru; Quito, Ecuador; and Coral Gables, Florida.

Why Is There a Cadillac Named El Dorado?

El Dorado means "the gilded one" in Spanish. In the six-teenth and seventeenth centuries, the Spanish *conquistadors* learned of a South American Chibcha Indian legend that told of a country swimming in gold somewhere between Bogotá, Colombia, and Lima, Peru.

The legend probably stems from a ritual performed by the Chibcha in the highlands of Colombia that involved anointing each new chief with resinous gums and swaddling his body in gold dust as an offering to the earth gods, while the people threw gold bars and jewelry into the water. This ritual had died out before the arrival of the Spanish in the sixteenth century, but the belief in a city of gold buried somewhere in the deep persisted.

The Spanish expeditions in search of El Dorado started around 1569 and continued as late as 1617. One of the most important expeditions was that of **Gonzalo Jiménez de Quesada,** who had conquered the Chibcha and founded the city of Bogotá. The search for El Dorado spread from the Bogotá highlands all the way into the deep valleys of the Am-azon and Orinoco rivers. The Englishman **Sir Walter Raleigh** also got into the act and actually led two expeditions, one in 1595 and another in 1617, in search of the fabled city of gold.

Although El Dorado was never found, the search for it resulted in the exploration and conquest of much of north-ern South America. Today, El Dorado has come to stand for a golden dream, which is probably how the Cadillac got its name.

Why Do Latinos Have Two Last Names?

In Spain, every newborn bears both the father's last name and the mother's maiden name. Thus, if María's father's surname is Pérez and her mother's maiden name is López, María's name is María Perez López. However, if María becomes a mother, it is her father's name (Pérez) that she passes on to her offspring. If María has a child by a man whose last name is González, the child's surname will be González Pérez. Thus, the patriarchal line prevails. In the United States most Latinos drop their mother's surname, but in Spain and Latin America the two-surname tradition prevails.

THE "SPANISH" IN "HISPANIC"

If "Hispanic" Comes from "Spain," Where did the Spanish People Come From?

Obviously, the Spanish people come from Spain, a country that occupies five-sixths of the Iberian Peninsula in southwestern Europe (the last fifth is Portugal). Spain also owns the Balearic Islands in the western Mediterranean and the Canary Islands off the northwest coast of Africa. Altogether Spain governs an area about the size of Illinois, Iowa, and Missouri combined.

The Spanish people have one of the oldest and most diverse cultural and ethnic heritages in Europe, and thus can be said to come from many different places. They are descended from the ancient Iberians, who were invaded by the Carthaginians, Celts, Romans, Vandals, Visigoths, and Moors. Also, large numbers of Jews settled in Spain, particularly in the south, as the result not of an "invasion" but rather of a migration, and contributed vastly to Spanish culture.

Even before **Columbus** sailed the ocean blue, there was

no such thing as a typical Spaniard. There are five distinct cultural regions in Spain—Castile, Andalusia, Galicia, the Basque country, and Catalonia—and each region has had its share of outside and inside influence.

The people of Castile, on the Meseta Central, are thought of by most foreigners as the "real" Spaniards. The reason for this is that during the unification of Spain under **Ferdinand** and **Isabella** in the 1500s, Castilian Spanish was codified as the official state and literary language.

The people of Andalusia on the sunny southern coast, who, in addition to Spanish, also speak the Andalusian dialect, are known for their gaiety and love of horses and dance. They have Jewish and Moorish blood, and have incorporated both cultures, particularly the Arabic culture, into their everyday life.

On the lush, rainy northwest coast of Galicia live the Gallegos, who are closely linked to the Celts (as the name suggests). They are known for their hardworking, frugal ways. To this day, the Gallegos play bagpipes, dance the Spanish jig, and wear kilts on certain occasions.

Catalonia, the region along the northeastern Mediterranean, breeds brisk, artistic people. Amazingly, three of the greatest artists of the twentieth century all came from Catalonia—**Pablo Picasso, Salvador Dalí,** and **Joan Miró.** Besides Spanish, Catalonians speak Catalonian, a branch of the old Provençal dialect of southern France.

The three Basque provinces in the east seem almost a world away from the rest of Spain. The Basque people, who live on the northern coastline and in the Pyrenees, speak a language of their own, called Basque, whose origins are still unknown. Unlike Spanish (or "Castilian"), Basque is completely unrelated to Latin or any other Romance language. The Basque people call themselves Iberians, not Spanish, and have long sought independence from the rest of Spain.

How Did Boise, Idaho, Become Home to Many Americans of Basque Descent?

Although few in number, the Basques who came to America at the end of the nineteenth and the beginning of the twentieth century settled in the Great Basin area, the area between Salt Lake City and the Sierra Nevada in eastern California, which includes most of Nevada, southeastern Oregon, and southwestern Idaho. They also populated California during the Spanish and Mexican periods. The Basques dominated the Western sheep industry from the end of the nineteenth century, and today are involved in a wide variety of commercial and industrial activity throughout the United States. **Paul Laxalt,** the U.S. senator from Nevada, was descended from the Basques who came to America. That's why nobody knows what kind of name Laxalt is.

Are Latinos in the United States Descendants of People All Over Spain?

Spaniards from all five Spanish regions conquered and later settled Latin America. Thus, the different flavors of each region were added to the prodigious melting pot—or, more accurately, distinctive stew—that eventually gave birth to our New World Latinos.

What Is the Spanish "Lisp" and Where Did It Really Come From?

The Spanish "lisp" consists of pronouncing the letter "c" as "th" when it is followed by a vowel. "San Francisco," for example, would be pronounced "San FranTHisco." The "th" sound, contrary to popular opinion in the United States, does not come from a Spanish king who lisped, but from Greek influence on Latin and, later, on its first cousin, Spanish. Castilians and people from other regions of Spain "lisp" this way. But in many areas, such as Andalusia, the inhabitants do not. They pronounce "c" as an "s," much as we do in English. In Latin America, the "th" sound, like some wine, did not travel well and was completely dropped.

This does not mean that Latin Americans do not speak Castilian—they do, since Castilian is, after all, the official Spanish language, spoken throughout Spain and Latin America. There is no such thing as Mexican or Puerto Rican when it comes to language. Latin Americans all speak Spanish, even if they don't sound exactly alike—just as the people in Arkansas don't sound exactly like those in Ohio. Each Latin American country has its own distinct accent and its own indigenous or African words that have been incorporated into the language of each region.

Why Do Spaniards Say "Olé"?

Olé is the Spanish language adaptation of "Allah," the Arabic word for God. So when Spaniards cry *"Olé!"* at a bullfight, they are saying, "Praise Allah!", even if what they really mean is *"Viva,"* another Spanish word which simply means "Long live" or "Live" or, even, in some circles, "Man alive!" In a sense, no single word could be said to encapsulate as much history as that three-letter word *"Olé"*—seven centuries of history, to be precise.

The Visigoths ruled Spain from 415 to 711. In the seventh century, Arab armies swept across Northern Africa and conquered the Berbers, a white race of ancient origin. The Arabs converted the Berbers to Islam during the eighth century. In 711, the Arabs and the Berbers joined forces in conquering Spain, and a new mixed race, called Moors, emerged.

Moorish invaders from Africa overthrew the Visigoths at the Battle of Guadalete. Thus began seven centuries of Muslim domination in Spain, which are felt in Spanish and

Latin American culture, music, architecture, and philosophy to this day. Among Latinos, the numerical combination seven-eleven is considered lucky; this is widely believed to date to the year the Moors conquered southern Spain. It was certainly lucky for the Moors, at least while it lasted—and seven hundred years, by anyone's calculations, is a very long lucky streak.

The Moors transformed the city of Córdoba, in Andalusia, into a glorious Moorish caliphate that became a prominent center of learning. In Moorish Spain extraordinary scientists, philosophers, mathematicians, writers, and philosophers flourished, while northern Spain (which the Moors conquered sporadically but never settled) remained divided into small kingdoms.

The Moors devised ingenious methods of irrigation and transformed the arid coastlands and southern hills of Spain into lush, palatial gardens. They rebuilt the old Roman cities along Arabic lines, with elegant fountain courtyards and impressive, elaborate mosques. Fine silk, beautifully crafted leather goods, and Moorish tiles became the trademarks of the region. Metalwork, such as swords from Toledo, became famous throughout the known world.

Along the way, Arabic words and phrases influenced Castilian and other languages spoken in the various regions. *Olé* remained the benchmark word—a reminder that culture, language, and religion are often inextricably linked. *Moros y Christianos*—literally "Moors and Christians"—is a popular dish in the Caribbean, consisting of black beans and white rice. Its name reflects the extent to which these two Spanish cultures affected the New World.

Were There Any Jews in Spain?

There was an important Jewish population in Spain, and, at least for a while, the Moors tolerated it. In spite of their religious differences, the Jews and Moors of Spain worked together and often lived side by side. After the destruction of Jerusalem, many Jews settled in North Africa and in several Mediterranean cities. Later, they migrated to Western Europe, especially Spain.

Early on, the Christian Visigoths had practically wiped out the Spanish Jewish communities, which had existed on the Iberian Peninsula since Roman times. When the Moors conquered Spain, they established more liberal policies toward the Jewish population and did not oppose new Jewish immigration.

Spanish Jews spoke and wrote mostly in Arabic, and became an intrinsic part of the Arabic cultural renaissance. They were scholars, financiers, tradespeople, and philosophers who excelled in the art of rhetoric. They also produced important biblical commentaries, legal works, and beautiful Hebrew poetry. Among the Jewish scholars of the time were **Judah ha-Levi, Solomon Ibn Gabirol,** and the great **Maimonides.** Jewish literature, music, and philosophy became deeply imbedded in the Iberian tradition.

Around the twelfth century, a fanatical Arabic sect from North Africa known as the Almohads took control of Muslim Spain, and the Jews were made to choose among conversion to Islam, escape, or death. Many Jews fled to northern Spain, where Christian rulers who had begun organized efforts to reconquer the Iberian Peninsula found them useful allies—at least for a while, until a new Christian fervor sprang up.

Who Were the Marranos and Who Were the Sephardim?

Eventually, Christian fanaticism became as much a part of northern Spain as Almohad zeal was in the south. In 1391, thousands of Jews were massacred by Spanish Christians and thousands more were forcibly converted and baptized. The new "Jewish Christians" were known as Marranos (Spanish for "swine") and were suspected of practicing Judaism in secret. Many Marranos achieved high positions at court and in the Church, but they suffered persecutions, which began as spying but eventually culminated in autos-da-fé—gruesome celebrations in which heretics were burned at the stake. As a result of these pre-Inquisition policies in Spain, the mystical doctrines of Cabala became very important among Spanish Jews.

Spanish Jews and their descendants are known as Sephardim. Their customs, Hebrew pronunciation, and rituals differ somewhat from the Ashkenazic Jews, who came from other European countries.

How Did Queen Isabella and King Ferdinand Become the Most Powerful Rulers of Europe and the New World Combined?

You could call it a combination of dynastic fortune and a little bit of luck. In 1474, **Isabella** acceded to the throne of Castile. In 1479, her husband, **Ferdinand II,** became the rightful heir to the throne of Aragon. Thus, the two most important kingdoms of Spain outside the Moorish kingdom were joined. And, as luck would have it, both the queen and the king were exceptionally gifted leaders and believed in joint rule and equitable division of labor. Isabella loved governing internal affairs. Ferdinand liked tinkering around with foreign policy. Together, they began a massive Christian *reconquista* (reconquest) of Spain. In the process, they managed to unify Spain into one monarchy.

They were called "the Catholic Kings." Under the banner of Catholicism, Isabella and Ferdinand performed some of the most laudable feats and some of the most atrocious acts known to humankind. They also began looking around for some extra land they could pick up for Spain. Ferdinand conquered Naples and added Navarre and the territories on the French border to the family treasure. Then, as if by magic, one day **Christopher Columbus,** better known as **Cristobal Colón,** showed up at court. He had a bright idea, and Isabella and Ferdinand were bright enough to go for it.

How Bad Was the Spanish Inquisition?

Bad. The old song in *My Fair Lady* goes: "I'd prefer a new edition of the Spanish Inquisition/than to ever let a woman in my life." It was an example of Anglo Saxon flippancy in the mouth of an Englishman who obviously (a) did not understand history or (b) needed a sex therapist in the worst way.

At the behest of **Queen Isabella** and **King Ferdinand, Pope Sixus IV** endorsed the creation of an independent Spanish Inquisition in 1483, presided over by a high council and a grand inquisitor—the infamous **Tomás de Torquemada.** The main concern of Torquemada was the elimination, by any means necessary, of all Marranos (converts from Judaism) and Moriscos (converts from Islam) who might be suspected of religious infidelity. These "means" included the use of sophisticated instruments of torture, mass burnings at the stake, massacres, book burnings, and almost anything that would bring about the swift destruction of the "foreigners" within the newly unified Spanish walls.

What Happened to the Moors and the Jews in Spain?

Although Moorish territories had been wrested bit by bit from the Muslims by the citizens of Asturias and other northern regions since 1212, the marriage of **Ferdinand** and **Isabella** and the establishment of the Spanish Inquisition accelerated the reconquest of Spain by the Christians.

With Isabella and Ferdinand on the throne, the Moors were swiftly driven out of Spain and their lands settled by the

Spanish Christians within a few years. The final blow to Moorish power was the conquest of Granada by the Catholic Kings in 1492.

Once the last Muslim rulers had been driven into North Africa, all professing Jews were also forced to leave Spain, unless they agreed to be baptized and earnestly practice Catholicism. It was not until 1967 that Jewish synagogues and Muslim mosques were allowed to open their doors in Spain again.

Many Jews left as a result of the Inquisition, but many others chose to stay and become powerful influences on Spanish politics and finance. The son of one of these converted Jews was the Dominican friar **Diego Durán,** who came to live in Mexico at the age of six, around 1582, and whose work *Historia de las Indias de la Nueva España y Islas de la Tierra Firme* powerfully describes the glories of the Mesoamerican civilizations. It is an astounding history and one of the few remaining records of Aztec civilization.

What Else Happened in 1492?

Just as 1492 marked the fall of Granada, the final defeat of the Moorish Empire, and the successful unification of Spain, it also marked, ironically, the year that **Columbus** set sail for America—and thus the year that a new form of Spanish Inquisition (namely the subjugation and conversion of the Native American peoples) began. The rules of the Inquisition remained intact when it came to the treatment of the people of the New World: All those who were not Catholic (the only kind of Christian the king and queen recognized) were not human, and thus did not have to be treated as such.

THE AFRICAN PEOPLE

Why Are There More People of African Descent in Some Latino Groups than Among the Anglo Population?

African people were brought to the New World as slaves by the English, the Spanish, and the Portuguese. As early as the fifteenth century, the Portuguese pushed down the African coast and introduced the African slave into Europe. At first, Portuguese ships carried slaves to Spain. Then, when the New World was discovered, descendants of these slaves (born in Spain!), were brought to Haiti (Hispaniola) to work the mines.

The Spanish *conquistadors* attempted to use local Arawak, Maya, Aztec, and Inca to work in their New World plantations and mines, but when the Native Americans began dying off, the Spanish started importing slaves from Africa. The great ship companies of Europe bid against each other for the right to transport African slaves to the New World. The 1713 Treaty of Utrecht gave England the right to supply slaves to the Spanish colonies. In 1739, Spain tried to revoke the agreement, but England went to war to keep it.

Slavery had been a common practice in Africa, where African slave traders bartered humans for weapons, metal, cloth, and liquor. Only the best "specimens" were brought to the New World—and even then hundreds of thousands did not survive the terrible voyage across the waters, during which they were shackled in close quarters, with barely enough water or air to last the trip.

Most African slaves in the Spanish colonies came from eastern Nigeria, the Gold Coast, and particularly the Congo basin. The rise of the Ashanti, Dahomey, Oyo, and other peoples in the Congo basin was a direct result of the prosperity that the European slave traders brought to that area. It is estimated that as many as 15 million Africans came to the Americas between the sixteenth and the nineteenth centuries. During the eighteenth century, when the slave trade reached its peak, about 6 million slaves were brought to both North America and Latin America. In 1807, England abolished slavery and persuaded Spain, France, and Portugal to follow suit. However, much illegal slave trading went on in the Americas well into the nineteenth century.

The African peoples who populated the Spanish colonies, particularly the Caribbean and parts of Central America and northern South America, as well as Brazil, brought with them strong religious and cultural traditions, which the Spanish were unable to suppress.

The African people kept their foods, their gods, their music, their colorful crafts, and then, slowly, gave it all to their new countries—to the point where it was hard to determine where one culture started and the other one ended. Even African languages became blended into the speech of the New World's Spanish people, particularly the Caribbean people. Words and phrases such as *kimbombo,* a Yoruba word for okra, and *fulano y mengana,* with the colloquial meaning "Mr. and Mrs. So-and-so," among dozens of others, are still part of everyday language in the Spanish Caribbean.

As to the reason behind a greater *mestizaje* (racial or ethnic mixture) in the former Spanish colonies, there are two prevalent theories. The first is that proportionally (i.e., according to the ratio of people to square feet in populated areas), more African people came to the Spanish New World than to the English colonies. The second is that the Spanish *conquistadors* and many settlers left their wives back in Europe when they first ventured across the seas. The English, Dutch, Germans, and other North American settlers tended to bring their families with them. In addition, Spanish people were said to find the African people generally pleasing in their physiques and personalities.

The Spanish forms of discrimination (and there were many) hinged more on class and religion than on race per se. The English, on the other hand, seemed to be very caught up in the question of race. Which, of course, is not to say that the English did not interbreed with Africans, as a cursory look across the North American continent will reveal.

As for the treatment of slaves in the fields, the English and Spanish share equal blame. Museums throughout Latin America and Spain exhibit instruments of torture used against African slaves that are often more horrifying than some of the sophisticated weapons found in Hitler's dungeons after World War II.

TRES

Mexicans

Who are Chicanos?

Who are Anglos?

Who's a gringo?

THE *CONQUISTADORS* IN MEXICO

How long did it take the Spanish to conquer Mexico?

Did Mexico become Spanish right away?

How did the Spanish rule in Mexico?

What role did women play in all this and was there such a thing as a conquistadora?

Who was La Malinche, how did she help the Spanish win Mexico, and why do some people call her the first Mexican feminist?

NORTHERN EXPOSURE, OR HOW NEW MEXICO CAME TO BE KNOWN AS NUEVO MEXICO AND CALIFORNIANS AS CALIFORNIOS

What did the Spanish want with New Mexico?

What did Cabeza de Vaca do that was so revolutionary?

What was the Northwest Passage and what did Sir Francis Drake have to do with the Spanish Conquista of the Southwest?

Besides the Pueblo peoples, who were the real first settlers of the Southwest?

A brief historical footnote, or so much for missionary zeal

DID THE SPANISH GO TO TEXAS OR CALIFORNIA FIRST?

Parlez-vous Texan? No way!

Who were the Californios?

MEXICO VS. SPAIN

Where did Spain go wrong? (Don't blame it all on the Spanish Armada!)

So what was the defeat of the Spanish Armada all about?

What was the Grito de Dolores?

THE ANGLO CONNECTION

When did the Anglos and the Mexicans first meet?

What was the Santa Fe Trail?

How did the Santa Fe traders lead the way to Anglo expansionism?

What exactly was Manifest Destiny?

HOW TEXAS WAS WON—OR LOST

Who was Stephen F. Austin and why is he called the Father of Texas?

Who won at the Alamo?

Why should we remember the Alamo, anyway?

*Why do Mexican-Americans object to
"Remember the Alamo"?*

*What role did African-Americans play
in the history of Texas?*

THE MEXICAN-AMERICAN WAR

Why did we fight with Mexico, anyway?

How did the Mexican stand-off get its name?

*If all Taylor had was a small volunteer
army, how did the United States
win the war?*

*Was Abraham Lincoln a war dodger and did Ralph
Waldo Emerson really go to jail for opposing the
Mexican-American War?*

What was the Treaty of Guadalupe Hidalgo?

*What was wrong with the Treaty of
Guadalupe Hidalgo?*

*What was the Gadsden Treaty and why did
the Mexicans say they needed it like a hole
in the head?*

*What was the Bear Flag Revolt and how did
the Californios feel about joining the
United States?*

CALIFORNIA DREAMING

What was the Gold Rush and how did Mexico miss out on it by a couple of days?

What role did Latinos play in the success of California mining?

Did discrimination start in the gold fields?

Was the California constitution drafted and signed exclusively by Anglos?

Allá en el rancho grande: What happened to the Mexican-American cowboys?

DESPERADOS AND THE MEXICAN REVOLUTION

What is a desperado, anyway?

Was Pancho Villa a desperado?

Why was the Mexican Revolution of 1910 so important and how did the United States get involved?

THE SECOND AND THIRD WAVES

What did the Mexican Revolution have to do with Congressman Henry Gonzalez's becoming chairperson of the Banking Committee?

How did the second wave of Mexican immigrants differ from the old Californios and Tejanos?

How did U.S. immigration laws benefit Mexican immigrants but discriminate against Asians?

Why do Mexican-Americans say the railroads were built on their backs?

What's a barrio and what's a colonia?

Chicano go home?: Why were Mexicans and Mexican-Americans repatriated?

What's a bracero?

Why did Texas pass a law making all Mexican-Americans white?

Why was the bracero program finally stopped?

What were the Zoot Suit Riots?

Mojados: illegal or undocumented?

What was "drying out the wetbacks"?

What was the El Paso Incident?

Who are the commuters?

IDENTITY, ACTIVISM, AND *VIVA LA RAZA*

How did Mexican-Americans do
in the armed forces?

How did Mexican-American activism
get its start?

Who was César Chávez?

What is the Chicano movement?

Chicano mural painting: When is graffiti
not graffiti?

THE WOMEN: CHICANA MOTHERS, HEALERS,
ARTISTS, AND REVOLUTIONARIES

What exactly is machismo, anyway?

Is there such a thing as macha?

What's a curandera?

What's a partera?

So where were the women in Mexican
and Chicano history?

Where are the great Chicana artists?

*Who are some of the great Chicana and Chicano writers
of today?*

CULTURAL HERITAGE: A MOVABLE FIESTA

Did Montezuma II eat tacos?

Is chocolate really Mexican?

*How are Tex-Mex and Southwestern food different
from Mexican food?*

*Are tacos, tortillas, fajitas, and chile the Mexican
national dishes?*

What is mole poblano?

What is tequila, anyway?

What's a piñata party?

What are mariachis?

Why do Mexican-Americans celebrate Cinco de Mayo?

What's a charreada?

*How many different fiestas do Mexican-Americans
celebrate?*

The history of Mexico and that of the United States are so closely intertwined that they have been compared to Siamese twins who, before suffering a radical and painful separation, shared the same heart. When we speak about Chicanos, we do not speak of a cultural minority who crossed our borders and then by slow assimilation became part of the great American melting pot. We refer to a cultural minority who have lived within the boundaries of the present United States since long before the first English settlement at Jamestown.

Who Are Chicanos?

"Chicanos" (the name is an abbreviation of "Mexicanos," Spanish for "Mexicans") was originally used as a pejorative term by both Anglos and Mexican-Americans to refer to unskilled workers born in Mexico, particularly recent immigrants. But since prejudice seldom makes fine distinctions, all Mexican-Americans, no matter how many centuries they may have been living in the territory that is now the United States, are often labeled Chicanos.

Although for years many Mexican-Americans objected to the term, more recently, starting with the labor revolt led by **César Chávez** in the 1960s, Mexican-Americans have chosen to call themselves Chicanos as a symbol of pride and solidarity with *la raza*—the people.

Who Are Anglos?

To Chicanos, "Anglos" originally meant Americans of Anglo-Saxon descent. Today Anglos are more broadly defined as Americans who are neither African-American, Latino, Native American, Asian, or Brown. An Italian-American or a Hungarian-American, for instance, could qualify as an Anglo, even if she or he doesn't have a drop of Anglo-Saxon blood coursing through her or his veins.

Who's a Gringo?

"Gringo" is the Latin American term for a foreigner of English or Anglo-American descent. Although the term is sometimes interchangeable with "Anglo" among Mexican-Americans, it seems to be slowly falling into disuse. There are many theories on just how gringo became a word, since it's not of Spanish origin. Some historians have argued that it was part of a phrase Mexicans used repeatedly during the Mexican-American war, when U.S. soldiers wore green uniforms—"green go" home or "green go" away.

THE *CONQUISTADORS* IN MEXICO

How Long Did It Take the Spanish to Conquer Mexico?

From the time **Hernando Cortés** and his 550 men landed at the Gulf of Mexico near present-day Veracruz in the year 1519, the Spanish *conquista* of Mexico took only two and a half years.

The reason for this fulminant takeover can be attributed in part to **Montezuma II**'s belief that the *conquistadors* were gods and that their takeover had been divinely preordained to punish the Aztec for having previously conquered and enslaved the Toltec and other Indian groups. But success of the takeover had several other causes. The Spanish army, with its cannons, horses, and harquebuses, was decisively superior to the Aztec arrows, which, incidentally, were not poisoned. The Spanish introduced bacteriological warfare in the form of smallpox and other European diseases, which the Indians succumbed to by the thousands. Finally, the native Mexicans were themselves divided into many warring factions, among them the Tlaxcalans, whom the Spanish enlisted as powerful allies against Montezuma.

IMPORTANT DATES

February 1540	Francisco Vásquez de Coronado begins his explorations of the Southwest in search of treasure-laden cities.
March 30, 1609	The Spanish write instructions for the building of Santa Fe de San Francisco, better known today as Santa Fe. In spring 1610 a site is chosen and the buildings are planned.
April 30, 1803	The United States acquires Louisiana from the French for $15 million as part of the Louisiana Purchase.
September 9, 1850	California is admitted to the Union as the thirty-first state.
March 2, 1861	Texas secedes at the beginning of the American Civil War, forcing the ouster of its Unionist governor, Sam Houston.

Did Mexico Become Spanish Right Away?

In name, yes, but, in practice, no. **Cortés** conquered and settled Tenochitlán (present-day Mexico City) after a fierce war with the natives, but the rest of Mexico, which was conquered only gradually, remained much the same after the arrival of the Spanish. The Maya in the south, for instance, were almost impossible to subdue, and the Spanish left them alone for quite a while. Similarly, the Chichimec of the north continued in their traditional ways almost uninterrupted by the Spanish.

How Did the Spanish Rule in Mexico?

The Spanish imposed Catholicism right away, aided by armies of missionaries imported to convert the Native Americans. The Spanish crown, aware of **Cortes**'s desire to become the new **Montezuma** of Mexico, quickly began curbing his personal power. A royal court, called an *audiencia,* was established in 1528 and the first viceroy, **Antonio de Mendoza,** was put into power. The early Spanish settlers and followers of Cortés were given *encomiendas,* or grants which gave them ownership and control over Native American land, labor, and produce.

The principal goal of the Spanish in Mexico was to mine for gold and, later, silver. This was the Native Americans' chief occupation, other than cultivating the land and supplying the early colonists with exquisite foods, beautiful women, and comfortable lodgings built in the Spanish style.

The establishment of the *encomiendas* was, in fact, the first codification of slavery. It entitled the Spanish to control the lives of the Native Americans by intensely feudal local governments. This type of rule by "trusteeships" gave birth much later to the formation of *ranchos,* or ranches, which operated almost like individual cities.

Many members of the clergy, such as Friar **Bartolomé de las Casas,** who was known as the "defender of the Indians," objected strongly to the *encomiendas.* The Native Americans themselves revolted against this control, both in 1541 and later in 1680, in the famous Popé Rebellion. **Popé** was a distinguished medicine man who launched a successful rebellion and attacked Spanish settlements, killing hundreds of people.

What Role Did Women Play in All This and Was There Such a Thing as a Conquistadora?

To begin with, unlike the early English settlers of Jamestown, the Spanish *conquistadors* brought no women with them. This was the fundamental reason for the swift interbreeding of the Spanish with the Native American populations and the emergence of the *mestizo,* or mixed, race that predominates not only in Mexico but throughout Latin America. Both the Spanish and the various Native American peoples had patriarchal systems, and women, by and large, were considered chattel.

Thus, decades later, when Spanish women began arriving in Mexico and the Americas, they were held accountable for the atrocities committed "at arm's length," although they themselves had nothing to do with the enslavement, forced conversions, and brutalization of Native Americans by their husbands, brothers, and fathers. That is not to say, of course, that Spanish women didn't share the belief in the white man's superiority over the Native American, or that they did not disdain Native American religions and dismiss their infinitely sophisticated cultures as primitive. They did, of course, in the same way most Englishwomen, while not participating actively in the decimation of Native Americans, seemed, on the whole, to hold with the general beliefs of their European society.

The following account, written by **Michele de Cuneo,** a member of **Columbus**'s second expedition, encapsulates the treatment of native women by the Spanish from the very beginning. It also provides a rare insight into the universality of both sexism and racism:

> While I was in the boat, I captured a very beautiful Carib woman, who the aforesaid Lord Admiral gave to me, and with whom, having brought her into my cabin,

and she being naked as is their custom, I conceived the desire to take my pleasure. I wanted to put my desire to execution, but she was unwilling for me to do so, and treated me with her nails in such wise that I would have preferred never to have begun. But seeing this (in order to tell you the whole event to the end), I took a rope-end and thrashed her well, following which she produced such screaming and wailing as would cause you not to believe your ears. Finally, we reached an agreement such that, I can tell you, she seemed to have been raised in a veritable school of harlots. (M. de Cuneo, *"Lettre a Annari,"* 28.10.1495. *Raccolta columbiana,* III, Vol. 2, pp. 95–107)

Not only is the nameless Native American woman taken against her will and raped, but, once subdued, she is called a whore. She has not only become the object of a double rape—sexual and racial—but she, like the Native American peoples themselves, once overpowered, is accused of liking and accepting the European form of "civilization" with the alacrity of a harlot.

Who Was La Malinche, How Did She Help the Spanish Win Mexico, and Why Do Some People Call Her the First Mexican Feminist?

La Malinche, whom the Amerindians called **Malintzin** and the Spanish called **Doña Marina,** played a key role in **Hernando Cortés**'s conquest of Mexico.

La Malinche was Aztec, but she had been sold as a slave to the Maya during one of **Montezuma**'s forays into southern Mexico. When the Spanish landed in Yucatán, she was in turn offered as a gift to them by the Maya. La Malinche's native tongue was Nahuatl, the language of Montezuma, but she spoke the Maya language as well.

Hernando Cortés liked her the minute he saw her and

took her as his mistress, although he also "offered" her to one of his lieutenants soon after he "received" her and, later, married her to another *conquistador.*

La Malinche stayed with Cortés from the time he departed the coast to the fall of the Aztec capital and, according to **Bernal Díaz del Castillo,** one of Cortes's chief soldiers, "Cortés could not understand the Indians without her." She spoke several Indian languages and learned Spanish in a matter of weeks. La Malinche interpreted for Cortés not only the Indian languages, but the native people's psyches. She served as ambassador and spokesperson during the fateful meeting between Cortés and Montezuma, when the latter was taken captive and his empire seized.

Some speculate that La Malinche persuaded Montezuma that his reign was over not only because she was in the service of Cortés, but because she held a grudge against the Aztec (her own people) for having sold her as a slave to the Maya in the first place.

In the minds of some historical revisionists, La Malinche is the first Mexican feminist, giving her original oppressors a taste of their own medicine. It is also thought that she may have saved thousands of Native Americans who otherwise might have gone to their deaths because she had enormous clout with the Spaniards. However, ever since they first sought their independence from Spain in 1810, Mexicans have regarded La Malinche as the symbol of betrayal and servile submission to the European invaders.

To this day countless myths revolve around La Malinche. One claims that she drowned her son when Cortés wanted to take the child back to Spain with him and leave her behind. Supposedly, La Malinche is still crying over it. She's been called "La Llorona" (the weeper), and rumors persist that her cries are heard all over the Southwest. In the late 1980s, a group of Chicano teenagers who were talking with their friends from public phones were reported to have heard the cries of La Llorona coming through the telephone lines. Their mothers banned them from using public phones.

NORTHERN EXPOSURE, OR HOW NEW MEXICO CAME TO BE KNOWN AS NUEVO MEXICO AND CALIFORNIANS AS CALIFORNIOS

What Did the Spanish Want with New Mexico?

President **John F. Kennedy** remarked when explaining our reason for space travel: "We choose to go to the moon and do these other things, not because they are easy, but because they are hard." The Spanish, too, began a northern *conquista* not because it was easy, but because it was hard. But, as usual, there were other political and military considerations as well.

All in all, it took the Spanish from 1530 to 1800 to complete their exploration and development of the northern territories—i.e., the land north of Mexico. The principal regions of Spanish settlement were New Mexico, Texas, and California, although parts of the territories they claimed extended to present-day Arizona, Colorado, Nebraska, and Oklahoma.

In 1528, **Pánfilo de Narváez** set sail for Florida. His expedition ended in complete disaster, but **Álvar Núñez Cabeza de Vaca,** one of the handful of survivors of his shipwrecked group, wandered on foot for eight years across the southwestern United States and northern Mexico before he finally met up with his fellow *conquistadors* in central Mexico. When he got there, he brought news that changed the course of history in the Southwest.

As a result of his dealings with the native populations, Cabeza de Vaca had experienced a remarkable spiritual awakening that gave him an entirely new outlook on life and on so-called "different" peoples. But this aspect of his discovery was of no interest to the gold-hungry, Eurocentric Spanish of the time.

What did cause a great stir in his reports (written in the form of letters to the King of Spain) was the fact that while wandering naked, hungry, and alone at the mercy of "savages," Cabeza de Vaca was told about the fabulous Seven Cities of Gold (Cibola). This prompted **Fray Marcos de Niza** in 1539, **Francisco Vásquez de Coronado** in 1540, and **Hernando de Soto** in 1541 to begin exploring the Southwest in earnest. None of them found Cibola or gold, but they did find a most charming land populated by the various Pueblo Indians.

Subsequently, rich silver mines were discovered in Michoacán, Zacatecas, San Luis Potosí, and Guanajuato, all near Mexico City. These discoveries spurred the Spanish to give up the idea of conquering the Southwest for the next fifty years.

What Did Cabeza de Vaca Do That Was So Revolutionary?

Shipwrecked, naked, and hungry, the mighty *conquistador* **Álvar Núñez Cabeza de Vaca** was captured by Pueblo Indians living along the Gulf of Mexico and in what is today New Mexico and Texas. Since the Pueblo believed the white man possessed divine powers, Cabeza de Vaca was ordered to heal the sick in exchange not only for food, but for his life. At first, he argued that he was a soldier and could not perform such "supernatural" feats.

But under penalty of death, he fell on his knees and prayed sincerely and earnestly for the recovery of the sick. Amazingly, the sick were healed. He was then taken from town to town by the various Pueblo Indians to perform his "miracles." In the process, Cabeza de Vaca was transformed from a bloody soldier into a mystic and a lover of the Pueblo people.

He wrote the King of Spain in his *Naufragios* (*Shipwrecks,* 1542) that he realized what he was doing was nothing more than practicing primitive Christianity and its lost element of healing—something which the strictly priestly and hierarchical Catholic Church of his time considered heretical. In fact, the *iluminados,* or mystics, had been burned at the stake by the Spanish Inquisition right along with the Moors and the Jews, for having unauthorized religious experiences.

Even more startling, perhaps, than his healings and his bold confessions to the king were the following lines: "I said to Andrés, 'if we reach Spain, I shall petition His Majesty to return me to this land, with a troop of soldiers. And I shall teach the world how to conquer by gentleness, not by slaughter.' "

What Was the Northwest Passage and What Did Sir Francis Drake Have to Do with the Spanish Conquista of the Southwest?

The Northwest Passage, a route from Europe to Asia through the northern extremities of North America, eluded European navigators for centuries. It was the carrot in front of the donkey for Englishmen, Frenchmen, and others who sought an easy route to China, bypassing the New World altogether. However, it was not until the twentieth century that a Scandinavian navigator named **Roald Amundsen** was actually able to traverse the Northwest Passage by following the Canadian coast westward. This route has been deemed impractical, since the northern waters remain icebound most of the year.

In the late 1570s, the famed English privateer **Sir Francis Drake** sailed through the Straits of Magellan, up the west coast of South and North America, across the Pacific, and around the world. The Spanish were sure that Drake had at long last found the mythical Northwest Passage, which in those days was believed to lie just north of Mexico.

The Spanish crown immediately decided to protect Spanish territorial interests by at last settling the Southwest. In 1598 **Juan de Oñate** led a large expedition northward and founded San Gabriel de los Españoles (known today as Chamita). It was nine years before the English would settle Jamestown.

In 1609, the Spanish established Santa Fe de San Francisco, an area covering present-day New Mexico, as well as parts of Arizona, Colorado, Texas, Nebraska, and Oklahoma.

Besides the Pueblo Peoples, Who Were the Real First Settlers of the Southwest?

Since Drake had not, after all, discovered the Northwest Passage, the only reasons the Spanish saw for settling New Mexico were, first, the small amounts of mineral wealth that had been discovered in the area, and, second, the need to Christianize the Pueblo. The Spanish took the latter mission very much to heart.

Thus, with the help of the Nahua-speaking Indians, Native Americans and *mestizos* from the Mexican territory accompanied the Spanish priests and *conquistadors* as soldiers and settlers into New Mexico, and settled the Spanish territories of the Southwest.

These native peoples and *mestizos* actually played the most important role in settling the American Southwest, since "uncivilized" frontier towns did not seem attractive places "fit to live" to the white ruling classes. By one of many twists of fate, the wife of the first governor of the province of Nuevo Mexico, **Juan de Oñate,** was actually the great-granddaughter of the Emperor **Montezuma II.**

A century later, twenty-one missions had been established, with some ninety thousand Indians concentrated in approximately ninety villages. In addition, countless numbers of settlements sprang up along the Upper Rio Grande. One of these settlements, established in 1680, was Nuestra Señora del Pilar del Paso del Río del Norte. Today, it is Ciudad Juárez, just across the river from El Paso, Texas.

Thus, Spanish rule, culture, and religion were firmly established throughout the present-day American Southwest. Along the way, the Spanish built or re-created towns and villages in their own image with the help of the Native Americans and *mestizos* whom they had brought from central Mexico. The *conquistadors* made it a practice to rename each town they settled with the Spanish name of a Catholic saint.

A Brief Historical Footnote, or So Much for Missionary Zeal

During the Mexican Revolution of 1910, when Mexican Native Americans stormed Catholic churches and overturned religious statues, much the same way the early Spanish missionaries had smashed the Aztec gods centuries earlier, small sculptures of the native Mexican gods were found encrusted in the statues of the Roman Catholic saints. It seemed that, rather than conversion, a type of cultural and religious syncretism had been going on from the very beginning.

DID THE SPANISH GO TO TEXAS OR CALIFORNIA FIRST?

Parlez-Vous *Texan? No Way!*

In 1582, a Frenchman named **La Salle** sailed down the Mississippi and began the French crown's efforts to establish a colony at the mouth of the river. French interest in the area led the Spanish to establish a mission on the Neches River in Texas. The following year Texas was made a Spanish province, and then six missions and a *presidio,* or fortress, were founded. By 1718, San Antonio de Bexar was settled. (Today San Antonio is the hometown of former mayor **Henry Cisneros,** President **Bill Clinton**'s secretary of housing and urban development.)

Expansion and settlements by the Spanish all across Texas aggravated long-existing conflicts between the French and the Spanish. Finally, the question was settled in 1763, when Spain acquired Louisiana from France and kissed the French *adieu*—until 1800, when Louisiana was ceded back to France in a series of maneuvers that were ultimately to end Spanish ownership of most of the Southwest.

"Texas," incidentally, means "a red tile or terra-cotta roof," such as you find in early Spanish colonial architecture. But the name is also thought to derive from a Pueblo Indian word meaning "friends." The letter "x" in the word "Texas" (and in "Mexico") was pronounced like an "h" in the seventeenth century. Subsequently, the Spanish abandoned the letter "x" for "j." Thus, the Spanish, Native American, and *mestizo* settlers of Texas called themselves Tejanos.

Who Were the Californios?

In the 1760s, word came to the Spanish king that the Russians were coming southward from Alaska and that the English had suddenly acquired a great yen for the Pacific coast. In typical fashion for a European empire of the time, the Spanish hastened to settle California. The first expedition was led by **Junípero Serra** and **Gaspar de Portolá** from Baja California. Father Serra was appointed to establish missions (his first being San Diego de Alcala in 1769), while Portolá's job was to found the Presidio of Monterey the following year. By 1823, twenty-one new missions had been added to Baja California, and three presidios and three towns were established between Baja California and San Francisco Bay. The early settlers of California, who were mostly either Caucasians of Spanish descent or *mestizos,* were called Californios.

Both the Tejanos and the Californios were farmers and ranchers, whereas the early Spanish and Native American settlers of New Mexico and the surrounding southwest territories were mostly miners and missionaries. Besides *mestizos,* Native Americans, and Caucasians, there was also a population of mulattoes (partly Caucasian and partly of African descent) who came to California. These mulattoes were the by-product of the slave trade the Spanish had introduced into the Americas between the sixteenth and the nineteenth century, particularly in the Caribbean.

The first Franciscan mission was founded in California in 1769—at San Diego de Alcala—by Father Junípero Sierra. During the next fifty-four years, a string of twenty-one missions, ranging all the way from Sonoma, just north of present-day San Francisco, to San Diego, were founded. Many of these missions still exist today, both as religious sites and as tourist attractions.

MEXICO VS. SPAIN

In 1775, the English colonies led a successful revolt against European control. By 1810, the Mexican *criollos,* or Creoles (native-born citizens of Spanish descent), were ready to do the same.

Early on, when American revolutionaries started organizing strategic battles against the English, they turned to England's ancient rivals, France and Spain, for support. The Spanish governor of Louisiana, **Bernardo de Gálvez,** sold munitions to the American rebels and allowed them to cross Spanish Louisiana and use the port at New Orleans. Many of Gálvez's militiamen were actually Mexican *criollos,* and most

of the money to help the early American revolutionaries
came from Mexico.

Where Did Spain Go Wrong?
(Don't Blame It All on the Spanish Armada!)

Latinos throughout the United States, Spain, and Latin
America tend to view the English and American explanation
for the eventual decline of Spain as another example of naive historical jingoism. For centuries, Anglo historians have
argued that if the Spanish Armada had not been defeated
by **Queen Elizabeth**'s English "sea dogs" in 1588, under **Sir
Francis Drake**'s command, Spain would not have gone down-
hill as a world power a century later.

But the reasons for Spain's fall from power—and for England's loss of its colonies, for that matter—are so varied and
complicated that they cannot be explained away by gloating
over a single victory at sea.

By the late 1700s, the Age of Reason was dawning in Europe and the Americas. Absolute control of distant lands by
monarchies was being seriously questioned. As early as the
seventeenth century, the Spanish economy had begun to collapse as a result of economic inflation caused in part by mis-
management and in part by the very wealth Spain had
amassed from its American colonies at the height of its powers. There were also extreme economic burdens involved in
governing more than half a hemisphere a whole ocean away.

Disease and overwork had reduced the Native American
population of New Spain from 11 million or more in 1520 to
a mere million. The cattle and sheep the Spanish had imported to the Americas, in an effort to develop ranching,
drank all the irrigation water and left the Native American
population unable to grow adequate food. Without people
to mine the silver and ore deposits or cultivate the land,

there was little Spain could do to reverse the recession that had gripped its enormous empire.

There were still more contributors to the downfall of Spain in Mexico—as in the rest of its colonies: social unrest, racial tensions, and, of course, the chorus of voices calling for freedom.

So What Was the Defeat of the Spanish Armada All About?

Simply put, **Philip II,** King of Spain, was a zealous Catholic who viewed the English Protestant Reformation with aversion. He also viewed **Queen Elizabeth I** of England, the Protestant queen, not only as a preposterous heretic, but as a military rival who might just be fixing to give him trouble with his American colonies. So, in 1588, Philip II threw his support to the Catholic **Mary, Queen of Scots,** Elizabeth's British rival.

Elizabeth seized the moment to turn her "sea dogs" loose to raid and destroy the Spanish treasure ships. The Spanish Armada (or "Armed Navy") fought back valiantly, but was masterfully defeated by the English. This single act, although it caused great psychological damage and cost a great deal of money, did not by any means break the rich Spanish bank or terminate Spanish power in Mexico or the rest of the Americas. It took another century and a great deal of internal social and political unrest to finally topple Spain—and the English had little to do with it.

What Was the Grito de Dolores?

The fundamental reasons for the Mexican Revolution of 1810 had perhaps as much to do with Spain's internal economic troubles as with the social and economic injustices that had plagued Mexico from the beginning of Spanish domination.

In 1541, there had been a major uprising led by the Zacatecas Indians in protest of the brutal treatment by the Spanish of the Native American tribes of Michoacán, Jalisco, Nayarit, and Sinaloa. The battle was fierce, and the Spanish, although they emerged the winners, lost hundreds of men. The final battle, fought in the Mixton hills, near the city of Guadalajara, resulted in the elimination or enslavement of most of the rebellious Native Americans. However, this act of suppression itself led to greater discontent and a stronger resolve on the part of the native populations to get rid of Spain.

Even more critical than the Native Americans to the success of the Mexican independence movement was the group known as *los criollos.*

The Mexican *criollos* (American-born persons of Spanish parentage) had felt great discrimination by the Spanish, not only in the form of "taxation without representation," which had also plagued the Americans in the English colonies, but in the form of rampant social discrimination. *Criollos* seldom got the top jobs; the best lands were always reserved for the Spanish-born rulers, who also had the last word when it came to local governmental affairs. Even though they were Caucasian, the *criollos* were looked upon as second-class citizens—higher than the Native Americans and *mestizos,* but lower than the *peninsulares* (Spaniards).

On September 16, 1810, **Father Miguel Hidalgo y Costillo,** a *criollo* and pastor of a small village called Dolores, uttered the famous Grito de Dolores (Cry of Dolores), which ignited Mexico's revolution for independence. "Long live our lady of Guadalupe!" he cried in the town square. "Down with bad government! Down with the Spaniards!"

The *mestizos,* or people of mixed Native American and Spanish parentage, who had been aggressively discriminated against, emerged as a catalytic social force in Mexico. Led by Father Hidalgo, fifty thousand Native Americans and *mestizos* captured Mexico City. In Morelia, south of Mexico City, **Father José María Morelos y Pavón,** a *mestizo* himself, called a congress and declared Mexican independence in November 1813.

Eventually, Morelos was captured and executed, and a loyalist government held sway for a while, but in 1823 the patriot **Antonio López de Santa Anna** deposed the loyalist government and took control. Santa Anna would become a main player in the Texas secessionist movement of 1836, as well as in the war with the United States and, later, in the Gadsden Purchase in 1853, when Santa Anna sold southern Arizona to the United States for ten million dollars.

THE ANGLO CONNECTION

When Did the Anglos and the Mexicans First Meet?

Although the exhortation "Go west, young man" became popular much later for Americans in search of their own El Dorado, the westward movement of English-speaking people had begun as early as the English settlements themselves. As the lands along the Eastern Seaboard were added to the English crown, the new English colonists began moving their wagons west to places like Ohio, Indiana, and Kentucky.

When the U.S. government purchased Louisiana from the French (who had purchased it from the Spanish) for $15 million in May 1803, the United States instantly doubled in size. At that point, only two thousand miles of Spanish territory separated the aggressive young nation from the consummation of a dream in the making—Manifest Destiny, the eventual occupation of the entire continent.

President **Thomas Jefferson** believed that all rivers and seas should be free for people of all nations to travel on. He confronted Spain and won the rights to travel down the Mississippi River for Americans from Kentucky and other parts of the United States. This simple right eventually became a symbol of Anglo expansionism.

During Jefferson's time, beaver furs, used in men's hats, were in great demand, and beaver was plentiful all along the Upper Rio Grande in New Mexico. Around 1790, mountain men from Kentucky began entering New Mexico to trap as much beaver as they could. They trapped without licenses and traveled where they pleased. Often, their loot was confiscated—but no matter, they kept coming back to Taos for more, year after year. These frontier beaver trappers were dirty-looking, bearded, and uncouth; they cussed and spat and picked fights willy-nilly. Often, the Native Americans and *mestizos* took perfumed cloths to their noses just to stand next to them. Thus began the first contact between the Spanish-Mexican and the Anglo. To the Mexican, the frontier Anglo seemed a lawless, violent man, who loved to shoot, drink, and wreak havoc.

What Was the Santa Fe Trail?

After the trappers (eventually beaver hats, like all fashion, fell out of favor) came the merchants, who foresaw a new and untapped market in New Mexico. These traveling salesmen needed to find an easy route from Missouri to Santa Fe that would allow them to enter New Mexico without being spotted by Spanish authorities, who considered them interlopers.

By coming down from the north rather than from the east, these merchants sneaked into Spanish territory undetected with wagons full of goods—from snake oil to women's underwear. As early as 1773, a man named **John Peyton** followed the trail. Then, in 1806, Captain **Zebulon Pike** led a large mounted expedition, and the famous Santa Fe Trail was officially born.

How Did the Santa Fe Traders Lead the Way to Anglo Expansionism?

After the Mexican Revolution, the new Mexican government, unlike the Spanish crown, eased restrictions on commerce with foreign countries. This, of course, included the United States. Suddenly the Santa Fe Trail became the highway of opportunity. Business boomed for the Anglo-Americans. They had hit pay dirt in a territory badly in need of essential goods that the fledgling Mexican government could not supply. The first official Anglo traders in New Mexico had come with only $5,000 worth of merchandise. By 1846, the trade from Santa Fe was estimated at about $1 million.

Exotic and essential goods were not all the Anglo-Americans carried with them. They brought new fashions and exciting and innovative ways of looking at the world. Unlike the beaver hunters, these Easterners dressed well and were generally well mannered. New Mexicans welcomed them with open arms. However, Anglos also harbored certain prejudices, which would eventually surface and create a painful rift between the two groups. Almost immediately, the traders adopted a superior attitude toward the native peoples, whom they considered lazy and uncivilized. They displayed the same attitudes toward New Mexicans that the Spanish had shown to the Native Americans three centuries before, and treated them as childlike, inferior human beings who needed to be taught the ways of the world.

As more Anglos began pouring into New Mexico and, in some cases, married and stayed for good, the Mexican government began to worry about the long-term effects of so much foreign influence on a territory so far away from Mexico City. President **Antonio López de Santa Anna** outlawed the trade between Anglos and New Mexicans. But by then it was too late. The people, who had grown used to their new way of life and loved the excitement of their rich marketplace, protested loudly, and Santa Anna was forced to re-scind the law in 1844. The residents of New Mexico were be-ginning to feel separate from their government to the south, and Anglo economic domination of New Mexico, begun by the merchants on the Santa Fe Trail, was a done deal. There was no turning back.

What Exactly Was Manifest Destiny?

In the summer of 1845, an article appeared in the *United States Magazine and Democratic Review* that served to put into words what the citizens of the young American republic were already feeling. The anonymous author held that "our man-ifest destiny overspread the continent allotted by Providence for the free development of our multiplying millions."

In a nutshell, Manifest Destiny was an Anglo-American version of the national supremacy theory, and gave Ameri-cans permission to stretch U.S. territory from the Atlantic to the Pacific. The phrase took, and so did the sentiment. Politicians from both the Republican and the Democratic parties used the words "Manifest Destiny" in articles and speeches everywhere, and felt as full of zeal and purpose as the Spanish *conquistadors*.

The acquisition of Mexican territory after the Mexican War (1846–48), the dispute with England over the bounda-ries of Oregon, and the purchase of Alaska in 1867 all seemed to help fulfill Manifest Destiny. The more extreme exponents of Manifest Destiny even spoke of going as far north as the Arctic Circle and as far south as Tierra del Fuego.

Several Mexican observers have remarked that, looked at in a different way, Manifest Destiny could have been called "Mexican Fate," since the country that suffered the most from it was Mexico. More than half of Mexico's territory lay between the Pacific Ocean and the American frontier.

HOW TEXAS WAS WON—OR LOST

Who Was Stephen F. Austin and Why Is He Called the Father of Texas?

Stephen F. Austin (1793–1836) was an American frontiersman with a special interest in Texas. His father, **Moses Austin,** had asked for and been granted permission by the Spanish government in 1818 to settle Anglo-Americans in Texas. He requested on his deathbed that his son Stephen carry out his wishes. In 1823, the Mexican governnment gave Stephen Austin permission to establish a settlement in Texas, provided he and his American colonists obeyed all Mexican laws, became Mexican citizens, converted to Catholicism, and did not allow slavery within their borders.

Austin gave each family interested in farming the land 177 acres. Stock raisers were entitled to 4,428 acres—and most of his "recruits" were ranchers. Austin took almost 100,000 acres for himself as a reward for organizing the territory. The first group settled in the best lands along the Bernard, Colorado, and Brazos rivers. There were only 300 men at the start—women and children were listed as chattel, so in effect they did not count—but within ten years the number of Americans living in Texas as Mexican citizens grew to about 50,000. The proportion of Mexican citizens, however, remained at around 10 percent, a paltry few in comparison to the 50,000 Anglo-Americans, since Mexicans had not migrated to Texas in large numbers either before or after Mexican independence. The Apache, Caddo, and Comanche tribes that had inhabited Texas since the Middle American prehistoric times had been vastly reduced in numbers, but they remained a threat to Anglo colonization for years to come.

The Anglo-Texans did not always abide strictly by Mexican law. Many, including Austin, disregarded the rules against slavery and brought in hundreds of African-Americans to work the cotton fields.

As far back as 1827, the United States had shown interest in Texas and had offered Mexico $1 million for the territory, but the Mexican government responded by imposing tighter controls on the Texans and passing strict anti-Anglo laws, taxing only American-owned ships on the Rio Grande. In 1830 the fires were stoked further when General **Manuel de Meir y Terán** led a group of soldiers into Texas with the purpose of expelling Stephen Austin and all the Americans in his colony. The effort was unsuccessful, but the seeds of animosity between the Texan Anglos and the Mexican government grew.

By 1832, Texas was in total rebellion. Its citizens—both Anglos and Mexicans—did not want to secede from Mexico, but they wanted to establish a separate state within the Mexican federation. Up until then, Texas belonged to the larger Coahuila territory, but its citizens had begun to view themselves as inhabitants of a separate region.

A key factor in the Texas statehood movement on the part of the Anglo-American population was the fact that neither the Mexican constitution nor the Coahuila-Texas constitution granted such "inalienable" rights as trial by jury or the right to bail. Another major objection was that in order to become Texas residents, the Anglos were expected to convert to Catholicism, and most of them were Protestants.

When Texans applied for statehood at an 1833 Mexican convention, President **Santa Anna** misinterpreted their actions as a request for complete independence. Even after the confusion was cleared up, Santa Anna was so incensed that he refused to grant any of their wishes. Instead, he jailed Stephen Austin for eighteen months for simply asking. When Austin returned to Texas, he gave a speech demanding complete secession from Mexico. It was the bugle call that heralded the beginning of Texas independence.

Who Won at the Alamo?

The Mexicans won. The Texans lost.

Why Should We Remember the Alamo, Anyway?

Driven by the winds of independence, **William B. Travis,** one of **Stephen Austin'**s men, stormed the customs garrison at Anahuac during the fateful summer of 1835. Some months later, another group of Texans seized the garrison at Goliad, which contained valuable supplies. Finally, on December 5, Texan armies, made up of both Anglos and Mexicans, raided a military supply depot at the Alamo Mission, and San Antonio, the most important city in Texas, fell into the hands of the rebels. The Mexican government was humiliated and forced to agree to Texan demands for independence.

But not for long. President **Santa Anna** took the revolt personally and decided to retaliate. He organized an army numbering in the thousands (anywhere from two thousand to five thousand, depending on the historical source) and prepared to attack Texas himself.

The Texan rebels, believing that Santa Anna would strike through the city of Matamoros, withdrew most of their men from the Alamo garrison and stationed them in Matamoros. On March 6, 1836, Santa Anna led his impressive army right into El Alamo territory, killing 182 Texans barricaded behind the mission walls.

The besieged Texan forces, under the command of William Travis, held on to the fort valiantly for five days. Among the defending Texan heroes were **Davy Crockett** and **James Bowie.** According to Mexican-American legend, though, Crockett was nothing more than a mercenary soldier whom the Mexicans captured and executed.

Santa Anna had won a great victory by his preemptive strike, but he was unaware that an enraged Texan army, led by the legendary **Sam Houston,** was on its way from Matamoros, armed to the teeth.

The Houston army caught up with Santa Anna's men at the San Jacinto River and Buffalo Bayou, shouting, "Remember the Alamo!" When the smoke cleared, 600 of Santa Anna's men had been killed; only 6 Texans died in the battle. Santa Anna was imprisoned for six months and later forced out of office by the Mexican government for humiliating his country. (Much later, he was put back into office—a turnabout not uncommon in early Mexican politics.)

Independence had been won and Texas became the Lone Star State, a state without a country, under its newly elected president and war hero, Sam Houston.

Why Do Mexican-Americans Object to "Remember the Alamo"?

Once **Santa Anna** stormed the Alamo and killed the 182 Texans, Anglo hatred against Mexico and anything Mexican exploded with a vengeance, and the seeds of ethnic prejudice and intolerance that had been seething underground sprouted like prickly cactus across the Texan landscape. Suddenly, Mexicans who had been living within Texas's borders for hundreds of years were viewed as Santa Anna Mexicans. They had become the enemy within. The Mexican victory in El Alamo had wrought a great loss.

Over time, the phrase "Remember the Alamo!" became not so much a reminder of an old war cry, but a warning to Texans of Mexican descent. Ironically, most Texan-Mexicans had sided with **Sam Houston** all along, and had fought and died for Texan independence. The great majority believed the Mexican government had turned against them and had ignored their demands. They had pinned their hopes on the

Anglos, who, they believed, understood the needs of this vast, proud, and complicated land called Tejas.

What Role Did African-Americans Play in the History of Texas?

In March 1836, the United States, as well as Great Britain, Holland, France, and Belgium, immediately recognized the Texan republic as an independent nation. But even at the outset, it was hard for the young republic to survive on its own. For one, the Mexican government kept remembering the Alamo too, and raids were continually organized against Texan cities, particularly Goliad, San Antonio, and Nacogdoches, the three cities most heavily populated by Anglos.

In addition, the Apache and other tribes had declared war against the new Anglo *conquistadors* and commanded effective attacks that often claimed lives and valuable property. The Texan government also had vast financial troubles. The solution seemed clear to most of the Anglo-Texans: become part of the United States. In September 1836, Texans voted for annexation.

But there was a hitch. At that point in U.S. history, the issue of slavery weighed heavily in the balance. The states were evenly divided—50 percent in favor of slavery ("slave states") and 50 percent against. Since most of the Texan Anglo settlers came from Southern states and owned slaves themselves, Texas would tip the scale.

The battle was waged valiantly for ten long years, and during those years abolitionists managed to keep Texas out. However, on December 29, 1845, the U.S. Congress admitted Texas as the twenty-eighth state in the Union, with slavery permitted in its state constitution. In 1861, Texas would secede from the Union, but by March 30, 1870, it was readmitted after agreeing to ratify the thirteenth, fourteenth, and fifteenth amendments to the U.S. Constitution, which banned slavery and protected the rights of former slaves and all people of color.

THE MEXICAN-AMERICAN WAR

Why Did We Fight with Mexico, Anyway?

In March 1845, Mexico broke off diplomatic relations with the United States on the grounds that the annexation of Texas was an act of hostility toward Mexico. This was more a symbolic gesture that underscored the long-standing animosity between the two countries than an open invitation to war—but it served to raise the temperature on both sides. The United States was in the throes of Manifest Destiny fever, seeking to acquire California and other northwest territories by hook or by crook. Mexico, on the other hand, was feeling the mighty U.S. Army closing in on its borders.

In the meantime, a coup d'état in Mexico brought to power a nationalist dictator, General **Mariano Paredes y Arillaga.** The Paredes government scoffed when the United States sent a diplomat to Mexico and offered him $25 million for a Rio Grande boundary with all the lands west to the Pacific Ocean.

President **James Polk** reacted with the full zeal of Manifest Destiny. He ordered General **Zachary Taylor,** who had been stationed in Texas with a volunteer army as a show of force against the Mexican government, to proceed across the Rio Grande.

How Did the Mexican Stand-Off Get Its Name?

General **Zachary Taylor** arrived at the Rio Grande in March 1846. The Mexican Army, instead of attacking the invader, decided to wait and see what General Taylor's men were up to. Both armies settled down, facing each other across the river, examining each other, measuring each other's military capabilities. After a while, they played a cat-and-mouse game, shouting insults back and forth across the river and even joking. It was a war of nerves, with each side goading the other to react. Thus, the phrase "Mexican stand-off," meaning a confrontation that neither side can win, entered our vocabulary to stay.

If All Taylor Had Was a Small Volunteer Army, How Did the United States Win the War?

At first, the Mexicans, led by General **Pedro de Ampudia,** were confident of a swift victory. They were three times more in number and better trained than the paltry volunteer U.S. Army made up of adventurers, vagabonds, and escaped criminals. On April 23, 1846, war was officially declared and General Ampudia arrived in Matamoros demanding that the Americans retreat to the Nueces River.

But the United States was to invest unprecedented effort in what it called a "little war." Congress, in declaring war, authorized the formation of an army of 50,000 men and appropriated $10 million. There was no contest. By August 24, 1847—scarcely a year and a half after the famous Mexican stand-off—an armistice was announced. In the process, Mexico had lost Texas, New Mexico, and California, as well as present-day Arizona, Nevada, Utah, and half of Colorado.

Was Abraham Lincoln a War Dodger and Did Ralph Waldo Emerson Really Go to Jail for Opposing the Mexican-American War?

Yes on both counts. Both **Abraham Lincoln** and **Ulysses S. Grant** protested that the war against Mexico was unjust, based on the belief that a powerful nation should not flex its muscles at a weak one. Lincoln was a young man at the time, and refused to serve in an army that would "unfairly" fight the Mexicans.

Ralph Waldo Emerson went to jail rather than pay taxes to support the war effort. It was reported that when his friend **Henry David Thoreau** asked Emerson what he was doing in jail, Emerson replied by asking Thoreau what he was doing out of jail.

But in spite of organized efforts on the part of thinkers, patriots, and philosophers in the United States, the expansionist sentiment won the day and Mexico lost more than half its land to its eastern neighbor.

What Was the Treaty of Guadalupe Hidalgo?

The Treaty of Guadalupe Hidalgo (1848) was the formal agreement between Mexico and the United States which effectively turned over Texas, New Mexico, California, Arizona, Nevada, Utah, and half of Colorado to the United States. By a single stroke of the pen, Mexico lost 50 percent of its national territory, and the United States acquired a large group of new citizens who remained in their homeland and yet found themselves smack in the middle of a country whose laws, political and social institutions, and fundamentally WASP traditions were alien to them.

A crucial part of the treaty concerned the fate of the Mexican-Americans living in ceded U.S. territory. Mexican-Americans were given a year to decide whether they wanted to retain Mexican citizenship or become U.S. citizens. At the time of the treaty, nearly eighty thousand Mexican citizens living in the new American territory became U.S. citizens, and about two thousand moved below the Rio Grande in order to retain their Mexican citizenship.

Article IX of the treaty also specifically provided that Mexican-Americans living in the new U.S. territories would have the right of worship and that their property rights would be fully protected. Typical of the total disregard for

Native Americans at that time, no mention was made of the civil or political rights of the native peoples living in their ancient lands, who had previously been granted full rights of citizenship under Mexican law.

Another important provision of the treaty dealt with the real and personal property of Mexicans. It stipulated that the U.S. government would guarantee that the Mexican-Americans would retain their title to all property, together with rights of disposal and inheritance.

What Was Wrong with the Treaty of Guadalupe Hidalgo?

On the surface, the treaty, which was ratified by the U.S. Senate on March 10, 1848, seemed fair by the standards of the day. But the treaty signed by the Mexicans was not the same treaty eventually ratified by the United States, since most important paragraphs that did not suit certain U.S. senators were simply deleted without consultation. Even more to the point, the treaty failed to address the protection of social institutions that were a vital part of the Mexican-American tradition. And since no effort was made toward acculturation or assimilation of new peoples in the American Southwest into the United States in those days, the Mexicans remained an insular, marginalized group for many decades. In addition, the Anglo-Americans were disdainful of the Mexican system of property laws, with its lack of surveys and propensity for failing to register grants legally.

In utter disregard for Mexican traditions and the Treaty of Guadalupe Hidalgo, the new Anglo settlers ousted Mexican grantees from the most desirable lands, claiming that the new order gave them a right to homestead vacant lands. These lands, usually near water, were the most desirable agricultural parcels.

The Anglos also felt justified in taking over native property when, confused by a complicated Anglo-Saxon system of property laws, the Mexicans were unable to produce adequate proof of ownership, even when they had occupied their lands and their houses for many generations.

Aside from the myriad cultural differences that led to inevitable clashes between the two cultures in the postwar era, one single factor stands out: The new American frontiersmen believed in good old "rugged individualism" and in treating the land as "gains" for individual profit. According to Spanish-Mexican tradition (which, incidentally, was also in keeping with the native peoples' philosophy), individual rights were subordinate to the general interest of the community, and verbal agreements and long-standing traditions were as binding as legal documents.

As far back as the landing of **Cortés,** the Spanish had been astonished to discover the great "generosity" of the native peoples, who thought of the land as belonging to everyone (or no one), rather than to individual persons. This communal tradition was part of the *mestizo* and *criollo* way. It came to an abrupt end when the Anglos started claiming territories and building fences.

What Was the Gadsden Treaty and Why Did the Mexicans Say They Needed It Like a Hole in the Head?

In 1853, **James Gadsden** was sent to Mexico by the U.S. government to settle all final and minor territorial disputes between the two countries. President **Santa Anna** was once again in power and his government was badly in need of cash. The Gadsden Treaty ratified the U.S. purchase of a strip of land south of the Gila River. Ironically, this territory included the town of Mesilla, which had been founded by Mexicans who had opted to leave their lands in the Southwest when the United States won the Mexican-American war.

The Gadsden Treaty covered a number of other issues, such as the rights of Americans to cross the Isthmus of Tehuantepec and the reestablishment of commerce between the United States and Mexico. It also amended the Treaty of Guadalupe Hidalgo by reducing the money the United States had agreed to pay Mexico from $15 million to $10 million. By paying Mexico $5 million in claims for Native American damages resulting from protests on the part of native peoples against the loss of their homeland territories to the U.S. government, the United States secured the release of Article XI of the Treaty of Guadalupe Hidalgo, which made it liable for Native American raids on Mexico. The Gadsden Treaty did, however, reaffirm the civil rights of Mexican-Americans and guarantee their land titles—a covenant which, practically speaking, was not entirely heeded.

The Mexicans had no choice but to accept Gadsden's proposal, for to reject it would have meant another costly war and another defeat. So, much as it was touted as the treaty that finally ended the Mexican-American conflict, most Mexicans believed they needed the Gadsden Treaty like a hole in the head.

What Was the Bear Flag Revolt and How Did the Californios Feel About Joining the United States?

Like Texas and New Mexico, California had been receiving a large influx of Anglo-American immigrants. A formidable landmass lay between California and Mexico (there were no jets or even railroad lines in those days, and many mountains to cross). And the fertile California soil, in which the Spanish Franciscan monks had grown grapes and rich varieties of vegetables as far back as the sixteenth century, made California seem like a separate entity even before Mexico severed its ties with Spain.

During the Mexican war of independence against Spain,

many Californios sided with the Spanish monarchy, fearing that once Mexico became a separate country, the Mexicans might encroach on their independent way of living.

The first Anglo-American immigrants who came to California became an integral part of Spanish-speaking California society. Many married into Californio families, became Mexican citizens, and, in general, helped form the bedrock of pre–Mexican War California. Then, in the early 1840s, a new group of Anglos began arriving via the Oregon Trail. These newcomers brought their families, refused to become Mexican citizens, and began settling remote areas, far from Mexican supervision. They were inspired by Manifest Destiny, and lent the spark for the rebellion that broke out in California just before the Mexican-American war.

That rebellion was the Bear Flag Revolt, and its flag depicting a bear, which is still flown in California, became the symbol of anti-Mexican sentiment. **John Charles Frémont,** a U.S. Army captain who was in California on a "reconnaissance" mission, seized command of this disorganized revolt and signaled the U.S. government that California was ready to break with Mexico. This sentiment, incidentally, was felt by both Anglos and Mexican-Americans, who believed California would do much better on its own, or backed by the mint and might of the U.S. government.

When war with Mexico erupted, the Californios quickly flew the Stars and Stripes right next to their bear flag. Soon after, Commodore **John Sloat** and, later, **Robert Stockton,** took control of the area. There was one minor hitch during this transition which foretold potential animosity between the Anglo and Mexican groups here too. Stockton placed an insensitive captain named **Archibald Gillespie** in command of California. Gillespie disregarded Mexican-Spanish traditions in the area and imposed all sorts of restrictive regulations that led the Southern Californios to start a revolt of their own.

However, in view of the developments of the Mexican

War, peace was negotiated with the Southern Californios under the Treaty of Cahuenga in 1847, and California cheered when the Treaty of Guadalupe Hidalgo was signed. On September 9, 1850, California was admitted to the Union as the thirty-first state. It was ratified as a nonslavery state and, although there was much proslavery sentiment on the part of many Anglo residents of Southern California, the state remained part of the Union during the Civil War and was one of the states least affected by the war.

CALIFORNIA DREAMING

What Was the Gold Rush and How Did Mexico Miss Out on It by a Couple of Days?

As fate would have it, just as the United States and Mexico were negotiating the Treaty of Guadalupe Hidalgo, the very gold that had eluded both Spaniards and Mexicans for centuries turned up, unexpectedly and in such incredible quantities as to change the course of American history.

On January 24, 1848, a contractor named **James Marshall,** who was building a sawmill for **John Sutter**'s settlement in the Sacramento Valley, noticed some shiny yellow rocks along the millrace. He looked closer. What he found was not just a few gold nuggets, but the mother lode, the richest gold-bearing territory the world has ever known.

Sutter and Marshall decided to keep it a secret. They were greedy and hoped to keep the whole thing to themselves, but there were also important political considerations. They feared that if the news got out, Mexico would never agree to surrender its land—and they were probably right. After all, had not an entire hemisphere been fought and conquered, settled and resettled for gold and more gold?

A couple of days after the treaty was signed and Mexico had ceded its territories, the word spread like wildfire. Newspapers ran enormous headlines, and the discovery was reported in publications all around the globe. Men started coming from all over the world to claim their piece of the rock, which by all appearances seemed inexhaustible. By some accounts, the Californian population grew from 15,000 non–Native Americans in 1848 to 260,000 in 1852.

What Role Did Latinos Play in the Success of California Mining?

Ironically, the first miners who arrived in California were Peruvian and Chilean immigrants, who sailed up the Pacific coast and arrived in the summer of 1848. It seemed appropriate that descendants of the Inca, whose culture had both revered gold and been destroyed for it, would be the first Californian prospectors.

The Peruvians and Chileans were soon followed by miners from the Mexican state of Sonora, and later by Mexican-Americans from all over the Southwest. After that, Europeans and Anglo-Americans from the East began to head for California in droves, risking life and limb against Native American tribes, the elements, and the seemingly impassable mountains and plains.

The Anglo prospectors were strong, greedy men with firm resolve, and they soon outnumbered the Spanish-speaking immigrants who had preceded them. But they knew nothing about mining, so they had to turn for help to the Mexican-Americans and other Latino immigrants, who came from a long and distinguished mining tradition. The Spanish-speaking miners taught them what a *batea* was—a flat-bottomed pan with sloping sides, which they used to extract gold from the rivers and streams. They taught them how to use an *arrastra*—a mill that pulverized rock and made it possible to remove gold from quartz. And they taught them the ancient Spanish art of using mercury to refine the gold—a patio process which the Spaniards had devised to refine silver in northern Mexico three centuries before.

The success of California mining was owed directly to the sweat of the Mexican and South American miners. As a result, Spanish and Mexican traditions became part of California mining law. For example, the law that stated that a man's right to a property depended on the discovery and development of a mine, and not on purchase, had prevailed in Mexico from the beginning. (The law applied only to men, not to women, who had not yet and would not for many years to come have the right to own property anywhere north or south of the Rio Grande.)

It was this very concept of law which many Anglos used after the Mexican-American War to take away much of Mexican-Americans' property. If a Mexican-American could not show a deeded paper or a bill of sale, then the Anglo could decide that the land was not his after all. As far as California mining laws were concerned, though, just "staking a claim" was considered enough—the gold was yours for the taking.

Did Discrimination Start in the Gold Fields?

De facto discrimination, which was the direct result of prejudice, had existed in dozens of communities throughout the Southwest from the day the Anglo-Americans began arriving, but perhaps the first examples of institutionalized discrimination and segregation happened during the famous and infamous Gold Rush.

It appeared that as soon as the Anglo prospectors had learned mining skills from the Latinos in the area, they began resenting both the Latinos' know-how, which reminded the Anglos that they didn't know everything, after all, and their very presence, which might mean less gold for the Anglos.

Within a couple of years, the Anglos affirmed that since

California was American, all gold belonged to them, and not to the "Mexicans" (they called all Spanish-speaking people Mexicans in those days, even the Peruvians). The Mexicans objected. Soon the two groups separated, with the Mexicans and other Spanish-speaking groups settling in the southern part of the mother lode and the Anglos in the north. By and by, however, the Anglos began invading the southern mines. To lend them further support, California passed a law taxing all foreign miners heavily.

The Latinos protested and revolts broke out all over the mines. Many of those suffering discrimination were actually new Americans of Mexican descent, whose lands had been ceded during the recent war. But the Anglos prevailed because they were many more in number and because, as the Mexicans put it, they "stopped at nothing." During the ensuing years, dozens of Mexicans and other Latinos were lynched or otherwise murdered. Finally, many of the survivors gave up their rights to the gold and fled for their lives. Sadly, it was the first of many times when Mexican-Americans would meet bald-faced discrimination without legal recourse.

Was the California Constitution Drafted and Signed Exclusively by Anglos?

In spite of the trouble at the gold mines, many wealthy California ranchers of Spanish and Mexican descent had a great deal to do with the formation of California as a state separate from Mexico and with its entry into the Union on September 9, 1850. Among the delegates who helped draft the California state constitution were influential Mexican-Americans like **Pablo de la Guerra, Mariano Vallejo,** and **José Antonio Carillo.** Ironically, these men were able to get California into the Union faster than might otherwise have been possible because of the successful mining operations their fellow Latinos had started only two years before.

Allá en el Rancho Grande: *What Happened to the Mexican-American Cowboys?*

A popular Mexican folk song that lives on among Latinos to-day begins *"Allá en el rancho grande, allá donde vivía ..."* ("Back there on the big ranch, the place where I used to live ...") It's a song that celebrates life on the *rancho* (from which the word "ranch" is derived) and speaks to both sides of the border. It romanticizes a life in which big sombreros, beautiful *señoritas,* and wide-open spaces were the norm.

As a result of the Gold Rush, many Southern California towns became virtual ghost towns, with people leaving in record numbers to try their luck at a pot of gold. But at the same time, the *ranchos* flourished. An exploding Californian population meant people needed to be fed, and beef was the food of choice for most of the new and often suddenly rich citizens.

At their peak, Californian ranchers, many of whom were Mexican-American, could demand $100 a head for their cattle—not bad in the days when $100 could also buy you a whole house. These Californios adorned their houses lavishly in the manner of the early Spanish *hacendados* and ran their wide-open ranches like small fiefdoms. The Gold Rush had been good to them, if not to their less fortunate mining compatriots.

But the writing was on the wall. First, the cattle ranchers from the Plains began undercutting their prices and the demand for Californian cattle dwindled in a few years. Then, in 1861, sudden floods killed thousands of cattle. The floods were followed by two years of drought, which killed even more cattle.

As if these sudden catastrophes weren't enough, new anti-Mexican laws, which had begun taking root after the Mexican-American War, burgeoned. Whereas the Treaty of Guadalupe Hidalgo had recognized the legitimate land titles of Mexican-Americans, a new law, the Federal Land Grant Act of 1851, drafted with California very much in mind, ordered that all Spanish and Mexican land grants be presented for verification. All grants not submitted within two years would be automatically rendered null and void.

Since verification was a long and complicated process and most grants, established in the Spanish and Mexican traditions, were seldom recorded on paper and had been divided and subdivided as a result of centuries of inheritance, the Mexican-American ranchers had to forfeit much of their property. Adding insult to injury, the California Supreme Court upheld an English law of riparian water rights—i.e., single individuals, not communities, owned water rights—which meant that many a *ranchero* was forced to sell cheap or give up his land, because neighbors could dam up his water and parch his land as they pleased.

Very few *rancheros* were able to survive, and Anglo speculators bought their land for a song. Thus, scores of Mexican-Americans who had previously been thriving landowners became a homeless and bankrupt underclass overnight, forced to seek menial jobs across the vast new American frontier.

DESPERADOS AND THE MEXICAN REVOLUTION

What Is a Desperado, Anyway?

The English term "desperado" is a contraction of the Spanish word *desesperado*, meaning "desperate one." And during the frontier years of the mid- and late 1800s, there were many lawless desperados indeed, both Mexican and Anglo, roaming the great Southwest.

A case in point was **Joaquín Murieta.** According to legend, Murieta had been a peaceful California gold miner until Anglos took away his claim to the land and murdered his brother. In a desperate attempt to avenge the injustices committed against him and other Mexican-Americans, Murieta killed, robbed, and ransacked anything that got in his way. He was compared to **Robin Hood,** but his random lawlessness only served to deepen discrimination against Mexican-Americans. When it was suspected that he had raided Calaveras County in California and had been involved in the devastating fire that consumed the mining town of Stockton, the State of California put a price on his head: $1,000, dead or alive. After chasing countless bandits around California, some rangers reported that they had killed said Joaquín Murieta, but his identity was never confirmed.

Another antihero was **Juan Nepomuceno Cortina,** whom Mexican-Americans likened to **Daniel Boone** and other intrepid frontiersmen. The story goes that in 1859, Cortina saw a sheriff in Brownsville, Texas, unfairly arrest a *vaquero* (cowboy) on his ranch. Cortina was apparently so enraged at this act, which he considered the straw that broke the camel's back, that he shot the sheriff and then freed all the prisoners from the local jail.

Cortina became a scofflaw and an "avenging angel," who many believed was responsible for starting dozens of riots, including the angry riots at a salt mine in El Paso (the Salt War), which resulted in the deaths of three Anglos and thousands of dollars of damage.

These protest actions by Mexican-American desperados who felt disenfranchised and persecuted after the Mexican-American War gave rise to armies of vigilantes in California and Arizona, and to the feared Texas Rangers just north of the border. The Texas Rangers became notorious for their "law and order" violence against Mexican-Americans. Often, they would arrest or kill innocent citizens simply because they were suspected of being desperados. In the process, the rangers started a legacy of antipathy and suspicion that some say still lingers in the hearts of many.

Was Pancho Villa a Desperado?

Pancho Villa was a hero of the Mexican Revolution of 1910, which sought to depose the dictator **Porfirio Díaz** (who had been in power for almost fifty years) and institute a pluralistic democracy that would return the land to the peasants and food to the people.

Not unlike **Cortina** and **Murieta** to the north, Pancho Villa became disgusted with the establishment and sought to take the law into his own hands. When he was in his early twenties, he killed a man and took to the hills. There he started his career as both a guerrilla fighter for democracy and a bandit who terrorized northern Mexico, robbing trains and banks and ransacking mining towns.

Villa had supported the progressive politician **Francisco Madero** for president. Later, when he lost an important battle to a supporter of **President Venustiano Carranza,** Villa became enraged at the United States for supporting Carranza and influencing Mexican politics. In March 1916, Villa attacked a town in New Mexico and killed seventeen Americans in reprisal for American intervention in his country's affairs. In a matter of days, General **John J. Pershing** was deployed with a large, organized army to capture Pancho Villa and bring him back to the United States for trial. The clever guerrilla fighter, who knew the difficult Mexican terrain like the back of his hand, disappeared from sight and Pershing's army returned empty-handed. Pancho Villa became a hero overnight.

Why Was the Mexican Revolution of 1910 So Important and How Did the United States Get Involved?

The Mexican Revolution of 1910 was a lengthy, bloody, and devastating civil war which changed Mexico forever. Its root causes were both class and racial struggle. In many ways, it can be likened to the Bolshevik Revolution that followed in

Russia seven years later. The masses revolted. The peasants demanded ownership of their lands. The Native Americans and *mestizos,* who had been at the bottom of the ladder, discriminated against by an autocratic government, said, *"Basta ya!"* (enough is enough) and demanded equal rights in employment, salary, housing, and political representation. It was a complicated revolution, with many factions vying for power—some more liberal and inclusive, others more radical, virulent, and unforgiving. Much of the protest was waged against the Catholic Church because of its domination of many Mexican institutions. Groups of Native Americans and *mestizos* (as well as many *criollos*) ransacked churches and overturned statues of Catholic saints in the streets.

In the end, after both liberals and arch-conservatives had gained power and been deposed several times, all Mexican institutions became secularized, a representative government was established, and the foundation was laid for the present-day democratic Mexican government.

Emiliano Zapata, a Native American peasant, became one of the heroes of the Mexican Revolution. His motto was "land, liberty, and death to the *hacendados* (landowners)." He joined **Francisco Madero** in his effort to oust the dictator **Porfirio Díaz.** Later, however, Zapata did not want Madero, who he believed was too soft, and he joined forces with **Pancho Villa** in one of the most radical and systematic revolutions of modern times. The Mexican economy came to a standstill. The railroad system was destroyed, thanks greatly to Zapata's and Villa's revolutionary activities. Zapata's men also destroyed most of the nation's crops and livestock. The food shortage and the ensuing economic chaos led to mass starvation and uncontrollable epidemics. All hell had broken loose south of the border. In 1913, President **Woodrow Wilson** ordered an arms blockade against Mexico and began a policy of U.S. involvement in Mexico, in keeping with **Theodore Roosevelt**'s Monroe Doctrine.

The ostensible reason for U.S. intervention in Mexico

was the fact that the Mexican revolutionaries had been receiving weapons from European governments, especially Germany. It was the eve of World War I, and the United States believed that German meddling in the hemisphere could seriously threaten U.S. sovereignty.

In April 1914, a group of marines landed in Tampico, Mexico, to pick up supplies, and were promptly arrested. Admiral **Henry T. Mayo** demanded an apology from the Mexican government (then in the hands of transitional dictator **Victoriano Huerta**), but when Huerta refused to apologize or salute the American flag, President Wilson sent a fleet to Veracruz, where the marines had taken the city, and the United States got ready to invade Mexico and declare war.

At the eleventh hour, Argentina, Chile, and Brazil interceded and war between the two countries was averted. By then the Huerta government had been toppled, and the United States saw no reason for further overt hostilities against the Mexican people.

However, Mexican attacks by Villa, Zapata, and other revolutionaries continued on both sides of the border. Throughout the Mexican Revolution, which lasted until 1917, Mexican revolutionaries raided the Southwest. The Mexican Revolution also created the first Mexican political refugees in the United States and began a new wave of migration that eventually reshaped Mexican-American life.

THE SECOND AND THIRD WAVES

What Did the Mexican Revolution Have to Do with Congressman Henry Gonzalez's Becoming Chairperson of the Banking Committee?

In a roundabout way, there is a connection. Chairman **Henry B. Gonzalez's** parents were among the scores of middle-class Mexicans who were forced to flee their country during the Mexican Revolution. His family settled in San Antonio, where the future congressman and respected leader of the Mexican-American community was born. Along with Gonzalez's parents came thousands of other immigrants across the Rio Grande seeking shelter from the Mexican devastation. Many were middle- and upper-middle-class; many more were poor, uneducated peasants. Most waded across the shallow Rio Grande on foot, carrying their belongings on their back, walking hundreds of miles toward the promised land of Texas and California.

In a short time, the Mexican peasants who had fled the revolution became a major part of the economy of the Southwest. The cheap wages paid them enabled the commercial farms in the area suddenly to flourish. In turn, the Mexicans, who had been used to poor wages and appalling living conditions, were grateful for the jobs and became "ideal" workers—the type who didn't complain and were willing to plant and harvest crops from sunup to sundown without taking a break.

In Los Angeles, where another group of Mexican refugees settled, the urban economy began thriving with the new influx of cheap labor into the manufacturing plants, as well as into other jobs for "unskilled" workers which many Americans were unwilling to take.

In a matter of years, the Mexican-American population exploded. By 1925, Los Angeles already had the largest Mexican population outside Mexico City (it still does today). Although there was no exact count of the Mexican migration into the United States until 1924, when the border patrol was established, figures for legal immigration show that between 1930 and 1940, more than two thousand Mexicans applied for permanent residence in the United States annually.

It is estimated that between 1900 and 1930, more than half a million Mexican immigrants entered the United States legally. Considerable illegal immigration occurred simultaneously. The new Mexican-American population in the United

States was rapidly taking shape, giving birth to the Latino cultural heritage of the twentieth century—and to many future leaders in all walks of American life.

How Did the Second Wave of Mexican Immigrants Differ from the Old Californios and Tejanos?

Although the Mexican immigrants of the post–Mexican Revolution era had a lot in common with native Southwestern Mexican-Americans whose families had lived in Texas, California, or Arizona for generations, there were also many obvious differences. The two groups shared a heritage, religion, and language. But many of the customs of the people had changed over the years, and even the Spanish spoken by these two groups differed. The new Mexicans spoke a Spanish that betrayed European, African, and Native American influences, whereas the Spanish spoken in the Southwest had retained its sixteenth-century Spanish vocabulary and grammar. As a result of centuries of isolation, the original Mexican-Americans had created their own microcosm within their territories. In many ways, the two groups viewed each other as quite different. An unexpected prejudice was born: The native Mexican-Americans discriminated against the newcomers.

At the same time, by their sheer numbers, the new Mexican immigrants began changing the face of the Southwest and incorporating their strong Mexican flavor into the community at large. This second wave of Mexican immigrants in fact created the bedrock of most present-day Mexican-American communities scattered all over the United States, particularly in California and the Southwest. In turn, the second wave was followed by the third wave—the *mojados* (wetbacks) and migrant workers.

This tendency on the part of successive waves of immigrants from the same country to discriminate against each other has been a peculiar occurrence among many immigrant groups in the United States, almost from the beginning of our history as a nation. Often, it has more to do with the prejudices and beliefs of the dominant culture of a particular region (Anglo in this case) than with the differences between the waves of immigrants.

How Did U.S. Immigration Laws Benefit Mexican Immigrants but Discriminate Against Asians?

Mexican immigration to the United States between 1890 and 1965 has been called one of the most significant demographic phenomena in the history of the Americas. This Mexican migration took many forms. Over the years, the United States has had permanent immigrants, temporary immigrants *(braceros)*, legal and illegal immigrants, commuters, dailys ("day trippers"), business travelers, tourists, and students.

Several political scientists have argued that, in many ways, the Mexican migration did not involve the blending of one culture into another (as has been traditional for other immigrants), but rather a movement within the same culture to the north and south of an arbitrary international border. From the beginning, these "crossovers" happened without regard to borders or national laws. Mexican farmhands, shepherds, miners, and cowboys felt a call to go north in search of better and more highly paid work. Political refugees fleeing the many upheavals during Mexico's early formative years, especially during and after the 1910 revolution, thought "going north" *(al norte)* was the most logical step. Men and women, poor and unable to find decent work within their borders, braved the Rio Grande and the Texas Rangers, hoping for a land of milk and honey where they could raise their children properly.

By the mid-1800s, there had been two major waves of European immigration into the United States. The first had come from England and Northern Europe; the second had come from Southern Europe, starting around 1850. All these immigrants, along with African-Americans and Native Americans, had contributed greatly to the growth and development of the United States as a nation. Once the Southwest became part of the United States and its full potential as a paradise of mining, agriculture, and ranching was recognized, new sources of labor became necessary. At first, the U.S. government turned to China and Japan in the hope of encouraging their citizens to come to America. Thousands came and quickly set to work in the building and rebuilding of America into the strong industrial power it eventually became. However, a sudden epidemic of national and racial discrimination began sweeping the land, with many Anglos crying out against "the yellow terror" and contending that most Asians were not "trustworthy" and would not make good citizens.

The Chinese were forbidden entry into the United States by various exclusion acts of the 1880s, and the Japanese were discouraged from coming by the Gentlemen's Agreement Act of 1907. At that point, Mexico became the chief source of immigrant labor in the United States, followed by Korea and the Philippines, which had not been included in the new immigration laws.

In 1924, U.S. immigration laws established quotas for people entering the country from different parts of the world. Northern Europeans were favored; Southern Europeans could gain entry in limited numbers. Almost all Asians were excluded. However, no quotas were stipulated for immigrants from the Western Hemisphere—thus Mexico, our nearest neighbor to the south, became the largest supplier of cheap labor.

Until 1924, the border between Mexico and the United States had not been policed at all. Starting in 1924, proof of identity and other "documentation" were required for legal entry into the United States. Many Mexicans entered legally, but others regarded the paperwork as an impediment and began avoiding the border patrol. The term "illegal immigrant" became part of our vocabulary.

Why Do Mexican-Americans Say the Railroads Were Built on Their Backs?

Asians, African-Americans, Greeks, Poles, Italians, and other Europeans had, over the years, much to do with the building of our nation. In the early 1920s, with the expansion of the Southern Pacific Railroad, Mexican-Americans went to work as track maintenance workers. A 1929 government report showed that anywhere between 70 and 90 percent of all the workers on Southwestern railroads were of Mexican origin, and that they were rapidly supplanting African-Americans. The Baltimore and Ohio Railroad also recruited Mexican-Americans by the thousands. Northern steel companies, such as Bethlehem Steel in Pennsylvania, hired Mexican workers for their plants. National Tube Company, an affiliate of U.S. Steel, added many Mexicans to the staff of its plant in Lorain, Ohio.

Mexican-Americans began relocating from the Southwest to industrial cities all across the United States. Between 1920 and 1930, Chicago's Mexican-American population swelled from four thousand to twenty thousand. Mexican-Americans found employment not only in steel factories, but in meat-packing plants, utility companies, construction, trucking, and dozens of other industries in the Midwest. In addition, they worked the sugar-beet fields of Michigan and continued their agricultural traditions wherever they could.

Mexican-Americans also met with much discrimination in their new Northern homes, especially from earlier immigrants such as Italians, Poles and other Slavs, who by then considered themselves "real" Americans and looked on the Mexicans as foreigners. Mexican families often lived in sub-standard houses and congregated on the wrong side of the tracks in the overcrowded ghettos known as *barrios* and *colonias*.

By the 1920s, Mexicans had already become the single most important source of agricultural labor in California, replacing the Chinese and Japanese, who had worked the fields at the turn of the century. Many were also employed in manufacturing (twenty-eight thousand, according to a 1930 State of California report), and as a group they accounted for the largest number of railroad workers.

What's a Barrio and What's a Colonia?

A *barrio* ("neighborhood" in Spanish) is an urban area where Mexican-Americans and other Latinos settle. Like other immigrant ghettos, *barrios* provide an enclave of the "old country" in the heart of a strange new city. Although leaving the *barrio* and becoming more integrated into American society was the goal of many Latinos, in recent years new generations of Latinos have chosen to return to their parents' or grandparents' *barrios* to rebuild and reclaim part of their heritage.

Colonias (Spanish for "colonies") were originally communities of Mexican refugees where newcomers either stopped over on their way to other cities, such as Los Angeles, Cleveland, Chicago, and New York, or simply settled while going to work in the surrounding areas. Both the *barrios* and the *colonias* were little homes away from home where new immigrants could find out about jobs or simply pause for a warm meal and a friendly chat on their journey to "somewhere."

Chicano Go Home?: Why Were Mexicans and Mexican-Americans Repatriated?

As the 1920s came to a close, the Great Depression was nipping at the heels of the United States. Between 1930 and 1933, the number of unemployed Americans grew from 4 million to more than 13 million. Hourly wages dropped from thirty-five cents an hour to fourteen cents an hour. Stockbrokers and financiers were leaping out of windows in New York City and college graduates were selling apples in the streets.

Mexican-Americans, like most other Americans, found themselves out of work as the railroads, automobile manufacturing plants, meat-packing businesses, and steel mills came to a screeching halt. In the Midwest and other industrial centers, Mexican-Americans were fired from their jobs overnight. In New Mexico, the cattle ranchers laid off Mexican-Americans indefinitely, and many New Mexican Hispanos lost their lands because they were unable to pay taxes or the assessments of the Middle Rio Grande Conservancy Project.

Thousands of Mexicans, along with other Americans, began roaming the country in search of any type of work they could get. Anglo immigrants from the Dust Bowl and other areas started heading west and competing for the few jobs that had traditionally been available to Mexicans. By 1937, more than half of all the cotton workers in Arizona came from out of state. In Texas alone, the jobless Mexican-American population grew to more than 400,000. President **Franklin D. Roosevelt**'s New Deal policies established a number of agencies and projects specifically aimed at ameliorating the conditions of Mexican-Americans, who, because they had stood at the bottom of the opportunity ladder, seemed to be among the worst off. The Federal Emergency Relief Administration, among other agencies, provided temporary work and assistance to Mexican-American workers. And, thanks to the establishment of the Works Progress Administration in 1935, Mexican-Americans were granted jobs during the Depression years. The WPA created jobs for carpenters, masons, and unskilled laborers, who built bridges, libraries, and other municipal structures. In the midst of great anguish, this was a brief moment of pride for Mexican-Americans, who saw themselves publicly recognized for their great tradition as master builders—a tradition harking back to the days of the Maya and the Aztec.

But in spite of the president's and **Eleanor Roosevelt**'s efforts on behalf of Mexican-Americans during the 1930s, a repatriation movement, which demanded that Mexicans and Mexican-Americans be sent back to Mexico, began gathering enormous support. Many Anglos considered Mexicans foreigners or itinerant laborers who had no right to take the few existing jobs from "real" Americans at a time of such extreme economic distress.

Showing a complete disregard for the enormous civil rights violations involved in the repatriation of Mexicans, local government agencies began rounding up Mexican-Americans and sending them "home." Frequently, they rounded up recent undocumented immigrants, but they also sent first-generation Mexican-Americans to Mexico, as well as Mexican-Americans whose families had been living in the United States for centuries.

All told, during the decade of the 1930s, the number of deportees came to approximately half a million people of Mexican descent, counting illegal immigrants. About 132,000, the greatest number, came from Texas, which had the largest Mexican-American community. California was second, followed by Indiana, Illinois, and Michigan. Mexican-Americans in New Mexico suffered the least; only 10 percent of repatriates came from the state. This was partly because New Mexico was less industrialized and therefore less damaged by the Depression, and partly because Mexican-Americans from

New Mexico had the longest history of integration in the Southwest.

The Los Angeles Times reported that more than 200,000 Mexicans were repatriated from the United States in 1932 alone. Of these, around 75,000 came from California, with about 35,000 from Los Angeles County. Chicago, Detroit, and Denver also served as repatriation centers.

Some citizens were deported by immigration officials. Others returned or went to Mexico for the first time voluntarily. Still others were threatened with deportation and left before they could be loaded onto the Southern Pacific or other railroads and dumped at border towns along the Tijuana and Brownsville lines.

Mexican president **Lázaro Cárdenas** established resettlement camps for the new immigrants in Guerrero, Michoacán, Oaxaca, and Chiapas states, as well as a small colony in Matamoros, in the state of Tamaulipas. In the end, though, the Mexican economy could not assimilate these new immigrants, and the refugee colonies served only to reaffirm the outrage and disillusionment Mexican-Americans felt toward the United States, their own country, which they believed had betrayed them.

Very few "new" Mexicans became fully integrated into Mexican society. During World War II, when repatriation efforts were reversed, Mexican-Americans found their way back to their familiar towns in California and the Southwest. The bitter experience of being sent "home" when they were no longer needed and being sent for again when cheap labor was in demand magnified the mistrust many Mexican-Americans had felt toward the Anglo for countless generations.

However, this great injustice, which many compared to the internment of Japanese-Americans in concentration camps during World War II, also led many sociologists and politicians to take a fresh look at the Mexican-American "question," and to seek ways of bettering working and living conditions in the United States.

The sad "repatriation" experience also served as a spur to the cause of *la raza* and the desire on the part of many Mexican-Americans to enter the political mainstream and participate fully in all matters involving their community. Although Spanish-language newspapers had existed in the Southwest as far back as the nineteenth century, new, more politically active publications and radio stations emerged for the Mexican-American community throughout the United States. Today, Spanish-language media have multiplied a hundredfold; several national Spanish television networks operate from coast to coast.

What's a Bracero?

Bracero comes from *brazo*, which means "arm" in Spanish. So a *bracero* is literally someone who works with his arms—a hired hand. Although there are plenty of women hired hands, the generic (masculine) term, *bracero*, is used when referring to *braceros* of both genders. *Bracera* would refer to a particular woman worker.

But a *bracero* is much more than a hired hand. You might say it's the symbol of an entire institution. The *bracero* program involved thousands of Mexican nationals recruited as temporary workers in the United States under various labor agreements with Mexico. The *bracero* program spanned two main periods in American history. The first began in August 1942 and ended in December 1947; the second extended from December 1948 all the way to December 1964. The first *bracero* program was initiated by the United States as a direct result of World War II. American workers (mostly male) had gone to war, and the country was in desperate need of farm and industrial laborers to replace them. During that period, only 250,000 *braceros* were hired to work seasonally in the United States, as the crops required. A contract usually lasted one year. Some *braceros* went back at the end of the year; others stayed over until the following year. Sometimes the same people came back year after year to work in the same region and even for the same employer.

The second *bracero* program was much more ambitious. It was instituted under Public Law 78 and lasted from 1945 to 1964, from the end of World War II through the end of the Korean War and the beginning of the Vietnam War. During that time, more than 4.5 million Mexican nationals came to work in the United States. Most *braceros* worked in agriculture, but thousands drove trucks and delivered crops and goods to civilian populations and, in spite of opposition by U.S. labor, also worked on the Southern Pacific Railroad.

The idea behind the *bracero* programs was born during World War I, when the Mexican government began asking the United States to grant itinerant Mexican workers certain guarantees that would ensure minimum wages, fair labor practices, the health and well-being of the migrant workers, and legal recourse in case of noncompliance by U.S. employers.

Before the *bracero* programs, Mexicans worked under deplorable conditions and sometimes were not even paid—or were paid subhuman wages, like indentured servants. The labor shortage during World War II, coupled with the hue and cry over the illegal deportation of Mexican-Americans during the Depression, prompted the U.S. government to agree to abide by mutual treaties that ensured certain basic rights for the Mexican workers.

Even with the laws on the books, there were many violations of the *bracero* program by prejudiced employers. Mexicans workers complained of poor food (their provisions often consisted exclusively of such things as tripe, chitterlings, pigs' feet, chicken necks, and leftovers from earlier meals); excessive wage deductions, which left the workers with very little money to keep for themselves or to send to their families back in Mexico; physical mistreatment; housing that was often nothing more than enlarged chicken coops; rampant prejudice and discrimination, and exposure to deadly pesticides.

The second *bracero* period reached its peak in 1956, when 445,000 Mexicans were processed under Public Law 78 to work in U.S. agriculture. These *braceros* accounted for 25 percent of all farm workers in the United States, and their cheap labor benefited the states of Texas, California, Arkansas, Arizona, New Mexico, Colorado, and Michigan. Texas did not participate in the first *bracero* program, because Texas growers and ranchers believed in the "open border" policies and preferred drawing their own rules and setting their own wages. However, the complaints from Mexicans about mistreatment and discrimination in the Lone Star State had been so extensive that the Mexican government barred its citizens from working in Texas.

Why Did Texas Pass a Law Making All Mexican-Americans White?

In response to the Mexican government's protests against the subhuman treatment of Mexicans and Mexican-Americans in Texas, the Texas legislature in 1944 passed the Caucasian Race Resolution, which declared all Mexican-Americans white and endorsed equal rights in public places of business and amusement for all Caucasians.

The law declared Mexican-Americans Caucasians because, in a strictly segregated society, this seemed the only way to grant Mexican-Americans some rights. Today, the U.S. census lists all people of Spanish-speaking origin as Hispanics, whether they are of Caucasian Spanish descent, *mestizo*, Native American, African, or otherwise.

But the Mexican government believed the efforts of Texas were insufficient, and Texas, like all other states, was forced to comply with Public Law 78 before Mexicans were legally allowed by their government to work along the Rio Grande.

Why Was the Bracero Program Finally Stopped?

In November 1946, with World War II over, the U.S. government informed the Mexican government that it wished to terminate the *bracero* agreement. However, most farm bosses in the United States had come to rely on Mexican workers and lobbied to keep the *bracero* program alive. The House of Representatives introduced a law in 1947 that kept the *bracero* program in place for a while. Even after the program was officially terminated, *braceros* continued to work the farms into the 1960s; labor contracts were carried out directly between *bracero* and employer without government intervention.

Word of mistreatment of *braceros* reached the U.S. Congress by way of various human rights organizations, such as the National Catholic Welfare Council, Americans for Democratic Action, the National Council of Churches of Christ in America, the National Farmers Union, and the AFL-CIO. Secretary of Labor **Arthur Goldberg** established a $1 per hour minimum wage law for *braceros* in an attempt to right old wrongs and to discourage the unfair hiring of Mexicans. Earlier, **George McGovern** (then a congressman) had introduced a law to phase out the *bracero* program, which met with much opposition by farm lobbies and other interest groups.

By 1964, the advent of mechanization in the harvesting of tomatoes and cotton, coupled with organized labor's growing opposition to the hiring of Mexican aliens, led to the final dissolution of the *bracero* program. Still, the flow of Mexican "hired hands" to the United States continued by way of legal immigrants, *mojados* (wetbacks), day trippers, and other commuters.

What Were the Zoot Suit Riots?

Although Mexicans and Mexican-Americans have encountered prejudice in the United States for centuries, an incident that occurred in the 1940s often stands as the archetypal example. It also marked the first stirring of a new Mexican-American awareness that began after World War II and that, in many ways, reached its apogee in the 1960s and 1970s, under the leadership of a great Mexican-American named **César Estrada Chávez,** but known to millions simply as César.

During the 1940s, Mexican-American teenagers adopted a dress fashion known as "drapes," which resembled the zoot suits worn by young men in Harlem. To Anglos, the Mexican-American "drapes" were zoot suits—and zoot suits, they thought, were clothes that only hoodlums wore. Newspapers and other periodicals in Los Angeles began running stories about the sharp rise of crime in the city, and openly blamed Mexican-Americans, whom they labeled "zoot suiters." On June 3, 1943, eleven sailors on leave walked into a Mexican-American *barrio* in Los Angeles and became involved in a brawl with a group of men thought to be of Mexican descent. This "attack" on members of the U.S. armed forces outraged hundreds of Anglo residents, and goaded the rest of the ship's crew stationed in Los Angeles.

The next day, two hundred sailors hired a fleet of taxis and circled the Mexican-American neighborhoods in Los Angeles. Each time they found a young Mexican-looking man, whether in or out of a zoot suit, they stopped and beat him to a pulp. The young Mexican-Americans fought back, but were often outnumbered and outmaneuvered. The police looked the other way. By June 7, thousands of civilians had joined in the riot. African-Americans and Filipinos, as well as Mexican-Americans, were being savagely attacked.

Downtown Los Angeles was finally declared off limits to military personnel, but by then the riots had spread to the suburbs. Soon the rest of the country was caught up in an anti-Mexican wave that sparked attacks in Beaumont, Texas; Chicago; San Diego; Pasadena; Detroit; Evansville, Indiana; Philadelphia; and finally Harlem.

A citizens' committee appointed by then Governor **Earl Warren** (later a Supreme Court justice) and headed by Bishop **Joseph McGucken** of Los Angeles determined that the riots had been caused by racial prejudice and were further encouraged by police practices and inflammatory newspaper articles. In spite of this, the Los Angeles City Council seriously debated a proposal that would make it illegal to wear zoot suits.

Shortly after the Zoot Suit Riots, a Los Angeles Commission on Human Rights was established to study the "race question" and prevent future outbreaks of hate crimes.

Mojados: Illegal or Undocumented?

The second wave of migration was followed by the third wave—the *mojados* (wetbacks) and migrant workers. The *mojados* (the name means literally "the wet ones") came to be called this because they often swam across the Rio Grande to U.S. soil. *Mojados* have long been the objects of prejudice and ridicule because of their undocumented or "illegal" status. "Undocumented" is the preferred legal term, since "illegal" carries a connotation of criminality which, seen in its proper light, does not apply to these millions of poor workers who have migrated across the border in search of honest work, and who have been the backbone of U.S. agricultural prosperity in California and the Southwest. In the decades of the *bracero* program, *mojados* streamed in, unsupervised and unprotected by labor laws. Texas, which did not welcome the *bracero* program, was the greatest beneficiary of this source of cheap Mexican labor.

When the first *bracero* program period came to an end in 1947, *mojado* smuggling increased sharply, since American agribusiness depended on the Mexican labor class for the planting, harvesting, and distribution of crops. Although it is impossible to determine how many *mojados* came, between 1947 and 1955 alone more than 4.3 million undocumented workers were caught and returned to Mexico.

The numbers who eluded La Migra (a Spanish abbreviation for "immigration authorities") are estimated in the millions. Of those, many returned to Mexico, but many more stayed and became part of the growing Mexican-American community. As a result of the arrival of *mojados,* many Mexican-Americans from Texas and other parts of the Southwest began a northward journey toward industrial cities where they would not compete with *mojados* for the low wages of the frontier states.

This began a movement of "new" Mexicans into the Southwest and "old" Mexicans to Northern and Eastern cities. During the 1960s, the migration of Mexican-Americans leaving agricultural jobs for industrial jobs rose exponentially. For every *mojado* who arrived, one Mexican-American moved farther north.

The influx of *mojados* continues in many guises to this day. Some workers are smuggled in by people who profit by the millions in this human traffic, which has been likened to the African slave trade; others brave it alone and roam the dusty towns of the Southwest until they find work or meet a friend or relative who has secured a place for them.

What Was "Drying Out the Wetbacks"?

By hiring *mojados,* American growers avoided minimum wage laws, bonding and contract fees, and all the other legal and moral obligations stipulated in the *bracero* program. The need for workers during World War II prompted authorities to look the other way.

After the war, the U.S. Immigration Service decided to start what is known as a "drying-out" program. It consisted of handing out ID papers to *mojados* employed at U.S. farms, returning them across the Mexican border, and bringing them north again as "legal" workers. At one point, the Mexican and U.S. governments agreed that the thousands of illegal Mexicans in the border regions would be given a blanket "drying-out" sanction and would be legalized en masse.

What Was the El Paso Incident?

In the fall of 1948, as the cotton harvest drew near, the Mexican government demanded that Mexican workers crossing the border be paid a minimum wage of $3 per hundred pounds of cotton harvested. U.S. farmers refused to pay more than $2.50 to Mexicans—although they were paying the going rate of $3 to all other workers. The Mexican government stood firm and forbade their nationals from going north, guarding the border with armored tanks.

In October, the U.S. farmers informed the Immigration Service that their crops would rot in the ground if Mexicans workers did not start coming fast. La Migra responded by simply opening up the El Paso border to Mexican workers. In spite of the Mexican army blockade, Mexicans workers began crossing the border by the thousands, braving their own government's bullets. As the Mexicans crossed, they were loaded onto trucks by agents representing the Texas growers and delivered to labor camps with the full approval of the U.S. Immigration Service.

Eventually, the Mexican government voiced such loud protests that the workers were released from the labor camps and the U.S. government extended an official apology to Mexico—but not until all the Texas cotton was harvested.

Who Are the Commuters?

Commuters, or "dailys," represent yet another form of Mexican migration to the United States. Visitor permits, or "border crossing cards," are issued by the U.S. authorities to Mexicans seeking to come to the United States on shopping or business trips, or for a brief vacation. Card holders are supposed to stay within twenty-five miles of the border and return to Mexico within seventy-two hours.

Many Mexican women use the visitor permits to work as domestics during the day in the United States (earning as little as $5 per day) and then return to Mexico at night. Others use the visitor permits for extended stays. If they're caught, they claim they are *mojados* and get returned. The next day, they use their visitor permits and return to the United States—this time, if they're lucky, for good.

Still others buy a round-trip ticket to Detroit or Chicago. When they arrive, they join friends or relatives who may have found them a job. At that point, the Mexican traveler cashes in his or her return ticket, which provides enough money to live on until the first paycheck. The new arrival loses himself in the crowd and joins the vast underground American economy—but, of course, without legal recourse, and always under the threat of discovery and deportation.

Ironically, whole communities in Mexico are supported by *remesas,* or remittances, from migrant workers in the United States. These *remesas* add up to more than $4 billion per year, and are Mexico's second largest source of foreign income, after oil.

IDENTITY, ACTIVISM, AND *VIVA LA RAZA*

How Did Mexican-Americans Do in the Armed Forces?

Mexican-Americans have served proudly in all U.S. wars; their presence in the ranks has increased since World War II. In World War II, when Mexican-Americans were drafted on a large scale for the first time and also volunteered, they received the greatest number of Congressional Medals of Honor of any single minority in the United States. During the Korean and Vietnam wars, the number of Mexican-Americans on the front lines was greatly disproportionate to their number in the general population. Thousands fought and died valiantly defending their country, as detailed congressional records and the thousands of names carved on the Vietnam War Memorial testify.

World War II was the benchmark for Mexican-American self-awareness. This was due in part to the fact that many left the crowded, unsanitary *barrios* for the first time and were suddenly exposed to new ideas of fairness and equality, and to disparate and prosperous lifestyles.

They learned new skills they could not have developed in their rural communities. After the war, many took advantage of the GI Bill and enrolled in college. Wartime and postwar jobs moved these Mexican-Americans to Anglo and multiethnic urban centers all around the country, resulting in a large exodus of Mexican-Americans from New Mexico, Texas, and Arizona. In fact, most of California's recent Mexican-American population came from the Southwest. In contrast, most of the recent immigrants to Texas come from Mexico.

How Did Mexican-American Activism Get Its Start?

As the Mexican-Americans began to be integrated into the larger society, they met with new forms of discrimination in housing, jury selection, law enforcement, public accommodations, and even in employment, since they were competing with Anglos for better blue-collar or white-collar jobs.

Several Mexican-American organizations had formed since World War I, with LULAC (League of United Latin American Citizens) playing the most significant role. Before that, other societies existed at the local level, such as the Alianza Hispano-Americana, a group founded in Arizona in

1894 that paralleled the Masonic Order. After World War II, LULAC grew to two hundred councils, extending all the way from California to the District of Columbia, with a membership of fifteen thousand. LULAC fought for equality of educational opportunity and won several landmark legislation cases for Mexican-Americans.

Later, in the late 1940s the Community Service Organization (CSO) was formed and, together with other Mexican groups, began drafting Mexican-Americans to run for public office. The CSO based its theories on the organizational principles of **Saul Alinsky,** who later became **César Chávez**'s mentor and friend. CSO emphasized mass political involvement and was instrumental in engineering voter registration drives.

As a result of these fledgling political efforts, **Edward R. Roybal,** a Mexican-American from East Los Angeles, won election to the city council in 1949. It was the first example of what political organization could do for Mexican-Americans. Other organizations, such as the American GI Forum (formed by Mexican-American veterans to fight discrimination in the armed forces) and the Mexican-American Political Organization (MAPA), soon followed.

On the heels of President **John F. Kennedy**'s election in 1960, a group of Mexican-American leaders from MAPA, LULAC, CSO, and the Viva Kennedy Organization met in Phoenix to form a Mexican-American political party. Leaders from other Latino groups were also present, namely Puerto Ricans and Cubans. This historic meeting led to the creation of the Political Association of Spanish Speaking Organizations (PASO) led by **Albert Pena,** commissioner of Bexar County. PASO concentrated much of its effort in Texas, where it managed to defeat the entrenched Anglo machinery and elect an all Mexican-American city council and mayor in the town of Crystal City—a stunning first for Mexican-Americans, and a harbinger of things to come.

Who Was César Chávez?

César Estrada Chávez was a migrant worker and the son of a migrant worker who rose from the agricultural valley of Yuma, Arizona, to form America's first successful farm workers' union. **Robert F. Kennedy** described him as "one of the heroic figures of our time." **Edmund G. Brown, Jr.,** marched with Chávez and his United Farm Workers, and when Brown was elected governor of California in 1974, he passed the Agricultural Labor Relations Act, a landmark bill that established collective bargaining for farm workers.

César Chávez spent his early years on the family's 160-acre farm. After the Depression, when his parents had lost their land, César moved with them to California. He picked carrots and cotton and harvested grapes wherever he could find work. Once he counted sixty-five elementary schools he had attended—sometimes for a day, a week, or a month.

After serving in the Navy in World War II, Chávez settled in Delano, California, with his wife, **Helen Fabela.** It was here that he began helping his people out of the miserable working conditions they had accepted for generations. He joined **Saul Alinsky**'s Community Service Organization (CSO) and started registering Mexican-Americans to vote. He also served as their advocate before U.S. government agencies.

By 1965, Chávez had organized 1,700 families and had persuaded two large California growers to raise the wages of migrant workers. Soon after, eight hundred members of his group joined the AFL-CIO in picketing grape growers in Delano. This was the beginning of La Huelga ("The Strike"), the organized strike led by Chávez which lasted five years and helped raise America's consciousness of the unfair practices and conditions Mexican-American farm workers had endured for decades. Chávez battled the corporations of the San Joaquin Valley by means of hunger strikes and peaceful demonstrations, which he patterned after the teachings of **Gandhi.** Often, he had himself and his followers arrested to gain attention for his cause, which he named La Causa.

Although he was a rather meek and self-effacing man whose gifts were not so much in public speaking as in leading, he often addressed large crowds and was able to rouse the multitudes with his deeply felt convictions. He captured the imaginations of intellectuals and fair-minded people all over the country: 17 million Americans joined his boycott and refused to buy California grapes for five straight years. Priests, nuns, rabbis, Protestant ministers, college students, unionists, writers, and politicians all marched at his side demanding long-overdue justice for Mexican and Mexican-American farm workers.

On July 30, 1970, after losing millions of dollars to La Huelga, the California grape growers capitulated and agreed to sign a contract granting rights and higher minimum wages to the workers. It was the first of many successful boycotts that César Chávez was to lead on behalf of the lettuce pickers, grape pickers, and all the other disenfranchised groups so dear to his heart.

César Chávez believed in fairness and equality for all people, and lent his support to countless civil rights marches on behalf of African-Americans, women, and, in later years, gays and lesbians. He was a vegetarian and a deeply spiritual man. His symbols were the Virgin of Guadalupe, Mexico's patron saint, and a flag he created which depicted a black Aztec eagle poised over the American landscape.

Although La Causa was to suffer many setbacks over the years, César Chávez remained a beloved leader not only of the Mexican-American farm workers, but of all Latinos, who saw him as a Moses, bringing them across the desert into a land of possibilities, with greater justice for all.

César Chávez, whose untimely death at the age of sixty-six in 1993 elicited eulogies and expressions of bereavement from national and international leaders and warranted an obituary on the front page of *The New York Times,* was a third-generation farm boy from Arizona who had dared to dream.

What Is the Chicano Movement?

The Chicano movement emerged out of the unrest caused by the Vietnam War and the courage and aspirations of the African-American civil rights movement in the 1960s, led by **Martin Luther King, Jr**.

César Chávez spearheaded the farm workers' union, which in turn created a new consciousness among Mexican-Americans of all classes. In many ways, he has remained the symbolic leader of *la raza*. But several other early civil rights workers, with varying points of view, contributed to the formation of the Chicano movement.

Chicano student organizations, particularly in California, joined the movement with more vociferous, less peaceful demonstrations, demanding that their language, culture, and ethnic contributions be recognized in the schools, and garnering support at all levels, from the universities down to the elementary schools. In the 1960s and 1970s, the United Mexican Students (UMA), the Movimiento Estudiantil Chicano de Aztlán (MECHA), and many others set the pace for today's cultural revolution and awareness of "Mexicanism" and Latino heritage. The famous Brown Berets, patterned after the Black Berets, formed dozens of chapters throughout the Southwest. Their platform, while committed to nonviolence, vigorously emphasized inclusion of Mexican-American contributions in all school curriculums, as well as a permanent place for Chicano writers and artists in all cultural and civic institutions.

Reis López Tijerina, a Chicano activist born in Texas, organized a separatist movement called Alianza Federal de las Mercedes (Federal Alliance of Land Grants) in 1963, which demanded the return of millions of acres originally owned by the Hispanic-Mexican community of the Southwest. The Alianza grew to around twenty thousand members and proposed to make the "reclaimed land" part of a utopian Mexican-American separatist community.

There were many confrontations in the mid-sixties between Tijerina's activists and the Army and state troopers who sought to prevent them from "seizing" the lands they laid claim to in New Mexico, Colorado, Utah, Texas, and California. On July 4, 1966, Tijerina led a sixty-two-mile march from Albuquerque to Santa Fe, New Mexico. He presented Governor **Jack Campbell** with a petition asking for the passage of a bill that would investigate the land grants of Hispanic-Mexicans, and announced that he represented six thousand Mexican-Americans who, he said, were direct heirs to lands that had been unlawfully taken from their ancestors.

Eventually, Tijerina was jailed and given a two-to-ten-year sentence for attempting to take over part of the Kit Carson National Forest. Although he resigned the leadership of the Alianza by 1970 and his group's efforts were not successful, his speeches and demonstrations served to focus attention on Mexican-American rights and grievances.

Rodolfo "Corky" González, another Chicano leader, founded the Crusade for Justice in Denver. He is the author of the famous epic poem *"Yo Soy Joaquín,"* which appeals to Chicano youths to attain their goals by seizing their rightful place. This poem continues to inspire millions of Mexican-American and Latino youths, and is taught in most Latino history and literature courses in the United States. "Corky" González was a famous boxer, a Democratic political leader, and an active member of the antipoverty program in the Southwest. His motto was *"Venceremos"* ("We Shall Overcome"), and his aims were to raise the awareness of Chicano identity and to provide his members with a wide range of services from legal aid and access to medical services to educational opportunities and financial help.

González's movement, like that of Tijerina, was separatist. Among its goals was persuading the United Nations to hold a plebiscite in the Southwest to determine independence for *la raza* and the creation of a separate Mexican-American state.

Corky González's most significant contribution—other than *"Yo Soy Joaquín"*—was the formation of the Spiritual Plan of Aztlán (El Plan Espiritual de Aztlán).

Aztlán is the name Mexican-Americans have given to their ancestral lands in the Southwest. It is a mythical homeland where the Aztec, a nomadic tribe, first lived before going southward in 1325 and founding Tenochitlán, the capital of their empire, on the site of present-day Mexico City.

This Aztlán plan, which was voted on in 1969 by two thousand representatives of one hundred Chicano organizations, calls for a revival of Mexican-American values and the creation of a new political party based on self-determination. El Plan Espiritual de Aztlán has served as the platform for Mexican-American identity and self-respect, and as an inspiration to Mexican-American youths.

José Ángel Gutiérrez, another Chicano leader from Texas, formed the Mexican-American Youth Organization and, in 1970, established a new political party, La Raza Unida (Mexican-Americans United). La Raza Unida sought to end discrimination against Chicanos by gaining access to mainstream American politics and financial institutions. Gutiérrez was an advocate of bilingual and bicultural education, which he saw as a means of preserving Mexican-American identity.

Corky González, José Ángel Gutiérrez, Reis López Tijerina, César Chávez, and many other leaders of the Chicano movement succeeded in putting Mexican-American studies programs in place in colleges and universities. They also achieved the election of hundreds of Mexican-Americans to political offices, school boards, and civic organizations. They were instrumental in righting many wrongs affecting the Mexican-American community, from the establishment of sewage and water service in deprived areas to the inclusion of works by Mexican-Americans in libraries. They helped in the establishment of medical clinics; a Mexican Chamber of Commerce; and credit unions and legal aid for migrant workers. In the 1990s, the work of these early leaders still benefits the artistic, political, and humanitarian efforts of Chicanos.

Chicano Mural Painting: When Is Graffiti Not Graffiti?

Mural painting has long been a revered Mexican tradition, preserved by many internationally acclaimed artists like **José Clemente Orozco, Rufino Tamayo, David Alfaro Siqueiros,** and **Diego Rivera.**

Since the recognition of the Chicano movement in the 1970s, hundreds of young Mexican-Americans have taken to the streets of cities in California and throughout the Southwest to celebrate their cultural heritage and transform the bleak urban landscape of the *barrios.* Some of their expressions have taken the form of graffiti written across walls and underpasses.

The Estrada Courts in Los Angeles, directed by artist **Gato Feliz,** and Chicano Park in southern San Diego present examples of the vibrancy and richness of Chicano muralist contributions to American culture. The violent, striking art of **Carlos Almariz, Frank Romero, Beto de la Rocha,** and **Gilbert Luján,** members of a group who called themselves Los Four in the 1970s, are also part of the cultural affirmation and protest that graffiti painting has come to symbolize, particularly in East Los Angeles.

The Estrada Courts murals, painted on blind walls in this renewal project, depict larger than life pre-Columbian scenes that remind Chicanos of their noble origins. Aztec gods, figures from the Spanish conquest, and images of the cherished Virgin of Guadalupe, the patron saint of Mexico, make up a great mosaic executed as a joint project by young Chicano artists.

Chicano Park in San Diego, which cuts the Chicano *barrio* in half where two freeways intersect, contains some of the finest Mexican muralist art in the tradition of the 1920s and 1930s. On two occasions, the residents of this *barrio* were evicted and their houses and apartments expropriated for the building of new roads. The tenants mounted countywide protests, backed by several Chicano organizations. Finally, the City of San Diego abandoned its efforts to install a scrap iron depot in the neighborhood, and restored the district to the Chicanos.

A historic monument was born. What had been a jungle of ugly concrete blocks became a park decorated with colorful murals depicting the history and struggle of Mexican-Americans. Two frescoes adorning the freeway entrances portray **César Chávez** addressing Chicano crowds and depict the struggles of Mexican workers and peasants from the past, such as **Zapata**'s guerrillas, and Latin-American heroes of the twentieth century, including not only **Fidel Castro** and **Che Guevara** but also the Spanish artist **Pablo Picasso.** These murals, which the Chicanos call "living museums," represent both the artistic expression and the cultural aspiration of a people whose voices are just now beginning to be heard.

A Chicano artist who has come to symbolize the struggle for justice is a railroad worker named **Martín Ramírez.** Ramírez was a migrant worker who was put in an insane asylum in California because he had lost his ability to speak. Since he could not speak, he painted, and for thirty years before his death in 1960, he created his "mute" and extraordinary paintings.

THE WOMEN: CHICANA MOTHERS, HEALERS, ARTISTS, AND REVOLUTIONARIES

What Exactly Is Machismo, *Anyway?*

Machismo comes from *macho,* which means "male gender" in Spanish. But, of course, *machismo* is much more than that—it is the symbol for the values of a patriarchal culture, where the term is imbued with dominant qualities like strength, importance, bravery, and power. The phrase "macho man," coined by the Village People in their hit song, refers to a tough *hombre* (another word borrowed from Spanish, meaning, of course, "man") who struts his stuff and takes no guff.

With *machismo* at the helm, it is no wonder that the history of Mexicans and all Latinos gives short shrift to women's contributions. In this respect, it is no different from Anglo history, in which men are almost always the protagonists. In the case of Chicanos and other Latinos, the cult of *machismo* makes sexism easier to spot.

Is There Such a Thing as Macha?

There is one aspect of *machismo* that seems to have eluded the Anglo definition of the word, but that is very much part of Mexican-American thought and, to a lesser extent, Latino thought in general. This is the fact that a woman, too, can be very *macho (muy macha).* This does not mean that she is masculine or imitates men, but rather that she is brave, strong, and resolute, and probably drinks tequila straight and eats her chile peppers whole—all *macho* virtues, not necessarily limited to the male gender. Thus, Mexicans and Mexican-Americans often refer to a gutsy woman as *muy macha,* without challenging her femaleness in the least. If anything, being *muy macha* adds to it. After all, if a society holds a certain quality in high esteem, doesn't it figure that each individual would want to possess that quality? There are dozens of Mexican and Mexican-American popular songs in which *mariachis* sing about how very *macho* (*"Es muy macha!"*) their women are.

Still, institutionalized *machismo* has relegated Chicanas and other Latinas to secondary status. Chicanas have only recently emerged to claim their rightful place both in history and in everyday life.

In her 1985 book, *To Split a Human: Mitos, Machos y la Mujer Chicana*, **Carmen Tafolla,** a feminist scholar from Texas, bemoans the fact that "the Chicana may thus find herself curiously placed on a borderland between two forces. In one camp, her struggle against sexism is trivialized. In the other, her struggle against racism is ignored."

What's a Curandera?

A *curandera* is, literally, a healer. Among Mexicans and Mexican-Americans, women are generally the *curanderas,* or spiritual and herbal "folk" healers who practice an ancient Native American art. Throughout California and the Southwest, there are thousands of documented cases in which *curanderas* have cured both infants and adults of every illness known to humanity—from whooping cough to cancer and mental illness. Many *curanderas* practice a kind of religious syncretism, combining their faith in the Virgin of Guadalupe with knowledge of herbology and a reverence for the ancient Maya and Aztec gods. *Curanderas* often work on the therapeutic staffs of clinics in the Southwest and are consulted in psychiatric cases. Some *curanderas* have gained so much recognition that they hold workshops and give lectures on the ancient and modern art of *curanderismo.*

What's a Partera?

A *partera* is a midwife—and much more. In an economically deprived society where, increasingly, children are born into households headed by single women, *parteras* deliver babies at home and then serve as *curanderas,* members of the extended family, and even baby-sitters. Delivering a child at home is still preferred by many rural and urban Chicanas, and the *partera* plays an essential role in the community.

So Where Were the Women in Mexican and Chicano History?

Mexican and Mexican-American women were present and pivotal all throughout their history, and even when their voices were silenced, their influence was profoundly felt.

During **Francisco Vásquez de Coronado**'s early expeditions, a woman, **Francisca de Hozas,** accompanied him and showed him the way. She drew Coronado a map and told him how to organize the expedition. He took her directions reluctantly—and she was proved right. Other women explorers who accompanied Coronado in his dangerous forays into the Southwest were **María Maldonado** and **Señora Caballero.**

During Mexico's struggle for independence, a fighter named **Manuela Medina,** nicknamed "La Capitana," led an entire company of rebels and fought and won seven crucial battles. Another woman, **Doña Josefa Ortiz de Dominguez,** dubbed "La Corregidora" ("The Chief"), also fought valiantly and distinguished herself by flawless marksmanship. Another woman, **Gertrudis Bocanegra,** organized revolutionary armies and took part in the Grito de Dolores in 1810. She was later taken prisoner and executed by Spanish loyalists.

Such warring women came to be known as "Las Adelitas" ("Little Adeles") during the Mexican Revolution of 1910, where they fought side by side with men and performed extraordinary acts of heroism. The original **Adela** was **Pancho Villa**'s lover, who often rode with him on the same horse, blasting away the *hacendados* (landowners) with a shotgun fired one-handed.

Adelitas became a symbol of feminist empowerment for both the Mexican and Chicano movements after the 1970s. Side by side with the Adelitas, Mexican and Chicana feminists elevated **Sor Juana Inés de la Cruz** to their pantheon of heroines. Sor Juana was a Mexican nun who lived in the seventeenth century. She was a mystic poet and the first known female voice to protest men's violence toward women. She dared question the leadership of men and still managed to remain a beloved saint for women as well as men—who regarded her as *muy macha.* Her essay *Contra Las Injusticias de Hombre al Hablar de la Mujer* ("Against the Injustices of Men in Talking About Women") is considered a classic.

In the Southwest, hundreds of Chicano women struggled bravely for their rights. During the frontier days in Texas, **Doña Chipita Rodríguez,** who fought off the advances of an Anglo, was accused of murdering him and went down in history as the only woman ever hanged in Texas. In California, **Josefa Segovia** was lynched for stabbing an Anglo.

During the 1930s, **Ema Tenayuca** organized the first successful strike of pecan-shellers in San Antonio, and lit the flame of possibility that was later to burn in **César Chávez's** heart.

During the 1940s, **Josefina Sierro** was active during the mass deportation of Mexican-Americans to Mexico and began an "underground railroad" in the tradition of **Harriet Tubman,** bringing back hundreds of Mexican-Americans to the United States. She was also single-handedly responsible for negotiating with Vice President **Henry Wallace** to make Los Angeles out of bounds to military personnel during the Zoot Suit Riots—thus effectively putting an end to the violence in Los Angeles in the 1940s.

One aspect of the Zoot Suit Riots that is seldom discussed is the fact that the riots were not only racist, but sex-ist. The naval officers and other Anglo men who went looking for Chicanos to beat up also raped dozens of Mexican-American women. This ignited the *macho* spirit of the Chicanos, who did not want to share "their women" with the gringos.

Among the leaders of the Chicano labor movement of the 1960s and 1970s, **Marcela Lucero Trujillo,** an activist in **Corky González**'s Crusade for Justice, **Virginia Musquiz,** a leading organizer of the Raza Unida Party, and the UFW's **Dolores Huerta** achieved prominence.

Huerta is perhaps one of the greatest Chicana activists of all time. As vice president of César Chávez's United Farm Workers, she helped him organize and win hundreds of victories. In 1988, Huerta was attacked by police officers in front of a hotel in San Francisco where President **George Bush** was attending a campaign dinner party. Huerta was conducting a peaceful demonstration in response to the president's statement that he would not support the UFW boycott of California table grapes. The UFW's position was that several farm children had died of cancer in McFarland County, where lethal pesticides were being used indiscriminately. Huerta wanted to focus attention on what she and hundreds of other Mexican-Americans perceived as unfair. It was not the first time her peaceful protests had landed her in the hospital.

Where Are the Great Chicana Artists?

The answer, of course, is everywhere. In the Southwest, where hundreds of ethnic jokes aimed at Mexicans make the rounds, there is one that goes: "Why is there no Mexican literature? Answer: Because spray paint only went on the market two years ago!" This double-edged joke, which relegates Mexican muralist art to the level of graffiti and also insinuates that Mexicans are a people devoid of culture, makes the point for Chicanas as well. They, too, have been ridiculed for their art, and then accused of not having any.

In a 1988 issue of *Time* magazine, revered art critic **Robert Hughes** devoted an entire article to Latino artists without reviewing a single woman artist, Chicana or otherwise. In New York City, two museums dedicated to the work of Latino artists, the Museo del Barrio and the Museum of Contemporary Hispanic Art, both have supported Chicano art, but have seldom exhibited women artists. This, of course, is no different from Anglo institutions, which have ignored women artists for centuries. According to Chicana and other Latina artists, these exclusionary policies make their plight particularly poignant, since these museums were expressly created to right old wrongs and end discrimination.

In response to systematic exclusion, **Maurene Acosta** and many other women artists have organized traveling shows of Chicana art, in which the works of Denver artist **Charlotta Espinoza** and muralist par excellence **Margo Oroña,** among others, can be appreciated and discussed. Other Chicana artists whose work has also won recognition in the past decade include **Santa Barraza, Thelma Ortiz Muriada,** and **Carmen Garza.** Artist **Frida Kahlo,** who was Mexican (not Mexican-American) and married to the muralist **Diego Rivera,** is the only woman artist of Mexican descent who has achieved superstar status in the United States.

Today, thanks to the perseverance of Chicana artists and writers, as well as to political support from organizations such as the Mexican-American Women's National Association (MANA), the Mexican-American Legal Defense and Education Fund, and many others, Chicana artistic contributions are increasingly being recognized.

Among Mexican-American writers, as among all Latino writers, women are leading the way. In fact, although there are many examples of excellent literature written by Chicanos, Chicanas are in the majority in more recent anthologies.

Who Are Some of the Great Chicana and Chicano Writers of Today?

There are too many to count, but here is a sample. Among the women: **Patricia Preciado Martín,** author of *Images and Conversations: Mexican-Americans Recall a Southwestern Past;* poet **Cherríe Moraga,** who writes on feminist and lesbian themes; **Sandra Cisneros,** author of *Woman Hollering Creek and Other Stories;* **Gloria Anzaldúa,** editor of a number of anthologies, including *This Bridge Called My Back: Writings by Radical Women of Color;* **Alma Villanueva,** author of *Bloodroot;* **Helena María Viramontes,** author of *The Moths and Other Stories.*

Among the men: **Antonio Villareal,** author of *Poncho;* activist **Rodolfo "Rudy" Acuña,** author of *Occupied America: A History of Chicanos;* author, journalist, and TV essayist (on *The MacNeil/Lehrer Newshour*) **Richard Rodriguez,** known for his novels *Hunger of Memory* and, more recently, *Days of Obligation: An Argument with My Mexican Father;* **Tomás Rivera,** author of *And the Earth Did Not Part;* **Rudolfo Anaya,** author of *Bless Me, Ultima;* **Oscar "Zeta" Acosta,** known for *The Autobiography of a Brown Buffalo;* and, although his work is seldom included in lists of "ethnic" literature, **John Rechy,** author of *City of Night.*

CULTURAL HERITAGE: A MOVABLE FIESTA

Did Montezuma II Eat Tacos?

Montezuma II and his people ate many of the same delicious dishes we eat today in the thousands of Mexican restaurants and *taquerías* in every town, village, and hamlet throughout the United States. Mexican food rivals Chinese food as the most popular "foreign" fare in America and is considered a major cultural contribution to Anglo society.

Mexican food, like Mexican culture itself, combines Native American, Spanish, and, to some extent, African culinary influences. However, most ingredients and recipes remain the gift of the Maya, Aztec, Pueblo, and other Native American peoples who lived in Mexico and the Southwest when the *conquistadors* landed.

Among the many foods **Cortés** and his men discovered on the lavish tables of Montezuma were sweet tamales, tomatoes, a vast array of tortillas, dozens of varieties of chiles, avocados, coconuts, papayas, pigs, turkeys, ducks, and, much to the disgust of the Spanish, little Mexican hairless dogs, which the Aztec considered a great delicacy.

Is Chocolate Really Mexican?

The native peoples of Mexico made an art of husking, roasting, and grinding cacao seeds. Before the Europeans came to Mexico, chocolate was a beverage unknown to them. The Aztec liked drinking their chocolate with very hot chiles. Today, Mexicans and Mexican-Americans sometimes add a bit of spice to their chocolate, but their favorite way of preparing it is very thick and sweet with steamed milk.

How Are Tex-Mex and Southwestern Food Different from Mexican Food?

Mexico is divided into six distinct regions, each one with its own cooking style—Chilango, Tapatío, Jarocho, Norteño, Yucateco, and Oaxaqueño. Central Mexico (Chilango), for example, has a great mixture of Spanish and Native American dishes. The famous *mole poblano* sauce originates from this area. In Yucatán (Yucateco), where half the region rises from the Gulf of Mexico and half from the Caribbean, tropical dishes, such as pork cooked in banana leaves, abound.

The food most closely associated with Tex-Mex and Southwestern cuisines comes from the northern Mexico region (Norteño), where the Spanish introduced cattle to an arid land that was perfect for grazing, and grew wheat for the first time where the native corn did not grow. Here you find blue corn, tortilla chips made with wheat rather than corn, chile stews prepared with beef rather than pork, and the famous Texas *chile con carne* and traditional open barbecues (from the Spanish word *barbacoa*). However, thanks to travel and the many waves of Mexican immigration from all parts of Mexico, Southwestern cuisine and Mexican-American dishes contain elements from almost every other Mexican region, particularly in the condiments and preparation of the native foods.

Are Tacos, Tortillas, Fajitas, and Chile the Mexican National Dishes?

No way. All of the above are generally regarded as *antojitos* ("little whims") or hors d'oeuvres—or to put it in more contemporary terms, fast food. Actually, turkey served in a *mole poblano* sauce, combined with tortillas, enchiladas, and quesadillas, is considered the national dish on both sides of the border.

What Is Mole Poblano?

Mole poblano sauce is a delicious thick sauce said to encapsulate all the flavors of Mexico. It's made from many types of chile peppers, garlic, bananas, onions, cloves, cumin, coriander, and its "secret" ingredient—unsweetened chocolate.

EVERYTHING YOU NEED TO KNOW ABOUT LATINO HISTORY

CHILE PEPPERS

More than 150 varieties of chile peppers, in an array of shapes and sizes, have found their way into the U.S. kitchen. While they grow, chile peppers are usually green. When they ripen, however, most varieties turn red, orange, yellow, or brown.

Fresh Chile Peppers:

1. Habanero   The Habanero, meaning "from Havana," is the hottest of all chiles.

2. Serrano   The Serrano is the hottest chile pepper that is widely available in the United States.

3. Anaheim   Also known as the California or long green chile, the Anaheim is superb stuffed in chile rellenos.

4. Guero   Guero is the generic term for yellow chiles, which are used primarily in yellow mole sauces.

5. Jalapeño   The jalapeño is the best-known hot chile in the United States. In 1982 it became the first chile to travel into space.

6. Poblano   The Poblano is one of the most popular fresh chiles in Mexico.

Dried Chile Peppers:

1. Mulato   The Mulato is a type of dried Poblano.

2. New Mexico   Also known as the California, the New Mexico has a sweet, smoky flavor.

3. Chipotle	A Chipotle is a dried, smoked jalapeño.
4. de Arbol	The de Arbol is primarily used in powder form to make sauces.
5. Ancho	The ancho is a dried Poblano.
6. Cascabel	The Cascabel got its name from the rattling noise it makes when shaken. *Cascabel* means "rattle" in Spanish.

What Is Tequila, Anyway?

In recent years, tequila has beaten *pulque* as the official Mexican alcoholic beverage. *Pulque* is a strong drink, fermented from the sap of the maguey cactus, which was widely used as a ceremonial drink by the Aztec. Mescal is a liquor derived from a relative of the maguey cactus, and tequila is actually the mescal originally made in the village of Tequila, in the Mexican state of Jalisco. Thus, tequila is just a mescal drink, closely resembling the same cactus "juice" the native peoples drank many centuries ago. Tequila is often used as a chaser to cool down the hot chile peppers in food. Water is not recommended, since after an initial (but short) "cooling" period, it serves to make the mouth feel even hotter.

What's a Piñata Party?

A piñata party is a birthday or other special-occasion fiesta for children. The piñata (from *pino*, the pine tree) is a tree-like structure made of clay or papier-mâché that hangs from the ceiling. Once the party gets going, the children break the piñata with long sticks, releasing the toys, candies, and other surprises hidden inside. The best part is scrambling for the goodies strewn across the floor. Mexican and Mexican-American children have been holding piñata parties since before **La Malinche** met up with **Cortés.**

What Are Mariachis?

Mariachis are strolling bands of Mexican and Mexican-American musicians dressed in traditional Spanish costumes adorned with sequins, mirrors, glass, and other shiny materials, and sporting large-brimmed, richly decorated sombreros. Mariachis play the guitar and the violin and serenade the crowds with traditional romantic Mexican songs.

Why Do Mexican-Americans Celebrate Cinco de Mayo?

Cinco De Mayo (the Fifth of May) commemorates Mexican independence from Napoleonic domination. The day of Mexican independence from Spanish rule is September 16. Both holidays are celebrated in Mexico. However, in the United States, Cinco de Mayo has come to be known as the official Independence Day. Mexican-Americans hold fiestas and parades to celebrate their cultural heritage in hundreds of towns, particularly in California and the Southwest. You might say it's the equivalent of St. Patrick's Day for the Irish—and, just as on St. Patrick's Day everyone is suddenly Irish, so it is on Cinco de Mayo, when even Anglos turn Mexican overnight.

What's a Charreada?

The *charreada* is Mexico's national sport—and a very popular one among Mexican-Americans. *Charros* are Mexican cowboys, and *charreadas* are rodeos, only they tend to be slightly more dangerous than the regular Southwestern kind. Skilled horsemen (and women) practice "steps" such as *el paso de la muerte* ("the pass of death"), in which the *charro* shimmies off the saddle and leaps onto the back of a speeding wild horse that has just been whipped into a frenzy by three other *charros*. *Charros* and *charras* also perform intricate rope tricks while standing on a moving horse, rope cows, bust steers, and do just about anything else imaginable on and off a bronco. The American rodeo was derived from the Mexican *charreada*. Incidentally, *rodeo* is also a Spanish word, meaning a gathering place for cattle.

How Many Different Fiestas Do Mexican-Americans Celebrate?

Too many to count, since each Southwestern and California town has its own *santo* (saint) or other holiday celebration, which often combines Spanish, Aztec, Maya, and Pueblo cultural and religious observances.

The Virgin of Guadalupe, the patron saint of Mexico and the symbol of its national identity, is honored on her day, December 12, by Mexican-Americans throughout the country. El Día de los Muertos (the Day of the Dead) is the Mexican version of Halloween (All Saints' Day), celebrated on the first and second of November. Mexicans and Mexican-Americans decorate their homes with skeletons symbolizing the spirits of the dead, who are thought to visit their relatives on these two days. The celebrants often go to the cemetery and bring food and flowers to the departed, who are believed to regain their taste and hearing for the two days. Candies, flags, hats, cakes, and even T-shirts decorated with skeletons are part of this solemn yet festive celebration, in which both children and adults participate.

Among many other fiestas and religious observances are the Corn Dance Fiesta and the Buffalo Dance Fiesta. The first pays homage to the main staple of the people, and the second celebrates the unity between the hunters and the game hunted for meat.

In Santa Fe, New Mexico, the Burning of Zozobra feast celebrates the destruction of "Old Man Gloom." A forty-foot marionette, taller than most buildings in town, is burned in the main square. After "gloom" has been consumed by fire, the people dance in the streets, shouting, *"Viva la fiesta!"* The next day, the town holds a "pet parade," in which children walk with a real or imaginary animal friend. The parade is so much fun that adults are known to borrow a child for the day so they can march too.

When it comes to the dozens of patron saints' fiestas around the country, the celebrations usually start in the main Catholic church or cathedral, where a special service is held. Then the people take the village *santo* to the main plaza and place it in a shrine or bower for all to see. They worship the saint by dancing all around it, playing hypnotic drum music and singing religious chants. At the end of the day, the *santo* is returned to the church. These fiestas, which go on almost year-round in towns with large Mexican-American populations, demonstrate the strong cultural tradition of the Mexican-American people and the remarkable blending of Catholic, Pueblo, Aztec, Maya, and other Native American religious traditions in their rich heritage.

From *Days of Obligation: An Argument with My Mexican Father* by Richard Rodriguez (1992)

Eventually I made my way through *Huckleberry Finn.* I was, by that time, a graduate student of English, able to trail Huck and Jim through thickets of American diction and into a clearing. Sitting in a university library, I saw, once more, the American river.

There is a discernible culture, a river, a thread, connecting

Thomas Jefferson to Lucille Ball to Malcolm X to Sitting Bull. The panhandler at one corner is related to the pamphleteer at the next, who is related to the bank executive who is related to the punk wearing a FUCK U T-shirt. The immigrant child sees this at once. But then he is encouraged to forget the vision.

CUATRO

Puerto Ricans

What is Puerto Rico?

EARLY HISTORY

Why do Puerto Ricans call their island
Borinquen?

How did San Juan come to be called Puerto Rico, and
Puerto Rico San Juan?

Why did Ponce de León bring African slaves to
Puerto Rico?

What do Puerto Ricans mean when they say negro?

How did Sir Francis Drake get his comeuppance in Puerto Rico?

Who was Marshall Alejandro O'Reilly?

A GROWING NATIONAL IDENTITY

How did Puerto Ricans feel about Spanish rule?

What's a machete?

What's a jibaro?

Who was Luis Muñoz Rivera and why is he called the George Washington of Puerto Rico?

Was Puerto Rico really free for only seven days?

What were the Monroe Doctrine and the Roosevelt Corollary?

What was the Spanish-American War all about, and why do we call it the first media-staged war?

Who were Teddy Roosevelt's Rough Riders
and what did they have to do with winning
him the U.S. Presidency?

Who was Eugenio María de Hostos and why is a school
in New York named after him?

How did the Puerto Ricans feel about becoming a U.S.
protectorate?

Who was the first elected Puerto Rican governor and
what did he do that was so important?

How did Puerto Rico become a commonwealth . . . and
what's a commonwealth, anyway?

Why did the independentistas try to assassinate
President Truman?

Why is Puerto Rican migration not immigration and
how did it get started?

How many Puerto Ricans are there and where do they
live?

Why is New York considered so important for the
future of all Puerto Ricans?

Commonwealth vs. statehood: what's the big
deal?

PAHRY TIME!

What's a pahry?

So what do Puerto Ricans on the mainland do when they have a pahry?

What's a santo?

What's a botánica?

What's a compadrazco?

What's the Puerto Rican national dish?

What Is Puerto Rico?

Quick, name a place that's improperly called a country; whose residents are American citizens but are barred from voting in U.S. elections unless they happen to live on the mainland; whose capital city is a hundred years older than Jamestown; and whose people are fiercely proud of their land, heritage, and Afro-Spanish traditions.

If you answered "Puerto Rico," you're familiar with some of the many contradictions that characterize the history and political status of this earthly paradise, which lies 1,000 miles southeast of Miami and measures 111 miles long by 36 miles wide.

EARLY HISTORY

Why Do Puerto Ricans Call Their Island Borinquen?

"Borinquen," meaning "the land of the brave lord," was the name the Taino Indians gave Puerto Rico. Taino, by the way, was not really their name. It was the name **Christopher Columbus** gave this group of Arawak Indians because *taino,* meaning "peace," was the first word out of their mouths when they saw him.

The Taino were peaceful people indeed. They fished, hunted, and gathered berries and pineapples in their plentiful land. They slept in *hamacas,* whose name has survived to this day both in Spanish and in English, as "hammock." So has *huracán* ("hurricane"), the god of ferocious winds whom the Taino understood no one would ever tame.

"Boricua," from "Borinquen," is what Puerto Ricans call each other, particularly on the U.S. mainland. Using the name is a form of bonding that reaffirms ancient roots.

How Did San Juan Come to Be Called Puerto Rico, and Puerto Rico San Juan?

It all began on September 23, 1493, when **Columbus,** back in the New World on his second voyage and exploring the island of Guadeloupe, met several Taino (Arawak) Indians from Borinquen who had been taken as slaves by the ferocious Carib people. The Taino begged Columbus to return them to their island, and he agreed.

When they reached Borinquen on November 19, 1493, Columbus was impressed with the wealth of the island, with its lush vegetation and more than two hundred species of birds. He let the Taino he had brought with him off the ship and immediately took possession of the island in the name of **Isabella** and **Ferdinand**. He named it San Juan Bautista, after **John the Baptist** and Isabella and Ferdinand's son, **Juan**. At first, the island of San Juan Bautista was mostly ignored by the Spanish, who had big gold fish to fry in Mexico and Peru. But fifteen years later, in 1508, the Spanish nobleman **Juan Ponce de León** was sent with a crew of fifty to explore the island and find out whether any gold lay there. None did to speak of, as they found out much later, but the minute Ponce de León viewed the bay at San Juan, he exclaimed, *"Ay que puerto rico!"* ("Oh what a rich port!") From that moment on, the island became known as Puerto Rico, and the port where Ponce de León landed as San Juan (short for San Juan Bautista). San Juan, of course, became the capital of Puerto Rico and remains so to this day. Ponce de León became the first governor of Puerto Rico. A large city on the southern coast, the hometown of thousands of Puerto Ricans on the U.S. mainland, still bears his name—Ponce.

Why Did Ponce de León Bring African Slaves to Puerto Rico?

The Taino welcomed the Spanish with open arms, believing them to be gods. However, they soon regretted their friendliness. The Spanish began their quest for gold by enslaving the native people and taking their lands. In exchange for working the gold mines and tending the fields to feed the *conquistadors,* the Taino were given lessons in Catholicism and Spanish history and culture. Hundreds of Taino died of exhaustion, malnutrition, and mistreatment. Still others died because they had no defenses against the European diseases the Spanish soldiers had brought with them. In 1511, the Taino rebelled after their pleas for better working conditions went unheard. Ponce de León responded by having 6,000 Taino shot on the spot. Those who survived took to the mountains or rowed away to neighboring islands.

Ponce de León was in a predicament. There were few

Spanish on his island—mostly soldiers—and even that population would soon dwindle, since the quest for riches in Puerto Rico had proved hopeless and Mexico and Peru had become the mecca for the New World gold diggers. Ponce de León's solution was to ask **Ferdinand** of Spain for permission to bring African slaves. In 1511, the first shipload of Africans arrived in Puerto Rico. With them also came a smallpox epidemic, which wiped out the rest of the Taino population. By 1515, fewer than four thousand Taino remained in Puerto Rico—compared to the forty thousand **Columbus** had found.

Since the search for gold had proved fruitless, Ponce de León decided to turn Puerto Rico into an agricultural paradise, to feed and support the Spanish crews who stopped over on the way to and from Mexico and Peru. From the beginning, the Spanish crown had envisioned Puerto Rico as a fortress, to help protect and maintain the hundreds of Spanish galleons that came across its shores.

The solution was sugar cane, and the Spanish government built sugar mills by the dozens. There African slaves and the few remaining Taino would cultivate and harvest the crop by hand from dawn till dusk under the hot tropical sun.

The Africans proved sturdier than the native people; their population increased while the Spanish and the native populations dwindled. By 1531, the Spanish numbered 426 in Puerto Rico, the Africans 2,264.

The Spanish government soon granted free land to Spaniards who wished to settle in Puerto Rico. Between 200 and 1,400 acres were given to each settler who agreed to farm the land (or, more accurately put, to oversee the slaves farming the land) and stay more than five years. Soon coffee and spices were added to sugar cane as the principal crops of the island; all three were in great demand back in Europe. By the seventeenth century, tobacco and ginger had become the most important crops. With the wealth acquired on the backs of the Taino and the African slaves, Puerto Rico began to thrive. Mainland Spaniards started to view the island differently. Suddenly, Puerto Rico was indeed a "rich port," a good place to settle, farm, and grow rich.

African slavery continued in Puerto Rico until 1873, when **King Amadeo** of Spain legally abolished it. By then African culture had grown deep roots in the fertile tropical soil of Puerto Rico, where West Africans had found flora and fauna much resembling those of their homeland. Africans believed their ancient Yoruba deities had followed them to the island and lived on there. Intermarriage and interbreeding among all three ethnic groups—Taino, Africans, and Spaniards—were common, and out of these practices emerged the great racial diversity of today's Puerto Ricans. Puerto Rican art, music, philosophy, literature, and religion all reflect the rich cultural legacy of these three diverse peoples.

What Do Puerto Ricans Mean When They Say Negro?

The word "negro" comes from Spanish. It means "black." Black color. Black race. Black sky. But in Puerto Rico, where skin color ranges from black to fair, there are many ways of defining appearance or ethnicity.

A dark-skinned or black person is usually referred to as *de color,* meaning "of color." A person with light brown skin is called *trigueño* ("brunette" or "swarthy")—and this describes the majority of the Puerto Rican population. *Indio* refers to someone with Native American features. *Blanco* ("white") is used for light-skinned persons.

However, *negro/negra* or *negrito/negrita* (a diminutive term) is not used to define a person's color. It is simply a term of endearment, and it can be used when addressing anyone, including a blond, blue-eyed person. Furthermore, Puerto Ricans make a distinction between African-Americans in the United States and black Puerto Ricans of African descent. African-Americans are called *morenos* ("brown"), while African–Puerto Ricans are called *de color.*

How Did Sir Francis Drake Get His Comeuppance in Puerto Rico?

In 1588, when the Spanish Armada was defeated, in part because of the maritime skills of **Sir Francis Drake** and in part because of a ferocious storm raging in the Atlantic, the Spanish colonies were in danger of being taken by the English. Spain knew it needed to fortify its colonies in the New World to keep them from English raiders, pirates, and privateers. Puerto Rico had grown rich as a result of the phenomenal stamina and farming skills of the African slaves. Coffee and sugar were traded illegally, since Spain forbade its colonies to trade with any other country. England and other European countries were aware of the great potential that lay within Puerto Rico's shores, and carried on contraband trade with the island in plain sight of the Spanish soldiers. Mindful of this presence, and of the fact that Puerto Rico was a stopover port for Spanish galleons filled with gold and other treasurers, the governor of Puerto Rico, **Diego Menéndez de Valdéz,** built a new fort, El Morro (now one of San Juan's tourist attractions). Other fortifications, such as La Fortaleza, a fortress at the edge of the shoreline, and La Casa Blanca (the White House), were strengthened to keep the English out.

Sir Francis Drake, in the meantime, had convinced **Queen Elizabeth I** that he had a foolproof plan to capture Spain's Caribbean colonies. The queen had some misgivings, but allowed Drake to proceed, intrigued by his descriptions of silver and gold treasures, which Drake knew were brought from Mexico and Peru to Puerto Rico en route to Spain. In 1595, Drake sailed for the Caribbean with twenty-seven ships and forty-five hundred troops.

But by the time he reached Puerto Rico, fifteen hundred Spanish sailors had joined the three hundred stationed on the island. They purposely sank two Spanish ships to block Drake's entrance into the harbor. When Drake's fleet arrived in San Juan on November 22, 1595, it was met by an unceasing artillery blast. Drake quickly withdrew out to sea and later circled the island to find a point of entry. But the Spanish were too well fortified to be penetrated. Drake gave up and returned to England empty-handed.

A few months later, both the English and the Dutch tried their luck at wresting the island from the Spanish. On June 16, 1597, the English **Earl of Cumberland** landed in Puerto Rico. By then an epidemic of smallpox had stricken the Spanish soldiers. Cumberland seized San Juan and flew the English flag from El Morro. However, his victory was short-lived. The Puerto Ricans did everything in their power to make the English *conquistador*'s life miserable, and in the end the English, too, succumbed to smallpox. Cumberland and his crew left Puerto Rico within two weeks of their arrival.

Two years later, England's new king, **James I,** signed a treaty with Spain agreeing to cease and desist from raiding Spain's South American colonies. Instead, James turned his sights northward, toward Virginia, where the first English colony was founded in Jamestown.

IMPORTANT DATES	
November 22, 1595	Sir Francis Drake, the English buccaneer and explorer, sails into San Juan.
June 16, 1597	The Earl of Cumberland reaches Puerto Rico.

February 1823	Mexico wins its independence under Colonel Antonio López de Santa Anna.
December 10, 1898	Under the Treaty of Paris ending the Spanish-American War, Puerto Rico becomes a U.S. protectorate.
March 2, 1917	President Woodrow Wilson signs the Jones Act, granting all Puerto Ricans U.S. citizenship.

Who Was Marshall Alejandro O'Reilly?

By the mid-1700s, Puerto Rico was thriving on a vast illegal commerce which the people conducted behind Spain's back with European privateers and buccaneers. Only 5 percent of the land was being farmed. Trade between Spain and Puerto Rico had virtually ceased. Spanish taxes were supporting the island, but Spain was getting very little in return. In 1765, the Spanish king sent a brilliant soldier and civic planner to overhaul the system of government in Puerto Rico and help stimulate its economy.

Marshall **Alejandro O'Reilly** devised a plan, called "The O'Reilly Report," which came to be considered one of the most important documents issued by the Spanish empire to its colonies, because for the first time it recognized the intrinsic needs of the colony, not just the needs of Spain. O'Reilly devised a way to legalize all trade and ensure that the crown would benefit from it. He laid the groundwork for a system of land distribution whereby new Spanish settlers were freely given agricultural acres if they were willing to farm them. New schools were opened. New towns were started. Houses built in the Spanish colonial style, with thick stone walls that kept the interior cool, sprang up from coast to coast. As a result of Spain's new interest in Puerto Rico, a regional cultural life emerged. **José Campeche,** who is considered the first great Puerto Rican painter, did his work in this progressive era.

A GROWING NATIONAL IDENTITY

How Did Puerto Ricans Feel About Spanish Rule?

By the nineteenth century, as in other Latin American nations, citizens of Puerto Rico had begun to believe that it was time to leave "home" (Spain) and start a household of their own.

In 1791, the Haitian slaves revolted against French domination and declared Haiti the second free nation in the New World. By 1822, the great Venezuelan patriot and general **Simon Bolívar** had liberated today's Venezuela, Colombia, Panama, and Ecuador—the whole of northern South America—from Spanish rule.

José Francisco de San Martín, a veteran of the Spanish wars against Napoleon, aided by General **Bernardo O'Higgins,** had succeeded in liberating Chile and Peru and the rest of South America.

In 1823, Mexico bravely won its independence under Colonel **Antonio López de Santa Anna.**

Bolívar's Gran Colombia subsequently split into three independent countries—Venezuela, Colombia, and Ecuador—and borders were designated according to the interests of each national group. Ten new nations were born virtually overnight. Argentina, Uruguay, Paraguay, and Bolivia arose out of the old viceroyalty of La Plata; Colombia, Venezuela, and Ecuador out of the viceroyalty of New Granada; and Chile and Peru out of the viceroyalty of Peru. Portugal's New World territory became Brazil. Central America remained a single territory until it broke into five republics: Guatemala, Honduras, Nicaragua, El

Salvador, and Costa Rica. In 1844, the Dominican Republic declared its independence.

By the dawn of the nineteenth century, only Cuba and Puerto Rico remained Spanish colonies. But the cries for independence were being heard throughout; the scent of freedom was in the air. As with the United States a century earlier, the New World's Spanish colonies had finally come of age.

As the nineteenth century began, Puerto Ricans, who had by now a cultural and national identity distinct from Spain, began demanding autonomy from the "mother country." They sought educational reforms, the right to establish labor unions, and less taxation and more representation in the Spanish Cortes (Parliament). A key part of their demands was the appointment of Puerto Ricans, not Spaniards, to local governmental positions, which had been held strictly off limits to all *criollos.*

Ramón Power was among the first Puerto Ricans to raise a voice of dissension. He represented Puerto Rico before the Spanish Cortes and, in 1812, secured both a more liberal constitution for Puerto Rico and the right of Puerto Ricans to Spanish citizenship.

His provisions for greater self-rule, including the distribution of land to natives, freedom from taxation for those willing to work the land, and the opening of doors to new immigrants from other Latin American nations, were contained in the Ley Power (the Power Act), and, later, in the Real Cédula de Gracias of 1815. But this leniency didn't last long. When **José María Quiñones,** another early "father" of Puerto Rican independence, requested that Puerto Rico be granted complete independence, Spain responded by sending despotic military governors who demanded greater allegiance to Spain and higher taxes.

In 1868, a physician and patriot named **Ramón Emeterio Betances,** who had been expelled by the governor of Puerto Rico for his revolutionary ideas and had lived both in the United States and on several Caribbean islands, issued the Ten Commandments of Freedom. He called for Puerto Ricans to be granted rights akin to those in the American Bill of Rights. He pleaded for an end to slavery (which, in spite of having been officially abolished, was in full bloom), as well as freedom of speech and freedom of religion.

Thousands of his supporters marched into the small town of Lares, in western Puerto Rico, and took over with firearms and machetes in hand. This revolt, which was eventually squelched by the Spanish, came to be known as El Grito de Lares, and is celebrated as a national holiday among Puerto Ricans both on the island and on the mainland.

What's a Machete?

The machete is the traditional sword used by *jíbaros* to cut cane. But a machete is more than just a long sharp knife—it's the symbol of Caribbean farmers, much as the hammer and sickle were the symbol of Bolsheviks. In recent times, a group calling itself the *macheteros* (machete wielders) has advocated Puerto Rican independence from the United States.

What's a Jíbaro?

A *jíbaro* is a Puerto Rican field worker, who is usually an ace at cane hacking and machete wielding. The *jíbaro* is revered as the backbone of the early Puerto Rican agricultural economy. He is also mocked and vilified. In today's urban centers on the mainland, *jíbaro* is often a synonym for "hick."

Who Was Luis Muñoz Rivera and Why Is He Called the George Washington of Puerto Rico?

As a result of the Lares revolt in 1868, Puerto Ricans began organizing political parties for the first time. Among the many splinter parties, the Reform Party, led by **Luis Muñoz Rivera,** sought to gain political freedom by forging alliances with Spanish political parties. Muñoz Rivera proposed that his party and other splinter Puerto Rican political groups form a union with the party he believed would soon gain power in Spain, the Spanish Fusionist Party (which did rise to power shortly after his prediction). He envisioned that once that party got into power, a deal for Puerto Rican independence could be worked out.

Muñoz Rivera emerged as the leader of the Liberal Fusionist Party of Puerto Rico, while another Puerto Rican leader, **José Celso Barbosa,** formed the Orthodox Historical Autonomist Party.

Was Puerto Rico Really Free for Only Seven Days?

By 1897, an agreement was reached with Spain whereby Puerto Rico was granted local government control, the same rights as all Spanish citizens, and the right to elect native representatives to local government. These representatives would have full say over local taxes, budgets, and education. Both Muñoz Rivera and Celso Barboso ran for office; Muñoz Rivera won. It was the first time Puerto Rico would have its own independent governor—a great step toward complete independence. The date was July 17, 1898. On July 25, the United States invaded.

What Were the Monroe Doctrine and the Roosevelt Corollary?

When **James Monroe** was elected president of the United States in 1817, at the age of fifty-eight, he had a long and distinguished political career behind him that included service as secretary of state, as governor of Virginia, and, most notably, as an engineer of the Louisiana Purchase. Under Monroe, U.S. industry prospered, and Manifest Destiny reared its head well beyond the nation's borders.

The idea of the Monroe Doctrine sprang from a speech Monroe's secretary of state, **John Quincy Adams,** delivered before Congress in 1823; the phrase soon came to stand for a new U.S. expansionist experiment. In his speech, Adams declared that the United States would not tolerate European intervention in Latin America. The policy grew out of concern that England was flexing its economic muscle in Latin America (having seized chunks of territories by nibbling off Belize and the Mosquito Coast of Nicaragua), and that France, under **Napoleon III,** had designs on Mexico and intended to turn it into a client state by imposing a Hapsburg prince on a (briefly) restored Mexican throne.

However, the Monroe Doctrine did not promise that the United States would do the same—that is, refrain from intervening in the affairs of Latin American countries. In fact, while it appeared to be a simple exercise in isolationism and good-neighborly policy toward the fledgling new republics to the south, the Monroe Doctrine actually paved the way for the free ride U.S. imperialism took throughout the Western Hemisphere for many decades to come.

On the other hand, the doctrine provided a framework for various multinational treaties between the United States and its Latin neighbors, including economic programs that benefited many of the new nations, and mutual defense accords that served to unify the hemisphere during both world wars. The Monroe Doctrine also helped to lay the groundwork for the formation in 1946 of the Organization of American States (OAS).

The Roosevelt Corollary, issued in 1904 by President **Teddy Roosevelt,** served as an amendment to the Monroe Doctrine and went one step further (some say one step too far). The corollary gave the United States the right to act as "an international police power" wherever "chronic wrongdoing, or an impotence which results in a general loosening of the ties of civilized society" required intervention "by some civilized nation."

In the eyes of many Latin Americans, the Roosevelt Corollary packed a wallop. It not only allowed the United States to intervene unilaterally in the affairs of any country in the hemisphere, but it elevated Manifest Destiny to new heights by deciding who was civilized (the United States) and who wasn't (the rest of the nations in the hemisphere). This philosophy led to the Spanish-American War and to U.S. military intervention in various Caribbean and Central American countries for many years, including the overthrow of governments deemed harmful to U.S. investments and the installation of puppet rulers who would follow the policies outlined by Washington.

What Was the Spanish-American War All About, and Why Do We Call It the First Media-Staged War?

On the record, the reason for the Spanish-American War of 1898 was to help liberate Cuba from Spanish domination (Cuba and Puerto Rico were the only Spanish colonies left in the Western Hemisphere). The act that triggered the war was the blowing up of the warship *Maine,* which had been docked in Havana harbor to keep an eye on the Spanish in case they went too far with the Cubans. The word was that Spanish soldiers had blown the *Maine* to smithereens.

In fact, Cuban freedom fighters *(libertadores)* **José Martí,**

Antonio Maceo y Grojales, and many others had already made great strides toward liberating their country by the time the United States stepped in. It has been widely speculated that the *Maine* might actually have been blown up by American soldiers in search of a reason to go to war. A victory over Spain and "necessary" intervention in Cuba, Puerto Rico, and other colonies would ensure the expansion and protection of U.S. foreign markets in lush agricultural lands rich in sugar, coffee, tobacco, and minerals.

At first, President **William McKinley** was reluctant to enter a war against Spain, but overwhelmingly imperialistic sentiment had overtaken the country. **Henry Cabot Lodge,** the powerful senator from Massachusetts, and **Theodore Roosevelt,** who was then assistant secretary of the Navy, both lobbied intensely for U.S. involvement in the Caribbean. Roosevelt supposedly told a friend, "I should welcome almost any war, for I think this country needs one."

There was also another powerful lobby that seemed to want a war: the press—specifically, newspaper barons **William Randolph Hearst** and **Joseph Pulitzer,** both of whom had learned from the American Civil War that wars sell papers. The Hearst and Pulitzer papers began running stories (many of them true) about the atrocities the Spanish were committing against the Cubans and urging the president to step in.

At one point, Hearst was said to have dispatched artist **Frederic Remington** to Cuba to send back pictures of the atrocious war. When Remington didn't find anything really bloody to paint, Hearst got furious. "You furnish the pictures," he told the artist, "and I'll furnish the war!"

Who Were Teddy Roosevelt's Rough Riders and What Did They Have to Do with Winning Him the U.S. Presidency?

On April 25, 1898, the United States declared war on Spain, with **Teddy Roosevelt**'s Rough Riders in the vanguard. Roosevelt was commissioned lieutenant colonel and raised the First United States Volunteer Cavalry Regiment. He and his men were called Rough Riders because many of them were actually cowboys. Roosevelt was acclaimed a hero when he led the daring charge on Kettle Hill (wrongly called the charge on San Juan Hill) in eastern Cuba, in the province of Santiago de Cuba.

The same day, General **Nelson A. Miles,** under Roosevelt's command, landed in the southwestern Puerto Rican town of Guánica with sixteen thousand U.S. troops. There was no contest. The Spanish quickly surrendered and the Puerto Ricans warmly welcomed the United States. Most believed the invasion would be transitory and that this was simply putting a formal cap on 405 years of Spanish domination.

The Spanish-American War lasted only three months, and most of it was actually fought at the bargaining table. Spain was a dwindling empire on its last legs. There were more than five thousand American casualties in what Secretary of State **John Hay** had characterized as a "splendid little war," but only 379 were battle casualties. The rest of the deaths were caused by yellow fever, malaria, and other tropical diseases that plagued the U.S. troops.

When the war ended, the United States found itself in possession of Cuba and Puerto Rico, as well as Wake Island, Guam, and the Philippines. These last three had essentially been the last colonies controlled by Spain at the end of the century. You might say Spain was forced to throw in everything but the kitchen sink, and the United States wound up with a lot of land on its hands.

Cuba remained a U.S. protectorate until 1902, when it declared itself a free and independent nation. The Philippines eventually won complete independence from the United States in 1946; Guam and Wake Island remain under direct U.S. control today.

Puerto Rico, which had savored relative freedom for seven days after Spain had voluntarily granted it most of its rights of independence, found itself a U.S. protectorate. It was the beginning of a complex relationship, called by many different names over the years, that is still going strong today.

Teddy Roosevelt became extremely popular after his victory and was elected governor of New York. In 1900, when **McKinley** ran for reelection, he became vice president. Roosevelt was to preside over the Senate for only one week during a special session. Before the regular session of the Senate opened, McKinley was assassinated and Roosevelt found himself president of the United States. Four years later, he was still popular and was elected president in his own right by a resounding majority.

Under Teddy Roosevelt's presidency, the United States exerted great power over Latin America and beyond. It became instrumental in the creation of the country of Panama, forged from a lopped-off chunk of Colombian territory, the beginnings of the U.S.-controlled Panama Canal. Although Roosevelt characterized his foreign policy with the adage "speak softly and carry a big stick," he seldom spoke softly—and didn't need to. U.S. imperialism had reached its zenith.

Who Was Eugenio María de Hostos and Why Is a School in New York Named After Him?

Eugenio María de Hostos was a Puerto Rican journalist, philosopher, educator, and freedom fighter who organized the League of Patriots in New York City to aid in Puerto Rico's transition from a U.S. military government to a civil government. He maintained that the Puerto Rican people should have the right to decide, by means of a plebiscite, whether they wanted to be independent or be annexed by the United States.

However, when U.S. ambassadors met with Spanish delegates to negotiate the end of the Spanish-American War and the fate of the new territories, the few Puerto Rican officials whom Hostos had convinced the United States to invite to the table had no say in the final outcome. Under the Treaty of Paris of 1899, Puerto Rico became a U.S. protectorate with fewer rights of self-government than it had enjoyed in recent years under Spain.

Eugenio María de Hostos was born in Mayagüez, Puerto Rico, in 1839. He studied in Spain and became a lawyer. He believed that Puerto Rico should be independent and lobbied the Spanish government incessantly for independence, until he was forced into exile for his "liberal" opinions. During the struggle for Cuban independence from Spain, he joined forces with the Cubans and fought with **José Martí,** Cuba's "George Washington."

Hostos became part of the great Puerto Rican triumvirate of independence fighters—the others being **Ruiz Belvis** and **Ramón Emeterio Betances.** In 1874, Hostos moved to New York and published a famous newspaper, *La America Ilustrada.* Later he went to live in the Dominican Republic, where he published the newspaper *Las Tres Antillas,* which promoted independence and self-government for all three Spanish-speaking Caribbean countries: Cuba, Puerto Rico, and the Dominican Republic. He favored an Antilles Confederacy, in which the three islands would be united as a kind of commonwealth.

Aside from his political and journalistic career, Hostos was a dedicated teacher. He founded the first normal school in the Dominican Republic, where he became known as "El Maestro" ("the teacher" or "the master"). Later he moved to

Chile, where he was president of the Chilean Athenaeum, headed two schools, and taught constitutional law at the Universidad Chilena in Santiago de Chile. Among his many political and literary treatises, his *Derecho Constitucional (Constitutional Rights)* and *Tratado de Sociología (On Sociology)* are still studied in his native Puerto Rico, as well as other parts of Latin America.

Hostos believed that only through education can an oppressed people rise and take charge of their lives. He died in the Dominican Republic in 1903, one year after Cuba gained its independence. Hostos never saw his dreams for an independent Puerto Rico realized. Hostos Community College in the Bronx, New York, is named after him and memorializes his philosophy of "progress through education," which he so vigorously defended.

How Did the Puerto Ricans Feel About Becoming a U.S. Protectorate?

The transition to status as a U.S. protectorate was difficult for most Puerto Ricans. The language barrier, which necessitated the use of translators between Puerto Rican leaders and American military authorities governing the island, created tensions and many misunderstandings. The cultural barrier, which caused Americans to question even the most minute details of Puerto Rican criminal and civil laws—and, in many cases, to overturn them—went even deeper.

In 1900, almost two years after officially taking over, the United States declared Puerto Rico a U.S. territory under the Foraker Act. This meant that Puerto Ricans were neither U.S. citizens nor citizens of an independent nation. A civil administration replaced the transitional military government and allowed for the election of Puerto Ricans to a House of Delegates, where they could implement laws relating to internal affairs. However, the U.S. president was responsible

for appointing a governor to head the House of Delegates—
and that governor was to be an American, never a Puerto
Rican.

Besides granting the U.S. governor final say over the affairs of the island, the Foraker Act also put an extra economic squeeze on Puerto Rico by adding a heavy tariff on
products coming out of Puerto Rico. This was done to protect U.S. sugar and tobacco interests from Puerto Rican competition.

Many thinking Americans believed that the Foraker Act
was unfair, and the legality of the act was tested in the Supreme Court in what became known as the Insular Cases.
Luis Muñoz Rivera, who had become the leading Puerto Rican statesman, wrote to President **McKinley** that the Foraker
Act was "unworthy of the United States which imposes it and
of Puerto Ricans who have to endure it." As a result of the
act, the Puerto Rican Unionist Party emerged. The party
platform repudiated U.S. domination and supported any of
three options: statehood, nationhood, or semi-independence
under American protection.

Some called Muñoz Rivera the "spiritual governor" of
Puerto Rico; as fate would have it, his son, **Luis Muñoz
Marín,** became Puerto Rico's first native governor in 1948.

The U.S. Supreme Court ruled that Congress could set
up territories the way it had done in Cuba, Puerto Rico, and
the Philippines—and thus the Foraker Act was upheld. With
its underlying philosophy of "tutelage," a buzzword of the
time, the Foraker Act remained in effect until World War I.

"Tutelage" implied that it was the United States' duty to
instruct Puerto Ricans in how to behave like a progressive,
civilized nation. The idea of tutelage carried with it the seeds
of economic development and Americanization, and was
rooted in the philosophy expounded by writer and clergy-
man **Josiah Strong** in his best-selling book of 1885, *Our Country.* Strong argued that the United States was the torchbearer
of Anglo-Saxon virtue, and was therefore destined to "move

down upon Mexico, down upon Central and South America, out upon the islands of the sea, over upon Africa and beyond." And, he asked rhetorically, "Can anyone doubt that the result of this competition of the races will be the survival of the fittest?"

The rising threat of World War I, as well as unremitting pressure on the part of Puerto Ricans, led President **Woodrow Wilson** to sign the Jones Act on March 2, 1917. With one fell swoop of the pen, the president granted U.S. citizenship to all Puerto Ricans, unless they signed a document explicitly refusing it. Refusing citizenship meant giving up many civil rights, and there were few written refusals. Puerto Ricans immediately became subject to the U.S. war draft; but a U.S.-appointed governor would continue to rule over all internal affairs. During World War I, almost twenty thousand Puerto Ricans served in the U.S. armed forces. Thousands died on the front lines. The Puerto Rican people donated hundreds of thousands of dollars to the war effort and bought more than $10 million in war bonds. During the 1920s and 1930s, Puerto Ricans continued to ask for greater autonomy in local affairs. When **Theodore Roosevelt, Jr.** (**Teddy**'s son) served as governor of the island from 1929 to 1932, he launched several favorable economic and cultural programs and envisioned greater self-government for the people. In the late 1930s, a group of Puerto Rican nationalists, led by the Independentista fighter **Albizu Campos,** demanded Puerto Rican independence in the streets of the city of Ponce, and started a revolt that left nineteen dead and more than a hundred wounded.

As a result of this "unexpected" episode, two bills were introduced in Congress asking for Puerto Rican independence. Both failed on the grounds that Puerto Rican social and economic circumstances needed to be improved before independence could be seriously considered.

By 1946, the United States had decided to appoint the first native Puerto Rican governor of the island: **Jesús T. Pi-**

ñero. One year later, though, Congress passed the Elective Governors Act, granting Puerto Ricans the right to choose their governor and in turn granting this governor full rights to appoint all officials, except the auditor and members of the Supreme Court.

Who Was the First Elected Puerto Rican Governor and What Did He Do That Was So Important?

Luis Muñoz Marín, the son of the early patriot **Luis Muñoz Rivera,** was the first native son elected by the people of Puerto Rico. He took office in January 1949 and quickly began implementing many ideas he had been championing for years.

In 1916, Muñoz Marín had returned to Puerto Rico to edit the paper his father had started, *La Democracia*. He was elected to the Puerto Rican Senate in 1932, the same year **Franklin Delano Roosevelt** took office.

Marín's father served as Puerto Rican representative before Congress and fought for the revocation of the Foraker Act. He died one year before the act was repealed. Luis Muñoz Marín, who had grown up in Washington, D.C. (he was a teenager when his family moved to Washington), and who became a respected lawyer and a well-known man about Washington, had now inherited the mantle. He had been known as a poet and a contributor to such magazines as *The New Republic* and *The Nation*. He was the editor of a Latin American cultural journal, *La Revista de las Indias,* and had translated several books into Spanish, including the poetry of **Walt Whitman.** His wife, **Muna Lee,** was an American poet from Mississippi, and among his many friends and supporters was **Eleanor Roosevelt.** She had visited the rural areas of Puerto Rico in 1933, had voiced great concern over the poor state of Puerto Rican farms and the economy at large, and had lobbied for a radical change in the status quo. At her bidding, Franklin Roosevelt denounced "the hopeless drive to remodel Puerto Ricans so that they should become similar in language, habits and thoughts to continental Americans." The Brookings Institution echoed his words and issued a report on the horrible state of the Puerto Rican economy. Slowly, a new era was dawning.

Earlier, Franklin Roosevelt had appointed **Robert Gore** governor of Puerto Rico. Apparently, Gore was unfamiliar with the inner workings of the Puerto Rican culture and was not very highly thought of by the people. Muñoz Marín had used his friendship with Mrs. Roosevelt to have Mr. Gore removed.

Now that he was governor, duly elected by the people, under his newly formed Popular Democratic Party (PPD), Muñoz Marín would see to it that Washington, under President **Harry S. Truman,** supported him in his efforts to revitalize the Puerto Rican economy.

In 1947, the Puerto Rican legislature passed the Industrial Incentives Act, which provided freedom from taxes for ten years to any new business—thereby attracting a wealth of American industries that were grateful for the break and saw an opportunity to multiply their profits. The tax-free status Muñoz Marín dreamed up continues in a similar form to the present day, and has made it possible for hundreds of U.S. businesses to thrive in Puerto Rico.

Another program, Operation Bootstrap, which called for U.S. and Puerto Rican cooperation and was aimed at building an industrial economy to offset the strict dependence on agriculture, met with enormous success.

How Did Puerto Rico Become a Commonwealth . . . and What's a Commonwealth, Anyway?

As the economic situation began improving in Puerto Rico in the postwar years, **Muñoz Marín** began to consider the question of political status. Earlier in his career, he had rejected the notion of establishing a "Commonwealth State," known as the Irish Solution because it was patterned after Ireland's relationship with Great Britain. He thought commonwealth status would amount to nothing more than freedom "on a very long chain." But now that Puerto Rico's economy was starting to take off, severing ties with the United States would mean giving up no-tariff status and other important perquisites that were keeping the island industry percolating and had created a building boom and a strong tourist economy.

Statehood was another option, and although Muñoz Marín might have opposed it in principle, he was known to be a very practical person. However, he reasoned that it would take too long for the United States to accept this Latin island as another state. (He said: "If we seek statehood, we die waiting for Congress.") So his PPD party decided to adopt what he called the "intermediate solution"—commonwealth status.

Muñoz Marín was very popular in Washington, and when he spoke politicians listened. In 1950, Congress passed Public Law 600, calling for an election in Puerto Rico in which the people could determine whether the "free associated state" would be adopted. Muñoz Marín had created the phrase "free associated state" to please all three dominant political philosophies. To those who favored independence, the word "free" looked promising. To those who favored some association or dependence, the word "associated" sounded good. And, finally, for those who favored U.S. statehood, the word "state" struck a chord. In English, though, the new status just read "Commonwealth." The Independentista party, who wanted nothing but complete independence, did not participate in the elections. But as far as Muñoz Marín and the majority of the Puerto Rican voters were concerned, the new commonwealth status did grant a significant amount of independence. Legally, the new arrangement had a lot of holes, since it was a unilateral agreement that Congress could abrogate any time it pleased. For Muñoz Marín, the commonwealth agreement was something to work on over time, until Puerto Rico could achieve total independence from U.S. control, while benefiting from economic and social privileges the island could not otherwise have.

Muñoz Marín was elected governor three more times, winning by a landslide in both houses of government, and would probably have died on the job if he hadn't opted to retire in 1964 to let someone else have a shot at government. He died in 1980. Under him, Puerto Rico had not only won new and respected political status, but had flown its own flag for the first time, and, under the Puerto Rican Federal Relations Act of 1950, the island had been granted the power to write and enact its own constitution, as long as its provisions did not overstep the limitations placed on a U.S. territory. The constitution went into effect on July 25, 1952 (Constitution Day, a national holiday), exactly fifty-four years to the day from the U.S. landing in Guánica during the Spanish-American War.

Why Did the Independentistas Try to Assassinate President Truman?

Puerto Rican status has been a burning question in the minds of all Puerto Ricans ever since the Spanish-American War. Even today, under Governor **Pedro Roselló,** the question is more incandescent than ever.

On March 1, 1954, three Puerto Rican members of the pro-independence movement (Independentista) who had felt ignored by Muñoz Marín and the commonwealth partisans attempted to assassinate President **Harry Truman** by firing at him from the gallery of the U.S. House of Representatives. Nothing happened to the president, but several congressmen were wounded by the three terrorists, **Rafael Candel Miranda, Andrés Cordero,** and **Lolita Lebrón.**

They were sent to prison and, although they were not released until 1979, continued to work for Puerto Rican independence behind bars. A terrorist group calling themselves the Macheteros (the machete wielders) continued their revolutionary struggle. In 1983, a handful of Macheteros robbed an armored-car company in West Hartford, Connecticut, and drove away with $1.7 million to finance their organization.

Why Is Puerto Rican Migration Not Immigration and How Did It Get Started?

Although Puerto Ricans had been coming to the U.S. mainland ever since the island became a U.S. protectorate, the real migration happened after World War II. The reasons were many, but it all boiled down to one factor: economics. During World War II, a hundred thousand Puerto Ricans served in the armed forces. Military life exposed many islanders to mainland prosperity and encouraged them to move north. In addition, the population of the island doubled, rising to 2 million, in the first twenty-five years of the century, and continued growing very rapidly because of improved medical services brought in by the U.S. government.

However, the standard of living did not improve substantially, and the unemployment rate soared. By contrast, jobs on the mainland were plentiful, especially in the booming Garment District in New York City (where Puerto Rican women in particular proved a highly desirable labor force), as well as in the service industries that required unskilled or semiskilled workers. The migration in search of jobs and better living conditions continued steadily until the 1960s, when the movement of people began slowing down.

The stream of new Puerto Rican residents to the mainland has continued to the present day, ebbing and flowing depending on the number of jobs available. Tourism, agriculture, and the pharmaceutical industry have thrived on the island since it became a commonwealth. But in spite of significant U.S. investments in Puerto Rico, thanks to tax breaks for U.S. corporations, the standard of living has not kept pace with that of the mainland.

Since Puerto Ricans are U.S. citizens, they are not considered immigrants, and can (and do) travel back and forth regularly between the mainland and Puerto Rico. Many Puerto Ricans also travel to the mainland as contract farm workers under the auspices of the Office of the Commonwealth of Puerto Rico established in 1948. These workers come on a seasonal basis to harvest potatoes on Long Island, fruits and vegetables in New Jersey, tobacco in Connecticut, and sugar beets in Michigan.

But most Puerto Ricans coming to the mainland settle in urban areas. Over the years, they have brought their food, music, and way of life to many different cities, particularly New York, where El Barrio, or Spanish Harlem, is alive with their traditions and where Puerto Ricans are considered the most significant rising political group.

How Many Puerto Ricans Are There and Where Do They Live?

Today, of the 6.3 million Puerto Ricans, about 2.3 (or 43 percent) live on the mainland. According to the 1990 census, about 900,000 live in New York City alone (1.1 million total in New York State).

In recent years, Puerto Ricans have begun migrating to other parts of the United States, particularly Illinois (which has a population of more than 125,000 Puerto Ricans), Texas, and Florida. Of the Puerto Ricans coming to New York, only 6 percent have college degrees. By contrast, 24 percent of Puerto Ricans migrating to Texas, where there is a thriving, upwardly mobile Puerto Rican community, have college degrees.

Why Is New York Considered So Important for the Future of All Puerto Ricans?

One third of all Puerto Ricans on the mainland live in poverty. Despite the brilliant leaders and accomplished scientists, artists, and entrepreneurs in their community, as well as the seeming advantages of U.S. citizenship, Puerto Ricans represent the most socially and economically disadvantaged Latino group. Drugs, crime, and lack of educational skills are much too common among the population of New York City's El Barrio.

Some social observers have pointed to the fact that Puerto Ricans, because they are mostly of mixed African and Spanish descent, have been victims of the same type of institutionalized discrimination that other African-Americans have suffered. In addition, the language barrier and a feeling of being neither here nor there—straddling two cultures and two languages—have only helped to alienate Puerto Ricans further. Others, like **Linda Chavez,** author and former executive director of the U.S. Commission on Civil Rights, have pointed the finger at the breakdown of the Puerto Rican family unit; a majority of Puerto Rican households are headed by poor women. Still others argue that the reason comparatively few Puerto Ricans belong to the labor force is that manufacturing jobs, particularly in the garment industry, which have been traditionally held by Puerto Ricans, fell on bad times in the 1960s and 1970s. The scarcity of manufacturing jobs has been compounded by recent recessions.

However, it is also important to point out that large numbers of Puerto Ricans hold *career-track* white-collar positions, and that almost a third of working Puerto Rican males and two thirds of working Puerto Rican females hold professional, technical, managerial, sales, and other middle-management jobs. Also, whereas New York is still the home of the most economically underprivileged class of Puerto Ricans, in certain regions of the country they do better than their Latino counterparts. In Texas, for instance, Puerto Ricans graduate from college at a higher rate than Mexicans and have a higher per capita income. In Lorain, Ohio, and in San Francisco, Puerto Ricans boast very high median family incomes.

Still, it is obviously of major concern to Puerto Rican leaders that 31 percent of all Puerto Rican males and 59 percent of all Puerto Rican females over the age of sixteen are not in the labor force, and that a great many are dependent on their families or on government assistance. These problems are compounded by the fact that the majority of the more than twenty thousand Latino men currently in criminal custody in the state of New York are Puerto Ricans, and that AIDS and crack and heroin addiction threaten the very life of New York City.

With such pressing health and social challenges knocking at its portals, New York has become the testing ground for Puerto Rican political, social, and economic progress.

There are twenty-two Latino elected officials in New York—twenty-one of them Puerto Ricans. (The remaining one is **Guillermo Linares,** a Dominican council member representing an ever-growing population from the Dominican Republic.) **Fernando Ferrer** has been Bronx borough president since 1987 and is considered a serious contender and probable winner of the 1997 mayoral race. Congressman **José Serrano** has emerged as an important voice for Latinos in Washington, and is known to have the ear and respect of President **Bill Clinton.** Serrano was also among the leaders who helped redraw the political boundaries of New York City during the last presidential election, particularly the new Twelfth Congressional District, which increased the Latino voting power base and helped get Congresswoman **Nydia Velazquez** elected to Congress.

Labor leader **Dennis Rivera,** who represents 120,000 predominantly minority health-care workers, is also a powerful political presence. He has been nominated for the chairmanship of **Jesse Jackson**'s National Rainbow Coalition. And Puerto Ricans hold other very crucial jobs in New York. Until 1993, **José Fernández** chaired the Board of Education. (He was ousted because of the board's opposition to his "Rainbow Curriculum," which endorsed the distribution of condoms and a grade school curriculum that included teaching about nontraditional families, such as those with gay and lesbian parents and single parents). He was replaced by another Latino, Ramon Cortines, who is considered more "middle of the road." **Carlos Rivera,** a Puerto Rican, is the city's fire commissioner.

Herman Badillo, the first Puerto Rican ever elected to Congress (in 1970), is still active in New York politics, and holds an undisputed position of leadership in the Latino community. He is a law partner of Fischbein, Badillo, Wagner, and Itzer, and is a close advisor to New York City mayor Rudolph Giuliani.

Today, Puerto Ricans constitute the swing vote in many elections, including the mayoral election. "Nuyorican" leaders believe the tide has begun to turn, and that the next decade will see a rising and powerful middle class among their people.

Commonwealth vs. Statehood: What's the Big Deal?

The question of Puerto Rican status has been hanging in the balance for more than a century. Back in 1964, the United States–Puerto Rico Commission on the Status of Puerto Rico decided that both commonwealth status and statehood were legitimate options for Puerto Rico, and that the people of Puerto Rico must decide which way they wanted to go. However, the commission, chaired by **James A. Rowe, Jr.,** did point out that statehood might impose undue economic hardships on the island.

Right after the report of the commission became public, **Luis Muñoz Marín,** who favored commonwealth status, and **Luis Ferré,** who headed the opposition party (PNP) and backed statehood, went to the polls to try to resolve the question. In the end, 61 percent of the people favored commonwealth status, while 39 percent voted for statehood. However, four years later, in 1968, Ferre was elected governor of the island. Although his election might have appeared to signal a desire for statehood, the island remained polarized on the question, and no action was taken to bring the matter before Congress.

In 1978, President **Jimmy Carter** called for a new referendum on the issue; he was apparently concerned about an impending United Nations vote accusing the United States of colonialism in Puerto Rico. That referendum never took place. In his first speech before Congress, in 1989, President **George Bush** supported a call for a referendum, and said he was in favor of statehood.

The question remained open-ended until November 1992, when Puerto Rican voters elected Governor **Pedro Roselló,** a strong advocate of statehood. Roselló won 49.5 percent of the popular vote and announced that a plebiscite to decide the status of Puerto Rico would be held on November 14, 1993. The three choices on the ballot would be statehood, retaining commonwealth status, and independence.

When November 14, 1993, finally rolled around, the people of Puerto Rico went to the polls in unprecedented numbers. Forty-eight percent of the voters favored maintaining commonwealth status, and 46 percent favored statehood. It was a very close vote—but one that affirmed Puerto Rico's ambiguous relationship with the United States for many years to come. Only 4 percent voted for complete independence. A poll taken by the Latino National Political Survey among Puerto Ricans living across the United States showed 68 percent in favor of commonwealth status, 27 percent in favor of statehood, and 4 percent in favor of independence.

If Puerto Rico ever became a state, many significant and far-reaching changes affecting both the United States and the island would occur overnight. For one, Puerto Rico's population exceeds that of twenty-six states, which means that, along with two U.S. senators, Puerto Rico would get to send seven members to the House of Representatives. These new members would represent a state in which 70 percent of the (mostly Democratic) 3.6 million residents speak only Spanish. Presently, three Puerto Rican congresspersons represent New York City and Chicago, but there are no Puerto Rican senators.

According to **Carlos Romero Barceló,** the congressional delegate from Puerto Rico and a powerful political leader of the New Progressive Party, statehood is essential, and he vowed to continue to fight for it. According to those in favor of statehood, the vote in favor of keeping commonwealth status was too close to be called a mandate.

Making Puerto Rico, called "the shining star of the Caribbean" in advertisements, the fifty-first star in the U.S. flag will do much toward incorporating Puerto Ricans into this country, which will benefit Puerto Ricans and all others involved. After the 1992 presidential election, Barceló received the right to vote on the House floor. Previously, he and other nonvoting delegates to the House (those from Guam and the Virgin Islands) could vote only in committees.

However, had the island lost its commonwealth status, Puerto Ricans stood to lose many important economic breaks. For one, Section 936 of the Internal Revenue Code exempts mainland companies operating in U.S. possessions from most federal taxation. If Puerto Rico ever becomes a state, the law will no longer apply and U.S. companies will most likely flee to Mexico and other parts of Latin America, leaving more than 160,000 workers on the island unemployed. And, of course, all the small ancillary businesses that depended on the more than six hundred U.S. companies in Puerto Rico would be enormously affected as well.

A 1990 U.S. Congressional Budget Office study concluded that statehood would cost Puerto Rico 100,000 jobs by the end of the decade. With 73 percent of its mainland investment gone, the gross national product would tumble by 3.3 percent. All this translates into a doubling of Puerto Rico's unemployment rate from its current 16 percent to 30 percent. A recession with far more devastating effects than any recent hurricane would be almost guaranteed to hit the island.

Still, Section 936 has come under severe scrutiny by the administration of **Bill Clinton,** which holds that the code benefits mostly pharmaceutical companies. The administration has introduced proposals to phase it out, regardless of whether or not statehood passes. As for the new federal tax that would be imposed on Puerto Ricans, who presently pay no such tax, 80 percent of Puerto Ricans would be exempt because their wages fall under the taxable minimum. The average annual income for Puerto Ricans on the island is $6,200, or half that of residents of Mississippi, the poorest state in the Union.

Either way, the issue of statehood is a big deal. With statehood, Puerto Rico would have become the most powerful Latino political voice in the United States. The United States, in turn, would have moved one step closer to *hermandad*—brotherhood and sisterhood—with all the Spanish-speaking nations of the hemisphere. In spite of the vote in favor of retaining commonwealth status, the dream of statehood is still alive and well in the minds of millions of Puerto Ricans.

PAHRY TIME!

What's a Pahry?

A *pahry* is a fiesta—as in "party." Which is not to say Puerto Ricans don't use the word "fiesta" when they celebrate—it's just that *pahry* is part of their ever-increasing "Spanglish" vocabulary.

So What Do Puerto Ricans on the Mainland Do When They Have a Pahry?

They have salsa parties where the bongos keep pace with the maracas and the maracas chase the blues away. Often, Puerto Ricans celebrate at home or at social clubs, but the biggest fiesta of all is the Puerto Rican Day Parade in New York City in June, when *comparsas* (carnival dancing groups) and marching bands follow the floats, which are followed by politicians looking for votes. In recent years, the Puerto Rican Day Parade has attracted bigger crowds than the Saint Patrick's Day Parade.

The Fiesta del Apostol Santiago, or Fiestas padronales de Santiago Apostal (St. James's Day), also brings out the dancers in El Barrio and other Puerto Rican neighborhoods. Both men and women wear traditional island costumes reminiscent of African dress and dance down the middle of the street to the fast carnival rhythms, singing *bombas*—African couplets accompanied by drum music.

Besides the parties and street fairs that are held in every Puerto Rican neighborhood across the United States during the warm months, a number of street celebrations take place in honor of the various *santos* whose statues are carried by the faithful adorned with flowers and food offerings.

What's a Santo?

A *santo* is a saint of the Roman Catholic church who also represents a West African Yoruba deity. The celebration of the *santo* day is an example of syncretism of Spanish and the African religions brought to the island. For example, the Yoruba god Chango, is represented by St. Barbara; the Yoruba goddess Yemaya is represented by the Virgin of Regla, and so on. The practice of Yoruba religions is called *santería*. Although its most influential center was in Cuba and it is very much in evidence in Miami and other cities with large populations of Cuban-Americans, there are many Puerto Rican followers of *santería* both in Puerto Rico and on the mainland.

What's a Botánica?

A *botánica* is a store that sells herbs and "natural" medicines—and there are hundreds of them in every Puerto Rican neighborhood throughout the United States. But a *botánica* is also a religious store for followers of *santería*, where they can buy candles, religious medals, beads, and statues and consult with the *santera*, or priestess, who usually owns the shop. There are both priests and priestesses, although the majority are women.

LATINO HEARTTHROBS OF ALL TIME

1. Irene Cara	Dancer and singer who recorded the hits "Fame" and "Flashdance (What a Feeling)," and won an Oscar for writing the latter
2. Mariah Carey	Grammy winner, top recording star

---

3. Julie Carmen	Actress who won distinction for her role in the 1988 film *The Milagro Beanfield War*
4. Vikki Carr	Top singer who opened the way for feminist music among popular Latino performers; performed at the White House for Presidents Nixon, Ford, Reagan, and Bush
5. Charo	Known as the "Latin bombshell"; sings and plays the Spanish guitar
6. Chayanne	Singer; one of *People* magazine's Fifty Most Beautiful People for 1993
7. Victoria Corderi	News anchor, "Street Stories," New York
8. Trent Dimas	1992 Olympic gymnastics gold medalist
9. Plácido Domingo	One of the world's leading lyric-dramatic tenors; starred in the 1986 film version of *Otello*
10. Gloria Estefan	World-renowned Grammy winner whose recordings and videos have sold millions around the globe
11. Emilio Estevez	One of Martin Sheen's sons (another is Charlie Sheen); a highly acclaimed actor and director with a top box-office draw; appeared in the 1985 films *St. Elmo's Fire* and *The Breakfast Club*
12. Andy Garcia	Actor remembered for his parts in *The Godfather III* and *The Untouchables*

13. Cristina Gonzalez	Dancer with the Alvin Ailey Repertory Ensemble
14. Rita Hayworth	Born Rita Cansino; sang, danced, and acted with the likes of Gary Cooper and Glenn Ford; at the height of her career, she was known as Hollywood's "Great American Love Goddess"
15. Julio Iglesias	Grammy Award–winning singer and songwriter; romantic crooner in English and Spanish
16. Ricardo Montalban	Star of the popular television series *Fantasy Island,* as well as hundreds of films, television shows, and TV commercials; in 1979 won an Emmy for his role in *How the West Was Won*
17. Ramon Navarro	Heartthrob who acted in silent films and talkies
18. Jackie Nespral	Weekend coanchor of NBC's *The Today Show*
19. Rosie Perez	Oscar-nominated actress and choreographer; played Tina in Spike Lee's *Do the Right Thing*
20. Chita Rivera	Dynamic actress and dancer who won a 1984 Tony Award for her performance in *The Rink,* and a Tony for her dancing and acting in the 1993 Broadway hit *Kiss of the Spider Woman*

21. Cesar Romero	Popular actor of the 1940s and 1950s who played villains and leading men; also appeared in numerous TV shows and series, including his role as the Joker in *Batman*
22. Linda Ronstadt	Renowned singer whom everyone thought of as Anglo until she recorded an album in Spanish; won a Grammy as Best Female Pop Performer in 1976
23. Gabriela Sabatini	Top-seeded tennis player who was a finalist in the U.S. Open singles in 1989 and won the title in 1990
24. Jon Secada	Top contemporary Latino singer and composer who got his start in Gloria Estefan's band
25. Charlie Sheen	Emilio Estevez's brother and the highest-paid Latino actor in Hollywood
26. Ritchie Valens	1950s rocker whose life story was told in the movie *La Bamba*
27. Raquel Welch	Model, actress, and dancer who won a Golden Globe Award for Best Actress in the 1974 film *The Three Musketeers* and continues a successful movie, video, and theater career

What's Compadrazco?

Compadrazco, which comes from the Spanish word meaning "coparenting," is at the root of the Latino social and extended family structure. It's a system of *madrinas* and *padrinos* (godmothers and godfathers) in which friends select each other to be a second parent to a child for the rest of the child's life. Often, at a wedding, the *madrina* is the one to buy the wedding ring for her godchild. This holds for all Latinos, not only Puerto Ricans. Close friends often refer to each other as *compadre* or *comadre* (depending on gender) by way of reinforcing their ties.

What's the Puerto Rican National Dish?

Although American food is as Puerto Rican as *gandules* (Puerto Rican peas), Puerto Ricans share many delicious dishes with other Caribbean countries and have some special ones of their own. *Asopao,* a chicken and rice mixture similar to the paella of Valencia, Spain, is perhaps Puerto Rico's most famous dish. *Pasteles* (meat and vegetable patties), *empanadas de jueyes* (crab cakes), *sopa de quimbombo* (okra soup), *bacalaitos* (codfish fritters), and *lechón asado* (roast suckling pig) are among the best-known Puerto Rican culinary delights. *Pirulis* (sugar sticks), *granizados* (tropical fruit ices), and *churros* (deep-fried, sugared stick-shaped doughnuts) are the "fast foods" sold at street stands all over the *barrios*. Puerto Rican cooking combines traditional Spanish dishes, such as paella, with African delicacies and native Taino spices and vegetables.

Puerto Rican chefs sauté *achiote* seeds, which were an essential ingredient of Taino cooking, in olive oil to produce an orange oil similar to West African palm oil. Their foods are often seasoned with *adobo,* a marinade of lemon, garlic, salt, pepper, and other spices that tastes as good on suckling pig as on fried goat. Another mixture, known as *sofrito,* is composed of sautéed garlic, onions, and green peppers and often tops meats and fish.

All this good food is often chased with hearty dark rum from the island or light American beer called *rubia*—"blond."

CINCO

Cubans

BEFORE THE CUBA LIBRE WAS INVENTED

When did the history of Cuban-Americans begin?

What was Cuba like before Fidel Castro?

Did the Siboney and Taino invent Cuban cigars?

What did the Spanish want with Cuba and why was it so important?

How did Havana come to be swapped for Florida?

What part did the English play in African slavery in Cuba?

Does that mean the Africans didn't mind being taken to Cuba?

Why did it take Cubans so long to gain their independence from Spain and how was slavery a key factor?

How did Cuba almost become annexed to the United States in the 1840s?

What was the Grito de Yara and why did Cuban landowners change their minds and join the rest of the folks?

How did U.S. business interests profit from Cuba's Ten Years' War?

Who was José Martí?

Who wrote the song "Guantanamera"?

Is it true that the early Cuban revolutionaries would have won their war without U.S. help?

So why did the United States fight the Spanish-American War?

If lust for Cuba was the reason the United States went to war with Spain, how come Cuba got its independence by 1902?

What's a Cuba libre?

What was the Platt Amendment and why did it open a bucket of worms that helped fuel the 1959 Fidel Castro revolution?

What's Guantánamo Bay?

Who was Fulgencio Batista?

If Cuba was doing so well, how come a revolution was waiting in the wings?

Who is Fidel Castro and what happened to his idealistic revolution that made Cubans flee to Miami by the thousands?

What's a gusano?

What did Fidel do for Cuba?

Who was Che Guevara?

What happened at the Bay of Pigs and why did Cuban-Americans blame President Kennedy?

What caused the Cuban Missile Crisis?

Who were the Marielitos and why did so many people hate them?

HAVANA, U.S.A.: THE LAND OF THE FIESTA, BUT NOT THE SIESTA

What's Little Havana and why isn't it so Havana anymore?

What's a YUCA?

Are all Cuban-Americans rich?

What's Santería?

What's a Fiesta de Quince?

What do Cuban-Americans eat?

BEFORE THE CUBA LIBRE WAS INVENTED

When Did the History of Cuban-Americans Begin?

The history of Cuban-Americans, for the most part, began with **Fidel Castro**—or, rather, with the communist revolution which he masterminded and which put him in power in 1959.

Soon after Fidel's takeover, hundreds of thousands of Cubans began fleeing the island and settling in Miami. In just a few years, they changed the economy and the character of that beautiful Florida city forever. Today, there are three generations of Cuban-Americans living in the United States—more than half a million in Florida, and the rest scattered throughout the country, especially New York and the Northeast. Cuban-Americans are the product of two main immigrations: the one that took place in the 1960s and early 1970s, and the one (much smaller) that resulted from the Mariel Boatlift in 1976.

But there were Cuban-Americans in the United States long before these two significant immigrations. In the late eighteenth century, a large Cuban colony blossomed in Tampa, Florida, where Cubans imported the fine art of Cuban cigar-making and established tobacco manufacturing plants and shops that are famous to this day. Cuban immigrants have come to the United States as a result of the many waves of political unrest that have occurred in Cuba since before the Spanish-American War. But the post-Castro "exiles" (a label they gave themselves and which the U.S. government used) outdid previous immigrants in sheer numbers and in influence.

What Was Cuba Like Before Fidel Castro?

In 1492, when **Columbus** first landed on Cuba, the largest and westernmost island of the Antillean archipelago, this is what he had to say about it in his journals: "[I have] never seen anything so beautiful . . . [everything I saw] was so lovely that my eyes could not weary of beholding such beauty, nor could I weary of the songs of the birds large and small. . . . Flocks of parrots darken the sun. There are trees of a thousand species, each has its particular fruit, and all of marvelous flavor."

Arawak peoples belonging to the Taino and Siboney groups inhabited the land and lived by fishing, hunting, and farming. Although the exact number of Taino and Siboney living in Cuba when Columbus arrived is uncertain (some sources estimate a hundred thousand), it is certain that by the end of the fifteenth century, their population had been practically decimated by European diseases and the hard labor imposed on them by the Spaniards. Toward the end, before the Arawak peoples disappeared as a group, as a result either of genocide or of interbreeding with the *conquistadors,* they had been reduced to small settlements in isolated, inaccessible regions of western Cuba.

The Siboney lived in cone-shaped, palm-thatched multifamily huts, known as *bohios,* which are constructed to this day as the archetypal architecture of "native" Cuba. In fact, the deep-country songs known as *décimas guajiras* often use the term *bohio* when referring to someone's home. Siboney villages consisted of one to two thousand inhabitants, with twenty to fifty multifamily dwellings. There was a square in the middle of the village leading to the house of the *cacique,* or chieftain, and a town center known as the *batey.* The Siboney were monogamous, with the exception of the chief of the tribe (always male), who was allowed about fifteen wives. The people were skilled at many crafts, including woodwork, ceramics, and textile production. They used wild cotton and palm fibers to make hammocks, fishing lines, and many other useful tools. Chiles and the pulp of the annatto tree were used both as dyes and as condiments, and they farmed corn, *yuca* (cassava, a tuber that is still a popular food among Cubans and Cuban-Americans and is served at Christmas dinner), tomatoes, sweet potatoes, pineapples, and other fruits. Columbus observed in one of his letters that the women seemed to work more than the men, but he was unsure whether they were allowed to own property. Aside from the Taino and the Siboney, another Arawak group of Indians, known as the Mayarí, also lived in Cuba before the Spanish *conquista,* but, as with the Siboney and Taino, precious few of their artifacts and sites remain.

Did the Siboney and Taino Invent Cuban Cigars?

You could say so, since they cultivated tobacco extensively and taught **Columbus** and other *conquistadors* how to roll cigars and smoke them. The word "tobacco" comes from *tabaco,* a Taino word. Curiously, the process of rolling these popular leaves by hand has not changed much over the centuries.

What Did the Spanish Want with Cuba and Why Was It So Important?

At first, as was their custom, the Spanish prospected for gold. **Diego Velázquez,** a rich landowner from Hispaniola (the Dominican Republic) who had won many wars against the native peoples, was sent by the Spanish crown in 1511 to secure the Cuban territory and establish settlements for the purpose of mining for gold. Velázquez established Baracoa (1512), Bayamo (1513), Trinidad, Sancti Spiritus (1514), Havana (1514), Puerto Príncipe (1514), and Santiago de Cuba (1515). Some gold was, in fact, found in the central highland ranges of the Sierra Maestra in the western part of the island (the same mountain range from which Fidel was to launch his 1950s revolution). But gold production was short-lived (1517–19) because Cuba's wealth really lay in its rich agricultural soil and its strategic location.

The island allowed access to both the Gulf of Mexico and the Caribbean, and lay at the crossroads of three main maritime routes: the Straits of Florida to the north, the Windward Passage to the east, and the Yucatán Channel to the west. These were the three points where Spain was most vulnerable to foreign aggression—namely English, Dutch, and French pirates and privateers stalking the Spanish galleons coming from Mexico and Peru laden with gold and other goodies. For two centuries, the island served as home base and launching pad for some of the most important

Spanish expeditions in the New World, led by **Pedrarias Dávila** (Central America, 1513); **Francisco Fernández de Córdoba** (Yucatán Peninsula, 1517); **Juan de Grijalba** (Mexico, 1518); **Hernando Cortés** (Mexico, 1519); **Pánfilo de Narváez** (Mexico, 1520, and Florida, 1527); and **Hernando de Soto** (Florida, 1538).

Thus, from the earliest times, Spain valued Cuba as a vital strategic colony. The agricultural wealth and other advantages that followed when African slaves were brought by the thousands were merely considered a handsome side benefit of Cuba's essential role as the Spanish fortress of the Caribbean.

CLASSIC FILMS ABOUT LATINOS

1. *West Side Story* (1961)

2. *El Norte* (1983)

3. *Scarface* (1983)

4. *La Bamba* (1987)

5. *Stand and Deliver* (1987)

6. *The Milagro Beanfield War* (1988)

How Did Havana Come to Be Swapped for Florida?

Spain became involved in Europe's Seven Years' War (1756–63), which was essentially a war between France and England. Not so surprisingly after the maritime fiasco the English called the defeat of the Spanish Armada, the Spanish sided with the French. Spanish colonies in the New

World became an obvious target for English military interest. In 1762, the English decided that Cuba, where sugar, coffee, and tobacco thrived and the trade winds were always in the mariner's favor, would make a nice little colony. They struck Havana harbor and took control of the city.

Some good things came out of this for the *criollos* of Cuba, who until then had been forced to trade almost exclusively with Spain (or else deal in the black market with other European powers). Trade taxes were abolished. The port was thrown wide open for commerce with merchants and traders from England and the North American colonies. All at once Cuba, which had been regarded merely as a fortress colony, began to view itself as a viable island with great prospects for a thriving economy. With the English in charge, Cuba could buy and sell to a large part of the world, particularly the rich American colonies to the north.

But the English occupation was short-lived, since the Spanish could not bear to lose their Caribbean jewel and by 1763 ceded Florida to the English in exchange for Havana.

What Part Did the English Play in African Slavery in Cuba?

Among the many Cuban imports during the brief English occupation was a highly coveted commodity: African slaves. Encouraged by the English, slave traders from all over the world descended on Cuba for a share of the newly opened market. The Spanish had not opposed African slavery (in fact, they were among the first to engage in the slave trade), they just never saw great demand for it in Cuba. During the brief ten months of English rule in Cuba, more than ten thousand African slaves were introduced—many more than would ordinarily have entered Cuba under Spain over a period of ten or more years. The outcome of this unexpected windfall was cheap labor to help grow and harvest sugar cane, tobacco, coffee, and other crops. Sugar cane became the main crop of the island. It was indeed a momentous time for Cuba. Rich African-Cuban musical, philosophical, and religious traditions are rooted in this period; they would in time cast a spell on the island and eventually transform it. This period, too, marked the start of Cuba's reliance on a single-crop economy, which was to be both the joy and bane of the island's existence to the present day.

The sudden economic boom in Cuba, during which sugar mills and plantations began to sprout all over the island, led to an exponential increase in the population and the number of towns. By the end of the eighteenth century, Havana ranked as one of the largest cities in the New World.

There were some differences between the treatment of slaves in Cuba and in other Spanish territories. The number of "free colored" people in Cuba soon surpassed other slave-holding societies in the Caribbean. The reason for this was twofold. First, it was customary for the white Spanish slaveowners to free their many illegitimate children. Second, ever since the sixteenth century African slaves in Cuba had been able to exercise certain rights. The most important of these was *coartación*, an arrangement that enabled slaves to negotiate their freedom with their owners. Slaves could purchase their freedom or their children's freedom by agreeing to give the owner a down payment and then a fixed sum of money in installments. This arrangement was possible because the Spanish looked on Africans not as people they were born to possess, but merely as a commodity, a source of cheap labor.

This attitude perhaps helps explain the different views of race held by the Spanish and the English. For the Spanish, if you looked white, you were white, even if one of your parents or grandparents was a person of color. The Anglo concept of the "octoroon" was practically inconceivable to the Spaniard. This is not to say racial prejudice was absent in

Cuba and other regions of the Spanish New World—but the rules of the game were slightly different.

Does That Mean the Africans Didn't Mind Being Taken to Cuba?

The Africans longed for their homelands in Western Africa (as many of their soulful ballads remind us); they longed for freedom, and, of course, they very much minded being exploited. And exploited they very often were, especially in the deep agricultural areas, where their labor was sorely needed and slaveowners paid less heed to the laws of *coartación*. Significant slave uprisings occurred in Cuba. There were also thousands of *cimarrones* (runaway slaves). In 1727, three hundred slaves rebelled on one Havana plantation alone. Four years later, another slave uprising closed down the copper mines of Santiago de Cuba. Some slave rebellions took the form of sudden and violent destruction of property and the random killing of whites. Other revolts represented the struggle for emancipation and justice more than mere outbursts.

In 1811, a free African-Cuban carpenter named **José Antonio Aponte** organized a large rebellion in Havana, demanding the emancipation of all slaves. Aponte's cause was supported by whites, as well as free persons of color and slaves. It was a very powerful rebellion and awakened many intellectuals to the injustices of slavery. Aponte's rebellion, as well as the hundreds of others throughout the island—in Matanzas, Holguín, Puerto Príncipe, Manzanillo, and almost every village and hamlet in Cuba—resulted not only in new social awareness, but in a terrible backlash by *Criollo* and Spanish-born slaveowners. In retaliation for their insurrection, African-Cubans were slaughtered, tortured, tied to ladders, and flogged to death "to set an example." An uprising in Matanzas province in the early 1800s, involving more than three hundred slaves from fifteen sugar plantations, ended when a local squadron of Spanish lancers attacked, killed, and dispersed hundreds of brave fighters. However, the slaves' struggle was not in vain. By the mid-1800s, an African-Cuban was to become a leader in the uprising against Spanish domination. His name was **Antonio Maceo,** and it is thanks to him and three other important revolutionaries, **Carlos Manuel de Céspedes, Máximo Gómez,** and **José Martí,** that Cuba won its independence from Spain.

Why Did It Take Cubans So Long to Gain Their Independence from Spain and How Was Slavery a Key Factor?

Whereas the rest of Latin America (except Puerto Rico) had gained its independence from Spain by the middle of the nineteenth century, Cuba remained a Spanish colony until the Spanish-American War of 1898. There were many reasons for this delay in fulfilling the dreams of millions of Cuban *criollos* who had envisioned a nation separate from Spain since the middle of the eighteenth century.

At issue was the highly structured hierarchical Cuban *criollo* society, which was divided between the Cuban elite, who owned the sugar and tobacco plantations, and the rest of Cuban society. The elite sought reforms for themselves, disregarding the Cuban population at large. They wanted lower tariffs and freer trade with the rest of the world, but they feared that complete independence from Spain might be bad for business. By 1817, England was putting pressure on Spain to abolish international slave trade. In 1845, Spain enacted the Law of Abolition and Repression of the Slave Trade. This law stated that all slaves introduced in Cuba after 1820 were in illegal bondage, and thus were entitled to their freedom. Although the law did little to diminish the supply of slaves to Cuba, it certainly made doing business and growing sugar a lot more expensive. For one, slave mortality, which had been previously of little concern to slaveowners (because slaves could be replaced at the drop of a sombrero), now presented a problem. Plantation owners were forced to look after the health of slaves, since bringing in replacements was against the law and therefore the cost had skyrocketed. Between 1800 and the 1820s, the price of male slaves slipped from three hundred to sixty pesos, but by the 1860s, a slave might go for as much as fifteen hundred pesos. Ironically, slave trade increased during this time, and, in fact, the majority of slaves entered Cuba after May 1820. Between 1821 and 1831, more than three hundred expeditions landed an estimated sixty thousand slaves in Cuba. Between 1830 and 1850, an average of ten thousand slaves arrived in Cuba annually. This open defiance of Spanish law constituted an odd sort of insurrection by the *criollo* landed gentry, who decided it was best to be independent of Spanish rule— but did not advocate freedom for all and the pursuit of happiness.

IMPORTANT DATES

1763	Spain cedes Florida to the English in exchange for Havana, after the British victory in the French and Indian War.
May 19, 1895	José Martí, who fought for Cuba's freedom, dies at the Battle of Dos Ríos.
May 20, 1902	Cuba wins its independence and elects its first president, Tomás Estrada Palma.

| January 1, 1959 | Fulgencio Batista flees Cuba in the early dawn for safety in Spain after being overthrown by Fidel Castro. |
| October 22, 1962 | President Kennedy announces that Russian atomic-missile sites are being built in Cuba, a threat to the security of the region. He institutes a blockade of Cuba and demands the withdrawal of all offensive weapons. |

How Did Cuba Almost Become Annexed to the United States in the 1840s?

The Cuban *criollo* elite—i.e., the landowners, not the intellectuals—felt disaffected from Spain, which charged Cubans high taxes and sided with England on the issue of slavery. It occurred to the Cuban elite that if the United States annexed Cuba, slavery could continue, and Cuban sugar, tobacco, and coffee production could be stepped up to serve North American states duty-free. The Cuban elite saw the annexation of Texas as an example of what they had in mind, since Texas had been allowed to join the Union as a slave state.

To add fuel to the fire, the notion of Manifest Destiny had taken hold of the minds of American thinkers—and Cuba seemed like a natural target. In 1823, Secretary of State **John Quincy Adams** viewed the annexation of Cuba as something of a natural law. "There are laws political as of physical gravitation," said Adams, "and if an apple, severed by a tempest from its native tree, cannot choose but to fall to the ground, Cuba, forcibly disjoined from its own natural connection to Spain, and incapable of self-support, can gravitate only towards the North American Union, which, by the same law of nature, cannot cast her off from her bosom." An operative phrase in Adams's speech was "incapable of self-support." Over this idea alone wars were fought.

While annexation fever grew among the *criollo* elite, the United States continued its efforts to obtain Cuba. First, President **James Polk** offered Spain $100 million dollars for the island in the early 1850s, but Spain declined. Then, in 1854 President **Franklin Pierce** upped the ante to $130 million, but again Spain declined. That same year, the U.S. ministers to Spain, England, and France met in Ostend, Belgium, and proclaimed loudly and publicly that the United States wished to buy Cuba. The Ostend Manifesto, as it came to be known, also contained a warning to Spain that if it did not acquiesce, then "by any law human and divine, we shall be justified in wresting it from Spain if we possess the power." Anyone with a little foresight could have predicted that, sooner or later, a Spanish-American war would be fought.

But the United States suddenly became involved in domestic issues that pivoted on the issue of slavery. Within ten years, the country was embroiled in the Civil War, which brought international activity to a virtual halt. At the same time, Cuban *criollos* with justice and a hatred of slavery on their minds were becoming more organized, inspired in their efforts by Latin American leaders such as **Simon Bolívar** and **José Francisco de San Martín,** who were successfully creating independent democratic republics in South America.

What Was the Grito de Yara and Why Did Cuban Landowners Change Their Minds and Join the Rest of the Folks?

In May 1865, a *criollo* political group known as the Reformist Party, composed of many plantation owners and representing a vast majority of their sentiments, directed a memorandum to the Spanish Parliament with four basic demands: that Cubans be represented in the Parliament; that the tariff system be completely reformed; that Cuban natives *(criollos)* be given the same rights as *peninsulares* (the Spanish-born); and that slavery be permanently abolished in Cuba.

Many factors led to the sudden about-face on the issue of slavery. First, it was clear that slavery had to end sooner or later, regardless of the wishes of the *peninsulares*. Second, Cuban planters had turned their sights toward new forms of labor: Chinese contract workers. Between 1840 and 1870, about 125,000 Chinese men and women became indentured workers in Cuba. At the same time, white immigration began increasing in Cuba. These new immigrants (who continued flowing into Cuba even after it gained independence) were poor or displaced Spanish workers who were feeling the crumbling Spanish economy at home. These new white immigrants went to work at *ingenios* (sugar mills), *cafetales* (coffee plantations), and other places usually reserved for African-Cuban slave labor. This new white population came primarily from the Canary Islands, Galicia, and Asturias. Clearly, a new and noncontroversial source of labor had been found.

The Spanish government, in the throes of an economic depression caused by the loss of the New World colonies and other mishaps at home, began tightening the screws on Cuba and, in the view of many patriots, hammered the first nail into its imperialist coffin in Cuba. Instead of letting the Cubans be, the Spanish augmented the authority of their military tribunals. They denied Cubans any parliamentary voice. They banned political meetings, raised colonial taxes a whopping 6 percent, and imposed protectionist duties on all foreign products. In response to Spain's protectionist duties, the United States raised tariffs on Cuban goods by 10 percent. Cuban producers were caught in the middle, squeezed from both sides, with ever-diminishing profits and foreign markets.

Within a couple of years, cattle barons from Camagüey, sugar landlords from Oriente, and members of the Cuban elite from all over convened in the town of Yara to plan a mass rebellion against Spain. Whites, African-Cubans, small farmers, free men and slaves, and people of all classes joined in the protest by the thousands. The gathering on October 10, 1868, called El Grito de Yara (the Cry from Yara), proclaimed Cuban independence and the establishment of a provisional republic, and decried unfair taxation. The protesters called for free trade with all nations, a freely elected representative government, and "universal manhood suffrage." As you can guess, women were excluded from voting (and it was actually the 1930s before Cuban women could vote), but in the context of the times, it was clearly a step toward greater equality.

This first cry for independence launched a bloody civil war against the Spanish that lasted ten years. The Spanish, seeing their prized island slipping away—an island they had previously dubbed "Cuba most faithful" because it had remained loyal to Spain while Mexico, Venezuela, and others were breaking their ties—took no prisoners. They destroyed the sugar mills, torched the land, conducted mass executions. They left Cuba utterly devastated, unable to defend itself.

How Did U.S. Business Interests Profit from Cuba's Ten Years' War?

As a result of ten years of devastation, Cuban growers began relinquishing their ownership positions in their *ingenios* and *cafetales*. They began trading their property titles for stock options in U.S. corporations, which took over their land. In effect, Cuban planters became administrators of companies owned by U.S. corporations. In addition, U.S. companies, such as the E. Atkins Company in Boston, foreclosed on estates they had loaned money to for agricultural operations, and subsequently acquired vast sugar properties and other holdings from insolvent Cuban landlords. By 1895, less than 20 percent of mill owners in Cuba were Cubans. Almost immediately, more than 95 percent of all Cuban sugar exports found their way to the United States. The stage was set for what would eventually be one of Cuba's greatest tragedies: a single-crop economy with a single country to sell to.

Who Was José Martí?

José Martí y Pérez was Cuba's **George Washington** and **Thomas Jefferson** all rolled into one. Born in Havana of Spanish parents on January 28, 1853, he is remembered throughout the Spanish-speaking world not only as a brilliant political leader, but also as a great poet. He was the founder of the *modernismo* literary style in Cuba—a forerunner of the symbolist movement that stressed directness and simplicity and broke away from the florid style of the nineteenth century. Among his literary works are *Ismaelillo* (poems, 1882), *Versos Sencillos (Plain Verse,* 1891), and a collection of children's stories, *La Edad de Oro (The Golden Age,* 1898). His simple, direct style was also evident in his short but brilliant political career.

Martí answered the call to rebellion against the oppressive Spanish regime early in life. He was arrested for sedition at the tender age of sixteen, and subsequently sent into exile. His first exile (1871–78) took him to Spain, Mexico, and Guatemala (where he wrote his famous poem "La Niña de Guatemala"). His second exile (1891) took him to both England and the United States. He lived for several years in New York (on Water Street, near the Fulton Fish Market), where he helped conceive the plan for the Cuban War of Independence (1895–98). He wrote some brilliant political prose that many years later became the blueprint of the unofficial constitution of anti-**Castro** Cuban-Americans in Miami. Martí's writings also served Fidel Castro well in many of his political speeches and proclamations.

Martí had studied the Ten Years' War and another failed war, called la Guerra Chiquita (the Small War), and had concluded that Cubans had failed in their efforts toward independence for lack of organization. He wrote in 1882: "The revolution is . . . a detailed understanding based on advanced planning and great foresight." He argued that Cuban independence had to be a process in which the final outcome was inevitable. He understood independence to be only a first step toward a bigger goal. He wrote General **Antonio Maceo,** the brave African-Cuban who fought with him, "In my view, the solution to the Cuban problem is not a political but a social one." Later, in 1892, he proclaimed: "Our goal is not so much a mere political change as a good, sound and just equitable social system without demagogic fawning or arrogance of authority. And let us never forget that the greater the suffering, the greater the right to justice, and the prejudices of men and social inequities cannot prevail over the equality which nature has created." He also addressed concerns about the control of wealth by a few, and put forth an advanced democratic philosophy when he wrote: "A country with a few rich men is not rich—only the country where everyone possesses a little wealth is rich. In political economy and good government, distribution is the source of prosperity."

For Martí, as for the revolutionaries who fought at his side, Cuban freedom meant freedom from oppression, racism, and any foreign dominance, whether by the empire across the Atlantic or the empire to the north. Martí fought earnestly against the annexation of Cuba by the United States. In 1866, he warned Cubans that the United States had "never looked upon Cuba as anything but an appetizing possession with no drawback other than its quarrelsome, weak and unworthy population." He warned Cubans that "to change masters is not to be free."

José Martí died fighting in Cuba, at the Battle of Dos Ríos, on May 19, 1895, three years before Cuba was to win its independence from Spain. He served Cuba better as a thinker and a writer than as a fighter, but he believed it was his duty to take his post at the front lines.

Who Wrote the Song "Guantánamera"?

"Guantánamera/Guajira Guantánamera ..." The rest of the song, made popular by the group the Weavers, is based on a traditional Cuban ballad (sung to a *guajira*—farm girl—from Guantánamo) and contains lines from a famous poem by **José Martí:** *"Yo soy un hombre sincero/de donde crece la palma/y antes de morirme quiero/cantar mis versos del alma."*

Is It True That the Early Cuban Revolutionaries Would Have Won Their War Without U.S. Help?

Yes. By the beginning of 1898, the Cubans who under Martí's leadership had mounted a carefully planned war of insurrection were in complete control of the countryside. The final coup would come with the takeover of the cities. Late in 1897, massive artillery units began marching into urban centers. General **Calixto García** seized Bayamo with its twenty-one thousand residents. Later, he took Las Tunas and several other cities. At the same time, **Antonio Maceo** was storming Santiago de Cuba, the largest western city. In the central and eastern region of the island, General **Máximo Gómez** and other revolutionary leaders took cities like Las Villas and were preparing to capture the island's capital, Havana. "The enemy is crushed," wrote Gómez, "and is in complete retreat from here." The general called it a "dead war" and predicted that it would end by January 1898. It was obvious that Spain had decided its time was up, and that the zeal and dedication of the Cuban insurgents could not be

put down. All the Cuban people were behind the revolutionary efforts, and Spain could not possibly stem the tide of history. Cuban independence and Cuban rule were destiny
manifest.

So Why Did the United States Fight the Spanish-American War?

The United States had been trying to gain control of Cuba
for most of the nineteenth century. It was, in the minds of
most U.S. political leaders, part of Manifest Destiny to control a territory lying only ninety miles from the continental
United States. However, when the Cuban *criollos'* efforts began proving successful and it became evident that Cuba
would soon be not only free from Spanish domination, but
a sovereign nation, the U.S. government decided that unusual measures were needed. In a government memorandum, Assistant Secretary of State **William R. Day** wrote:
"[Cubans] occupy and control virtually all the territory outside the heavily garrisoned coast cities and a few interior
towns. There are no active operations by the Spaniards. . . .
The Eastern provinces are admittedly 'Free Cuba.' In view of
these statements alone, it is now evident that Spain's struggle
in Cuba has become absolutely hopeless."

In view of this unexpected circumstance, President **William McKinley** issued a war message against Spain (after asking Congress's permission to send troops to Cuba). The
message did not speak of helping the Cubans liberate themselves from Spain (as has been said, and as some of the press
altruistically reported). It was clearly military intervention
directed against both the Spanish and the Cubans. "The
forcible intervention of the United States," President
McKinley told Congress, "involves . . . hostile constraint
against both Spaniards and Cubans, the means to establish
grounds upon which to neutralize the two competing claims

of sovereignty and establish by superior force of arms a third." That "third," needless to say, was the United States of America.

Thus the warship *Maine* exploded in Havana harbor and the Spanish-American War was declared and won in a couple of months. In the fallout, the United States acquired Puerto Rico, the Philippines, Guam, and the Wake Islands (see Chapter Cuatro). The United States also held on to Cuba—but only for a little while, at least politically speaking.

THE TEN RICHEST LATINO BUSINESSMEN

1. Joseph A. Unanue	CEO of Goya Foods, Inc.; net worth of $330 million
2. John Arrillaga	With Richard Peery, one of Northern California's largest real estate developers; net worth of $320 million
3. Roberto C. Goizueta	Chairman and CEO of the Coca-Cola Company; net worth of $245 million
4. Arturo G. Torres	Former owner of 70 percent of Pizza Management, Inc.; net worth of $105 million
5. Amigo and Max D. Soriano	Brothers who started a marine transportation company, which they sold for an estimated $70 million; net worth of $90 million
6. Robert Alvarez, Sr.	Formed Coast Citrus Corp.; net worth of $85 million

7. José Milton	Made his wealth in real estate primarily in Florida; net worth of $50 million
8. Manuel D. Medina	Formed a commercial real estate development company; net worth of $45 million
9. Natan R. Rok	Made his fortune in real estate and now owns much of downtown Miami; net worth of $45 million
10. Daniel D. Villarosa	Top place-kicker for the Los Angeles Rams and the Dallas Cowboys (1960–68); amassed his wealth investing in the media; net worth of $45 million

Source: "The Hispanic Business Rich List," *Hispanic Business,* March 1993

If Lust for Cuba Was the Reason the United States Went to War with Spain, How Come Cuba Got Its Independence by 1902?

The Cuban rebels had studied **McKinley**'s declaration of war carefully, and having been forewarned by **José Martí** about what the United States' intentions would be, they mounted an unprecedented public relations campaign to ensure that the United States would agree to recognize "Cuba Libre"—an independent Cuba. The Cubans had won enormous sympathy among the people of the United States, who identified with their cause. Journalists and congressmen rallied to their side in spite of McKinley's wishes. Finally, a compromise was reached between the hawkish president and the more liberal wing: It was acceptable for McKinley not to recognize Cuban independence outright, as long as there was some sort of disclaimer. So Article IV of the Spanish-American War Resolution, known as the Teller Amendment, reads as follows: "[The United States] hereby disclaims any disposition of intention to exercise sovereignty, jurisdiction, or control over said island except for pacification thereof, and asserts its determination, when that is accomplished, to leave the government and control of the island to its people." With the Teller Amendment in place, the United States went to war. And, as soon as the war was over, U.S. ministers, politicians, businessmen, and missionaries descended on the island for the spoils.

What's a Cuba Libre?

Cuba Libre means "Free Cuba"; the phrase was part of the nineteenth-century Cuban revolutionary cry, *"Viva Cuba Libre!"* A Cuba libre is a popular alcoholic cocktail made up of one part rum and two parts Coca-Cola. The implications are obvious: Cuba became free thanks to one part Cuban effort (rum, the Cuban national beverage) and two parts U.S. muscle (Coca-Cola, the quintessential American drink). Although the cocktail was popular in pre-**Castro** Cuba and in the United States, the irony did not escape many Cuban nationals. To compound it, **Roberto C. Goizueta,** a Cuban-American who fled to the United States from Castro's regime, is currently the chief executive officer of the Coca-Cola Company. Under his direction, the company has grown by leaps and bounds and opened whole new international markets, including the vast one represented by China.

What Was the Platt Amendment and Why Did It Open a Bucket of Worms That Helped Fuel the 1959 Fidel Castro Revolution?

The Teller Amendment clearly stated that the United States wouldn't try to take over the island—but interpreted another way (the way the United States interpreted it after the war was won), it didn't mean that the United States should not "protect" Cuba from itself and help it on its way. Thus, in 1900, members of the **McKinley** administration picked some Cuban candidates whom, they believed, Cubans should elect as president of the republic and as other officials. But the Cuban people refused to elect the hand-picked candidates. This uppity attitude enraged McKinley and many members of Congress, who decided the Cubans had proved unwise in their choices and thus unable to rule themselves.

Finally, in 1906, Secretary of War **Elihu Root** proposed a comfortable "way out" to Secretary of State John Hay. Root's proposal, which became known as the Platt Amendment because it was drafted by Senator **Orville H. Platt,** agreed to let the Cubans go their own way, as long as "in transferring the control of Cuba to the government established under the new constitution the United States reserves and retains the right of intervention for the preservation of Cuban independence and the maintenance of a stable Government." The amendment also stipulated that "no government organized under the constitution shall be deemed to have authority to enter into any treaty or engagement with any foreign power which may tend to impair or interfere with the independence of Cuba." It stated, too, that the United States could "acquire and hold the title to land, and maintain naval stations at certain specified stations." Translation? The United States had the right to tell the Cuban people how to govern themselves, to establish naval stations on the island, and ultimately to interfere whenever it deemed necessary.

With the Spanish-American War over and the Platt Amendment in place, Cuba went about the business of electing its own government. Its first president, elected in 1902, was **Tomás de Estrada Palma.** Shortly thereafter, the United States installed a naval base in Guantánamo Bay and proceeded to keep close watch over Cuba. At the same time, U.S. business interests accelerated their investment in sugar, coffee, tobacco, and other crops in Cuba. The Cuban economy flourished as never before. And Cuba's place as the chief supplier of U.S. sugar was firmly established—but so was the one-crop economic system that would later cause so much distress.

The idea that Cubans were not masters of their fate, since the Platt Amendment restricted their agreements and commerce with other countries, remained a thorn in the side of Cuban patriots. That thorn became infected when, on three separate occasions—in 1906, 1912, and 1917—U.S. military forces invaded Cuba and took provisional charge of its government to protect American interests from internal political unrest and corruption. After those invasions, Cuban presidents and representatives ran on anti–Platt Amendment platforms, promising to have it repealed.

In 1944, on the day of his inauguration, Cuba's great democratic president, **Ramón Grau San Martín,** proclaimed the abrogation of the Platt Amendment. After **Fidel Castro** took office in 1959, he reminded the Cuban people that they had been under U.S. imperialist domination ever since the Platt Amendment was enacted. The Platt Amendment had become such a symbol of paternalistic domination by a large, rich nation over a small one that the mere mention of it (and the repudiation thereof) was enough to get governments elected and new dictators cheered into office.

What's Guantánamo Bay?

Guantánamo Bay is a large deep-water harbor on the south-eastern shore of Cuba. It is one of the best-protected bays in the world, covering thirty square miles. The British first used it as a naval station during their brief sojourn in Cuba. Then, in 1903, the U.S. government seized Guantánamo Bay under a treaty that cannot be annulled unilaterally. The American naval and military presence on what **Fidel Castro** and other Cuban nationals consider Cuban territory has long been a source of disagreement between the two countries. American naval operations also serve to remind Castro's government just how close the United States is. In 1992, Guantánamo Bay became embroiled in yet more controversy when the U. S. government confined hundreds of Haitians who had been fleeing the dictatorial regime in Haiti to Guantánamo Naval Base. The Haitians, detained indefinitely pending U.S. legislative action, are housed in makeshift barracks. Many of the refugees suffer from HIV infection or full-blown AIDS, and their confinement has aroused great controversy as to the morally correct path the U.S. government should take regarding their fate. In June 1993, a federal judge in New York ruled that the U.S. government's policy of detaining the Haitians indefinitely is unconstitutional and violates their right to due process.

Who Was Fulgencio Batista?

Fulgencio Batista y Zaldívar was a Cuban army officer who was the most powerful political figure in Cuba from 1933 to 1944, when he ruled both as president and behind the scenes under the patronage of the U.S. government. As an army sergeant, he participated in the ouster of **Gerardo Machado,** a much-hated dictator who ruled by graft, corruption, and nepotism (at one point during his regime, almost everyone in high office was related to him). In 1933, Batista led a coup that helped overthrow the provisional government of **Carlos Manuel de Céspedes** (a direct descendant of the great nineteenth-century Cuban revolutionary with the same name), which had been put in place by the U.S. government. But then Batista gained the confidence of the U.S. ambassador, who lent him unconditional U.S. backing. Batista ruled behind the scenes from 1933 to 1940, when he was elected president. During that time, Batista became a populist president who defended *los humildes* ("the lowly"), with whom he identified. He came from humble beginnings and was of mixed Indian, African, and Spanish descent—a first for any Cuban president, since they usually came from the ruling white elite. In 1944, Cuba elected **Ramón Grau San Martín** to the presidency, and Batista retired temporarily to Florida.

In 1952, he was back. This time he led a bloodless coup and seized the reins of government from the then democratically elected president, **Carlos Prío Socarras.** Batista held presidential elections in 1954 and 1958, which he won handily through graft and ballot fixing. Over time, Batista grew from a corrupt Latin American–style dictator to a power-hungry, ruthless politico who stuffed his pockets and bought his way through government. As **Fidel Castro** and other opposition leaders decried his dictatorship, Batista intensified his efforts to create a police state, sending countless members of the opposition to jail or to their deaths.

When he could not do away with the opposition, Batista unashamedly bought their favors. In 1957, *Revista Carteles,* a weekly news magazine, disclosed that twenty members of the Batista government owned numbered Swiss bank accounts, each with deposits of more than $1 million. From the proceeds of the national lottery, Batista took all the money he wanted for himself and then donated the rest in exchange for political backing. He gave $1.6 million to the Roman Catholic Church; $5 million to labor unions; and, unbelievably, $1 million a month to newspaper editors and reporters in exchange for their silence. No wonder that somewhere in the Sierra Maestra of Oriente province, a revolution was brewing.

In spite of the undeniable corruption of Batista's dictatorship, on the surface Cuba's economy seemed to be thriving. Cuba had one of the highest per capita incomes in Latin America (second only to oil-rich Venezuela) and one of the highest standards of living. Havana was as sophisticated and cultured a city as any European capital. By 1957, there were more television sets in Cuba (one per twenty-five inhabitants) than in any other Latin American country. Cuba was first in telephones, automobiles, newspapers, and railroads. It was looked on as an example by many other third-world nations that aspired to such creature comforts and general well-being.

If Cuba Was Doing So Well, How Come a Revolution Was Waiting in the Wings?

In the 1950s, Cuba was a mass of contradictions. Yes, the economy was among the strongest in Latin America. But Cuba's economy was tied not to other Latin American countries, but to the United States, which exerted enormous influence. Cuba subsisted almost exclusively on imports from the United States, and paid U.S. prices for them. In 1950, Cuba imported $515 million worth of goods from the United States. By 1958, that amount had risen to $777 million. During the same period, Cuba's per capita yearly income was $374, compared to $2,000 in the United States.

To add insult to injury, in the mid 1950s, the price of sugar, that old reliable single crop that made it possible for Cubans to survive, suddenly plummeted in markets around the world. **Fulgencio Batista** imposed no tariff protection and thereby discouraged the development of any other national industries since they would not be able to compete against U.S.-made goods.

Then, too, a seemingly unclosable chasm yawned between the haves and have-nots. Although Havana in the 1950s was one of the most expensive cities in the world, with the largest per capita number of Cadillacs, the vast majority of Cubans lived in poverty. Out of a population of almost 6 million, only 620,000 were considered middle-class, with another 200,000 civil servants and 200,000 service workers just slightly below the middle class. The rest of the population was made up of peasants and agricultural workers; large numbers of unemployed; and the very rich, who accounted for a very small percentage of the overall population.

The vast *latifundios,* or agricultural estates, were owned by a handful of Cubans and U.S. syndicates; these often kept the land idle, awaiting a sudden demand for sugar in the world market before bothering to cultivate or harvest the crop. More than 25 percent of all the land in production was held by U.S. sugar monopolies. And while 25 percent of the Cuban population was comprised of sugar workers, these laborers could find work only an average of one hundred days a year.

The daily wages of these workers seriously declined during the 1950s, and so did social services. The sharp differences between the rural and the urban populations intensified. For example, while 80 percent of the city dwellers had electricity and running water, only 15 percent of the rural population could count on such basic services. In Havana, the ratio of doctors to patients was 1 to 227, while in Oriente province (the westernmost rural province, where **Castro** came from) it was a dismal 1 to 2,423. Illiteracy was on the rise, and fewer children attended school in the 1950s than had done so in the 1920s.

In the face of this enormous disparity, most of the Cuban wealth was being siphoned out of the country, either by U.S. companies that took their profits home, or by wealthy

Cuban nationals, who, fearing a debacle in their very unstable society and a depression in their one-crop economy, put their money to work elsewhere—primarily in U.S. real estate, banks, and investment institutions. In the meantime, the Cuban middle class, one of the strongest in Latin America, saw its buying power dwindle and its white-collar jobs diminish. These middle-class people, as well as the rural poor, were unable to improve their lot, since they lacked the wherewithal to take their meager savings out of the country or to invest them in a safe vehicle such as real estate, which in a matter of years had tripled in price as a result of inflation.

Compounding the social and economic disparities and the dire consequences of an almost exclusive dependence on sugar was a deep moral malaise that afflicted the people of this beautiful island. Gambling casinos, controlled by U.S. organized crime and sanctioned by Batista (who took a hefty cut), became a thriving industry. Illegal drugs were sold openly. Pornographic theaters and clubs, as well as brothels, became attractive employers for hundreds of Cuban women from rural areas who could find no other means of supporting their families. By the end of 1958, an estimated 11,500 women earned their living as prostitutes. In addition, hundreds of underage girls and some boys (as young as eight or nine) were kidnapped into prostitution. Newborn children were being abandoned at the doorsteps of local orphanages by the hundreds. Juvenile delinquency, homelessness, and suicides had become the norm. The vast majority of the hardworking poor and middle class were caught in an unbearable vise.

While Cuba was falling apart, an idealistic political leader by the name of Fidel Castro was organizing an army of revolutionaries, demanding a clean sweep of government corruption and inefficiency, and promising to end U.S. economic domination and foreign criminal exploitation of women and minors. In the cities and throughout the countryside, the people had begun to revolt, to stage mass demonstrations, to plant bombs in movie theaters and other public places, and to demand that the dictator leave at once. Fulgencio Batista, seeing his control slipping, instituted a Gestapo-like police force that conducted witch hunts and shot people en masse. The foreign press—particularly the U.S. press—had become aware of the human rights violations of the Batista regime. Countless articles brought one very significant fact to light: The weapons Batista used to carry out his atrocities were being furnished by none other than the United States of America.

President **Dwight Eisenhower** found himself in a very serious dilemma. Although Batista's government protected the interests of U.S. companies and investments on the island and made it possible for Cuba to remain a military base armed against potential enemies, Batista's totalitarian measures were unacceptable in the light of U.S. principles. And while Ambassador **Earl T. Smith** had warned Eisenhower that Castro was believed to be a communist (a feared word in those terrible Cold War years), the U.S. president believed he could no longer justify the sales of arms to Fulgencio Batista for the purpose of oppressing his own people.

Toward the end of 1958, the United States withdrew all support of Batista by canceling the sale of tanks and other weapons to his government. In the dawn of January 1, 1959, the dictator, having seen the writing on the wall, fled Cuba for Spain (where he died a rich man in 1973). At about the same hour, Fidel Castro, **Che Guevara, Raul Castro, Camilo Cienfuegos,** and a host of other revolutionaries began their long descent from the Sierra Maestra toward the capital. They rode in open jeeps, sporting their trademark beards and khaki uniforms, greeting the droves of cheering, hopeful Cubans along the highways and byways who believed that, at last, democracy and fundamental ethical morality would be restored to their beloved country.

Who Is Fidel Castro and What Happened to His Idealistic Revolution That Made Cubans Flee to Miami by the Thousands?

Fidel Castro Ruiz, better known as Fidel to friend and foe alike, was born on a farm in the province of Oriente on August 13, 1926. He attended Jesuit schools in Santiago de Cuba, Oriente's capital city, and in Havana. In 1950, he graduated from the University of Havana with a law degree. His only marriage (to **Mirta Díaz-Balart**) ended in divorce. His only son, **Fidel Castro Díaz-Balart,** born in 1949, has served as head of Cuba's atomic energy commission. But Fidel's ex-wife and members of her family declared themselves loyal anti-Castro democrats and fled to the United States after the revolution. Today, Fidel's nephew, **Lincoln Diaz-Balart,** is a Republican congressman from Florida.

Fidel Castro was a political animal from an early age. He was a member of a social democratic party named Partido Ortodoxo in the 1940s and 50s, when he opposed **Batista**'s regime from the start. On July 26, 1953, Castro launched a dangerous attack on the Moncada army barracks. This assault on Batista's regime failed, and Castro was imprisoned and sentenced to a fifteen-year jail term, but his daring maneuver brought him instant prominence. From jail, he wrote his famous book, *La Historia Me Absolverá (History Will Absolve Me),* which presented his anti-imperialist, reformist, and nationalistic ideals. At that time, Castro did not reveal that he was a Marxist-Leninist or propose outright communistic ideas.

In 1955, Castro was granted amnesty by Batista, provided he left Cuba for good. He went into exile in Mexico, where he founded the Twenty-sixth of July Movement (celebrated in Cuba today with as much fanfare as the Fourth of July in the United States) for the purpose of overthrowing the Batista dictatorship.

In December 1956, Fidel Castro and eighty-one other

rebels, including the Argentine revolutionary **Ernesto "Che" Guevara,** returned to Cuba and set up military headquarters in the westernmost part of the Sierra Maestra. From there, he and his followers began organizing his revolution, recruiting thousands of disaffected peasants in the interior of Cuba and exciting the imagination of millions of Cubans of all social and economic classes, who began to view Castro as a New World Messiah who could restore their country to sanity, law and order, and prosperity.

When Fidel Castro took over Cuba in 1959, his revolutionary regime welcomed many middle-of-the-road politicians and democrats. In a matter of months, however, Castro began implementing socialist measures, which included the general confiscation of land and industry from private ownership and the establishment of Marxist ideology. Enemies of his socialist-communist regime were swiftly executed, and within one year Castro had not only fully aligned himself with the Soviet Union both economically and politically, but had assigned Communist Party members or sympathizers to run the media, the schools and universities, and every other important institution. Freedom of speech and the right of assembly were abolished, and anyone who criticized Fidel or his government was in danger of swift execution by one of his militias, which he had organized in neighborhood cadres in the Soviet style.

As early as 1961, Fidel Castro publicly declared, "I have been a Marxist-Leninist all along, and will remain one until I die." Soon after, he opened the doors wide to Soviet economists, technicians, and military strategists and, in effect, handed over the island to Soviet Prime Minister **Nikita Khrushchev.** As a by-product of his Marxist revolution, Castro set up concentration camps for every conceivable form of dissident or "moral deviant." His puritanical revolution included the internment of thousands of gay and lesbian people in a concentration camp known as Guanahacabibes, as well as the incarceration and execution without trial of thousands upon thousands of Cuban nationals who opposed his communist regime. Writers, filmmakers, singers, composers, and artists were put on notice: Let your art reflect the communist-revolution ideology or else.

Suddenly, hundreds of thousands of Cubans who had believed Castro to be a true democrat leader woke up to the realization that they had exchanged one dictator for another, and that their island had become a perilous beachhead for Soviet Russia, where any minute a nuclear war between the two great superpowers, the United States and the Soviet Union, could explode in their midst.

As early as 1960, hundreds of thousands of upper-class, middle-class, and lower-middle-class Cubans began fleeing the island for the United States, particularly Miami, where the U.S. government welcomed them as political refugees, and where they soon flourished. Within a year, some Cuban refugees who had come penniless to the shores of Miami owned businesses or were employed in white-collar jobs. The skills they had brought with them, as well as their obvious desire to do well, aided by the fact that the great majority were Caucasian and did not experience overt racial prejudice, enabled the first wave of Cubans to establish a successful Cuban-American enclave in Miami. In time, they transformed Miami from a beach-and-swamp retirement community to what international bankers, politicians, and businesspeople call the "Capital of Latin America."

What's a Gusano?

Gusano, meaning "worm" in Spanish, is what Castro Cubans call Cuban exiles, or Cuban-Americans. Many Latinos also call Cuban-Americans *gusanos*—sometimes in jest and sometimes not. Another phrase used among Latinos to refer to Cuban-Americans (particularly those who came in the 1960s) is *los tenia*—literally, "the I-used-to-have people," because they often spoke about all they used to have back in the old country.

What Did Fidel Do for Cuba?

Aside from aligning the country with the Soviet bloc and assisting Marxist-Leninist revolutions around the world (most notably in Angola, where hundreds of Cuban soldiers died), **Fidel Castro**'s greatest claim to fame is undoubtedly the successful consolidation of a communist regime within ninety miles of U.S. territory.

Castro put great effort into education; Cuba attained the highest literacy rate in Latin America. Besides improvements in education, Castro's government also placed great emphasis on social services (25 percent of his budget was devoted to education and public health). As a result, Cuban nationals have access to doctors, nurses, hospitals, and other social welfare benefits that had been denied them during the Batista years. Hundreds of Cuban doctors and clinical technicians have been dispatched to help in other third-world countries, and many people from around the world have gone to Cuba for special treatments they could not find in their own countries.

During his reign of more than thirty years, Castro has stressed technical and scientific education; one of his basic revolutionary aims was to transform Cuba from a single-crop economy into a more technological, service-oriented society. In practice, however, Castro did not succeed any more than his predecessors in bringing Cuba out of its single-crop economic nightmare. Instead, whereas previous Cuban governments sold sugar to the United States, Castro simply sold it to the Soviet Union—until, of course, there was no longer a Soviet Union and the Cuban economy, starting in 1989, began an even deeper nosedive.

Who Was Che Guevara?

Ernesto "Che" Guevara was born in Argentina in 1928. He was called "Che" because that's what Argentines (and only Argentines) say when calling each other—roughly equivalent to "Hey, buddy!" Calling Guevara "Che" identified him as Argentine, and, probably, he himself referred to people as "Che."

Che Guevara helped **Fidel Castro** bring about his communist revolution in Cuba, since he had been a member of the Communist Party in his own country and had faithfully studied Marxist-Leninist ideology. Although he was trained as a doctor, he started his political career early, when he led revolts against President **Juan Perón (Evita**'s husband). In 1953, he went to Guatemala, where he joined the leftist regime of **Jacobo Arbenz Guzmán.** When Arbenz was overthrown in 1954, Che joined Fidel in Mexico and fought as a member of the Castro army in the Sierra Maestra until the success of the Cuban revolution. Although Che held many important positions in the Castro government, such as minister of industry (1961–65), his revolutionary zeal to turn Latin America into a communist playground took precedence. In 1965, he went on a secret mission to Bolivia to train a guerrilla force. Two years later, Che was captured near Santa Cruz and executed. He is remembered for his goatee and his black Argentine beret, as well as for his guerrilla training manuals and Marxist-Leninist revolutionary books, *Guerrilla Warfare* and *Guerrilla Warfare: A Method.* His life story was made into a play and a Hollywood movie in the 1970s.

What Happened at the Bay of Pigs and Why Did Cuban-Americans Blame President Kennedy?

The mass exodus of Cubans, as well **Castro**'s ceaseless tirades against the United States, put the U.S. government on notice. In 1961, when Castro completely nationalized all American-owned property in Cuba and, in effect, declared an ideological war against his nearest and most powerful neighbor, the U.S. government decided to take some drastic measures. First, President **Dwight Eisenhower** broke off all diplomatic relations with Castro's government. Then **Allen Dulles,** who had worked as CIA director under Eisenhower and continued in his post during **John F. Kennedy**'s administration, developed a plan to invade Cuba and get rid of the dictator with the aid of Cuban refugees in Miami.

Dulles sold the newly elected president on full air and military backing of the Cuban Brigada (Brigade). The invasion strategy called for young Cuban refugees to land along the Cuban coast and execute a carefully orchestrated popular revolt with anti-Castro agents strategically positioned inside Cuba. Another facet of that plan, which was not revealed to the public until a Senate investigation of the assassination of President Kennedy brought it to light years later, was the CIA's plot to have the Mafia assassinate Fidel Castro with the help of **Sam Giancana** and **John Roselli**'s hit men. Giancana was assassinated before he could tell the Senate the inside story, and Rosselli testified, but his body was found decomposed and floating in an oil drum in Florida shortly thereafter.

E. Howard Hunt (of Watergate fame) was one of the CIA operatives involved in the U.S. invasion of Cuba, as were countless other government men. But the Cuban invasion was ill-conceived from the start. There was a serious lack of communication between the CIA and Cuban exile groups (who knew the Cuban territory well, and warned the United States that dangerous coral reefs at the proposed landing site would jeopardize the mission). The U.S. government apparently had vast quantities of misinformation in its files regarding the topography of Cuba and the military installations around the designated landing site, Bahía de Cochinos (Bay of Pigs) in western Cuba. Another "small" matter the CIA had failed to notice was that Fidel Castro had recently built himself a beach home very near the Bay of Pigs, and that the whole area was heavily guarded. In addition, the so-called "secret invasion" was leaked to the press—and no doubt to Castro's men, who were fully prepared to greet the Cuban brigade with armored tanks and heavy ammunition when they landed on April 17, 1961. The Brigada, composed mostly of fourteen hundred middle-class young Cuban men, most of whom had never held a rifle, was ill-trained, underequipped, and kept in the dark by U.S. intelligence as to what their move would be once they landed. Certainly, an avalanche of Cuban support did not greet them when they arrived. Instead, they were overrun by thousands of Soviet-trained Cuban soldiers and loyal militia who had no trouble capturing the invaders, killing hundreds, and taking the rest prisoner as proof positive to the world that the United States was invading their country.

In planning the invasion, the CIA had assured the Brigada that the United States would provide full air cover during the entire operation, and that should they be captured, the U.S. military would be there to defend them against the communist troops. Those were the only terms under which the Brigada agreed to go in, since they knew they didn't stand a chance on their own. The young Cubans were to be the "face" of the invasion, but the real muscle behind it would be full-scale U.S. Navy and Air Force support.

At the last minute, once the invasion had already been launched, President Kennedy changed his mind and ordered all U.S. support withdrawn from the Brigada. It was speculated that he became fearful that a direct confrontation with a Soviet bloc country would precipitate the next world war.

Whatever his reasons, 114 Cubans were killed and 1,189 others were held prisoner and later ransomed from Cuba by Attorney General **Robert F. Kennedy** in exchange for food and supplies, and for hard cash from the families of the young invaders in Miami. Some Cuban-American families wired their entire life savings to Fidel in exchange for the release of their sons.

In later years, as Cuban refugees became U.S. citizens and their numbers grew, the overwhelming majority registered Republican. Their preference for the Republican Party was founded on the belief that Republicans were more efficient in combating communism in Cuba and around the world—and on their unwillingness to forget "the Kennedy betrayal." Among older Cuban-Americans in Miami, to refer to someone as a *kennedito* ("little Kennedy") is to call him or her weak-spined and probably leftist.

What Caused the Cuban Missile Crisis?

The Bay of Pigs defeat signaled to Soviet Prime Minister **Nikita Khrushchev** that he might be dealing with a weak U.S. president. He saw this as an opportunity to establish a nuclear beachhead at **Kennedy**'s doorstep. At **Castro**'s behest, Khrushchev quickly ordered the assembly of launching sites for medium-range and intermediate-range nuclear missiles in Cuba. The aim was to protect Cuba from the possibility of further U.S. invasions and to guarantee the Soviet Union a more favorable balance of power—one that served at least the same purpose as U.S. military bases did in neighboring Turkey.

Once aerial photographs by U.S. military intelligence uncovered the frightening time bomb at our threshold, the Pentagon advised President Kennedy to launch a full-scale surprise attack on Cuba that would once and for all terminate Castro's domination. Instead, Kennedy decided to issue a public ultimatum to the USSR on October 22, 1962. He declared a naval blockade on Cuba and demanded immediate withdrawal of all offensive missiles. The life-or-death tension lasted two long weeks, as both countries stood on the edge of nuclear warfare. Finally, Khrushchev gave in to Kennedy's demands in exchange for an assurance that the United States would refrain from attempting to overthrow Castro's government.

The Cuban Missile Crisis seemed to close a very long chapter in history for Cuban-Americans. Although many still hoped to return to their homeland, the vast majority began realizing that the United States was truly their new home, and that Castro's downfall might have to come from within. Given the climate in those days, it was hard for many Americans to believe that a communist regime would be allowed to thrive only ninety miles from our shores, but, as **Bob Dylan**'s popular ballad proclaimed, the times they were a-changing. And President Kennedy had another war to wage just then—this time in a country called Vietnam.

Who Were the Marielitos and Why Did So Many People Hate Them?

In 1980, during President **Jimmy Carter**'s administration, **Fidel Castro** opened his jails and mental institutions and loaded 125,000 Cubans onto shrimp boats and other rickety vessels labeled "the Freedom Flotilla." Sailing from the port of Mariel, the flotilla sent the Marielitos (meaning "those who came from Mariel") on their way to Key West. The Carter administration agreed to take in the refugees and airlift them to different parts of the country where they could find housing and employment. There was only one hitch: While the vast majority of Marielitos had been legitimate political prisoners in Cuba, whose only crime was to oppose the communist regime, hundreds were common criminals with long felony records, "mentally defective," or legally insane. When it became clear that some of these new refugees might have been part of a dastardly ruse played on an amiable President Carter by Castro to get rid of his Cuban undesirables, all hell broke loose. Later, when dozens of Marielitos who had been cleared by the U.S. authorities began committing crimes around the country, things got even worse.

Miami's Cuban-Americans rushed to the aid of the new arrivals with the full weight of their highly organized private charitable institutions. But soon fears that this new wave of Cubans would tarnish the image the Cuban-Americans had diligently defended made many of them criticize Carter's decision to let the Marielitos in.

The U.S. government initially detained 22,000 out of the original 125,000 who arrived, but most of the detainees were found to have committed only political crimes in Cuba, and were set free. Finally, only some 3,700 Mariel Cubans were detained by the immigration authorities for past or present criminal records and deemed "excludable aliens." Excludable aliens, unlike illegal aliens, are not considered persons under the Constitution, and thus have no rights. However, because the immigration authorities in Key West believed they could not very well return the excludables to Cuba, they simply shipped them off to two penal institutions, one a regular prison in Oakdale, Louisiana, and the other a maximum-security prison in Atlanta that had once housed **Al Capone.**

These excludables remained incarcerated for seven years, until 1987, without standing trial or being heard from. Then a sudden change in Cuba-U.S. relations brought the whole matter to a head. In December 1987, the Cuban government announced it would let Cubans who had families in the United States leave the country and join their relatives. The United States agreed to this—provided Castro took the Mariel excludables back.

Before the prison authorities in Louisiana or Atlanta even knew about it, the imprisoned Marielitos had learned that the United States had negotiated their return, and went on a violent rampage. The inmates at both institutions staged bloody riots, took hostages, and demanded a hearing. They argued that they had been inhumanly incarcerated for seven years in violation of international human rights accords, and now faced certain death in Cuba. It became apparent that these Marielitos would rather stay in American jails than be returned to Cuba.

As a result of the riots and the media attention to the plight of the Marielitos, U.S. District Court Judge **Marvin Shoob** ruled in the Marielitos' favor, and their cases were heard individually. As many as nine hundred were eventually freed and allowed U.S. residence. The vast majority have led useful lives in their new country. A few hundred were eventually returned to Cuba, as part of the agreement with Castro to let law-abiding relatives of Cuban-Americans go. Those mentally ill or "mentally defective," who were forced to return along with the hardened criminals, remained the cause of much soul-searching and hand-wringing in Anglo and Cuban-American communities. Eventually, the Marielitos' plight was filed under the heading "all's fair in love and war"—the place where so many historical riddles wind up, for revision by future generations.

HAVANA, U.S.A.: THE LAND OF THE FIESTA, BUT NOT THE SIESTA

What's Little Havana and Why Isn't It So Havana Anymore?

Little Havana, in downtown Miami, was the first enclave of the first and second wave of Cuban exiles in the 1960s and 1970s. Its main street, Eighth Street, was officially named Calle Ocho ("Eighth Street" in Spanish). Calle Ocho, as well as the bustling streets, avenues, and alleyways in the vicinity, became the center of Cuban-American commerce. Stands selling Cuban sandwiches and *batidos* (tropical milkshakes) appeared overnight. Clothing stores, supermarkets, *botánicas*, and every conceivable type of Cuban-style Caribbean shop became institutions here. There are as many Cuban restaurants in a single strip of Calle Ocho as you will find in four districts in Havana, Cuba.

Centro Vasco, one of Miami's hundreds of popular Cuban-Spanish restaurants, reflects the taste, mood, and politics of the people in this picturesque neighborhood. In its open courtyard, you find pictures of **José Martí** propped up against a signed picture of President **Ronald Reagan,** who made it a point to stop by when campaigning in Miami years ago. The Cuban and the American flag stand side by side and beat each other like flyswatters, aided by ubiquitous little electric fans. **Gloria Estefan**'s music and Spanish guitars play so loudly you can hardly hear your companion speak, and the sumptuous food keeps coming till you forget there ever was such a thing as a *dieta* (diet)—fried bananas, fish *escabeche, yuca con mojo, lechón asado, moros y cristianos,* and, of course, guava paste and cream cheese to top the whole thing off.

Along the streets, where there are more signs in Spanish than in English (some even say "English Spoken Here"), men in their fifties and sixties gather around small card tables, smoking cigars and playing dominos. A game imported by the Spanish colonists in the seventeenth century, dominos is probably the favorite island pastime for Cubans, as well as Puerto Ricans and Dominicans.

While the men scramble the dominos, they talk politics, drink strong Cuban espresso in little paper cups, ponder when **Fidel Castro** is going to topple, and perhaps put down a bet on *la bolita*, an illegal lottery no one sees anything wrong with.

But that's the *old* Little Havana. It's still there, filled with older melancholy warriors, and now plenty of Anglo tourists, who come down to savor the flavor and visit a "foreign country" without having to trouble with a passport. But increasingly, the newer generations of Cuban-Americans have left Little Havana and now live in the elegant suburbs of Coral

Gables, Hialeah, Coconut Grove, Key Biscayne, and even South Beach, the little Art Deco strip of heavenly beach that Jewish retirees from points north developed and made famous in the 1950s.

Today, Little Managua, a growing community of exiles from Nicaragua, is slowly blending into the old Little Havana, and more recent Spanish-speaking immigrants now serve the food and even run some of the stores that younger generations of Cuban-Americans left behind.

Behind Little Havana and beyond the comfortable suburbs where many of the more than half a million Cuban-Americans make their homes looms Miami's thriving commercial center with its tall glass buildings, marble malls with fountains, and hundreds of banks from all over the world. This is the part of the city that Cuban-Americans are rightly credited with transforming. As the Cubans arrived, they began opening small shops and service businesses. Then, using the skills they had brought with them, they became the natural ambassadors between U.S. corporations and Latin American companies eager to do business with and in the United States. Venezuela's oil was gushing in the 1960s, and the bolívars, as well as the pesos from other Latin American countries, began pouring into Miami, with the aid of Cuban-Americans who understood both cultures and both languages, and could serve as representatives for U.S. banks and corporations.

The natural synergism and desire for enterprise between the Cuban-Americans and their contacts to the south and to the north transformed Miami, which had been an alligator-infested swamp (in the 1920s) and then a retirees' colony (from the 1950s to the 1970s), into the thriving "Capital of Latin America," as one of Miami's Cuban-American mayors, **Xavier Suárez,** renamed it.

This bustling commercial center is often what comes to mind when Cuban-Americans hear the words "Little Havana." They also insist that it's neither so little nor so entirely Havana anymore.

What's a YUCA?

A *yuca* is a cassava, a fibrous tuber grown by the Arawak Indians that is served at almost every Cuban meal. A YUCA is a Cuban yuppie—a young, upwardly mobile Cuban-American.

This thirty-something group, most of whom were either born in the United States or came at such an early age they only remember Cuba from their parents' photographs of palm trees and the Malecón wall in Havana, are a bilingual, bicultural, and economically successful lot. They speak English and Spanish with flawless native accents, and are likely to lapse into one or the other without realizing it. YUCAs are mostly Caucasian and considerably more liberal in their attitudes than their parents or grandparents. They prefer to listen to La Cadena Azul and La Cubanisima (two Miami Spanish-language and Cuban music stations) than to Radio Martí (a kind of Voice of America program aimed at Cuba, which President **Ronald Reagan** launched in 1985). A poll conducted by Spanish-language station WSCV showed that more than 60 percent of YUCAs under thirty-four years of age said they would never return (or go for the first time) to live in Cuba when **Castro** falls. Many more have tended to vote Democratic in recent elections, and to identify with the Latino community across the country as a whole. The great majority favors ending the U.S. blockade against Cuba. They advocate cultural exchanges and travel to the island and are eager to help the millions of people back in Cuba who are in dire straits as a result of the collapse of the USSR. Many YUCAs are in favor of the Cuban-American Committee, a group that seeks U.S. normalization with the Castro government as a means of eventually involving Cuba in a democratic process.

The generations coming after the YUCAs (those thirty

and younger) have even fewer ties to their old Cuban roots, and most prefer to speak English and play Nintendo rather than listen to their grandma's tales of Fidel and his revolution.

Are All Cuban-Americans Rich?

Although the very enterprising nature of this Latino group has led many to stereotype them as *los ricos* (the rich kids), Cuban-Americans fall into all social and economic categories. Cubans have the highest rate of incorporation into the work force of any Hispanic community in the United States, but their average family income still falls below the U.S. average.

This is due in part to the fact that many Cuban-Americans opted to remain in the ghetto, working for small businesses owned by other Cubans, rather than joining the fast-track society at large. Also, many of the older generation did not learn English or adapt readily to Anglo ways. For years, they believed that their stay in the United States was transitory and that **Fidel**'s regime would collapse at any minute. And, of course, the arrival of the Marielitos and other recent refugees, many of whom were of mixed African and Spanish descent, put a different face on the Cuban-American community as a whole.

In Chicago, almost 50 percent of the Cuban-American vote goes to the Democrats, and Cuban-Americans are closely aligned with all issues involving the Latino community in that city. In Union City, New Jersey, an overwhelmingly Cuban-American city, with a Cuban-American mayor and a Cuban-American U.S. representative, there is 16 percent unemployment, and those mostly working-class Cubans do not see themselves as the "rich kids." They share the concerns of many other Latinos in New York, Houston, Chicago, and East Los Angeles.

"Mulatto" Cubans often encounter the same prejudices

that Puerto Ricans and other nonwhite nationalities face—discrimination in housing, employment, and life in general. Even Caucasian Cubans have been known to discriminate against their own, and there are Cuban-American country clubs in Florida where mulattoes need not apply. Ironically, in the early 1960s, when the first wave of (Caucasian) Cubans began arriving in Miami, signs hung outside Miami apartment buildings that read "No Dogs, No Kids, No Cubans."

What's Santería?

Santería is a New World religion that emerged out of the syncretism, or fusion, of the ancient Yoruba religions brought to the Caribbean by West African slaves and Roman Catholic beliefs brought by the Spanish. *Santería* ("the religion of the saints") became very popular in Cuba, where not only slaves and the descendants of slaves, but even non-African-Cubans, believed in it (and still do, both in Cuba and the United States).

In the 1950s, it was recorded in a government gazette that President **Carlos Prio Socarras,** a white, democratically elected president, donated government money to both the Catholic Church and the *santería* religion. Today, in Miami, New York, and almost every city with a large Spanish-Caribbean population, *santería* is practiced regularly.

The gods, or *santos,* of *santería* are fused with the Catholic saints (so, for instance, the African god Babalú is also the Catholic St. Lazarus, and Yemayá, the African goddess of the waters, is the Catholic Virgen de las Mercedes). Practitioners of *santería* have both male and female priests, and an extensive pantheon of deities to worship, please, and appease. Those who practice *santería* believe in animal sacrifice (*not* human sacrifice) for the purpose of honoring their gods.

In June 1993, the Supreme Court ruled that a 1987 ban

in Hialeah, Florida, on animal sacrifice violated both African-Cubans' religious freedom and the First Amendment's guarantee of the free exercise of religion. This was viewed by the Cuban community and the Latino community at large, even by those who do not practice the religion, as a victory for ethnic understanding. The decision dated to a case brought by an animal rights group against a Cuban-American *babalao* (priest) for sacrificing chickens and goats. The *santeros* argued that they had the right under the U.S. Constitution to worship as they saw fit, and reminded their critics that many other ancient religions have practiced animal sacrifice. They also argued that they eat the animals they sacrifice (as opposed to discarding them), and that it is not done wantonly, but only under special liturgical circumstances.

The number of believers in *santería* is hard to estimate. In the beginning, it was a secret slave religion, carefully guarded against the Spanish, who sought to do away with these "primitive" and "superstitious" practices. Traditionally, it has been more a religion of the poor, and because the faithful think it is misunderstood, they seldom discuss their beliefs with outsiders. *Santería* is also very popular in Puerto Rico and the Dominican Republic. In Brazil, *santería* is known as *macumba,* and is practiced slightly differently.

What's a Fiesta de Quince?

This is the equivalent of a "sweet sixteen" party, only it happens at fifteen *(quince)*. *Quinceañera* parties are very popular in Miami, and often amount to debutante balls held in large ballrooms or country clubs, with Cuban-American parents spending thousands of dollars.

What Do Cuban-Americans Eat?

Cuban-Americans tend to mix regular "American" foods, such as hamburgers and hot dogs, with the flavors of their old country. The most popular Cuban dishes are roast pig *(lechón asado)*, *ropa vieja*, a shredded beef dish that means literally "old clothes," *yuca*, rice and black beans, fried bananas *(plátanos verdes* and *plátanos maduros)*, *bacalao* (codfish), and, of course, the ubiquitous Cuban sandwich, which has everything but the kitchen sink in it and is sold at little stands all over Miami and in every major U.S. city with a Latino population. Unlike Mexican food, Cuban food is not hot. Garlic and olive oil rule the Cuban kitchen.

SEIS

The Newest Immigrants: Dominicans and Central Americans

Who are the newest Latino immigrants?

Why is life harder for recent immigrants than for those who came before them?

What happened in the Dominican Republic?

What is the Columbus Lighthouse and why do Dominicans call it the Wall of Shame?

Why do Dominicans try to pass as Puerto Ricans?

What's the deal with the Panama Canal?

Who was Manuel Antonio Noriega and did President George Bush really invade a whole country just to get him?

Who rules Panama today?

THE REST OF CENTRAL AMERICA

Which countries make up Central America?

What happened in Nicaragua?

What did Iran have to do with Nicaragua?

What happened in El Salvador?

What about Guatemala?

Who Are the Newest Latino Immigrants?

While the roots of many Latino families go back centuries in this country—some much further back than those of their Anglo compatriots—the great majority of Latinos began entering the American mainstream in the late 1970s and 1980s. This new immigration has continued on a large scale in the 1990s.

The reasons for the steady flow of Latino newcomers are extreme political and economic distress in the Dominican Republic, Colombia, and Peru; and the devastating wars in

Nicaragua, Guatemala, and El Salvador, the homeland of the vast majority of these more recent immigrants. These new, "unexpected" waves of immigration augment the traditional stream of workers from Mexico and other countries south of the border.

In 1993 an estimated 800,000 people from the Dominican Republic (called Dominicans) lived in the New York metropolitan area alone. In Los Angeles, the Salvadoran community grew by 80 percent between 1980 and 1990, bringing the total population of the community to about 500,000. New York has the world's second largest Dominican population; Los Angeles boasts the world's second largest Salvadoran population. Add thousands of Colombians, Ecuadorans, Panamanians, Peruvians, and even some Argentineans, and you have a good idea of the rapidly changing demographics in the United States.

Why Is Life Harder for Recent Immigrants Than for Those Who Came Before Them?

The Latino immigrants of today encounter many more hardships than their European counterparts who came to America decades ago. Almost 100 million Americans are descended from immigrants who passed through Ellis Island. But by the end of this century, many more millions will be descended from immigrants who came either in slave ships or across the Caribbean or the Rio Grande by other means. By the year 2030, Latinos and nonwhites will comprise an estimated one third of the population. By the middle of the next century, the numbers will be even higher, and the census bureau will probably have to revise the term "minority."

Jobs were always difficult to find for new immigrants, but the Latino newcomers are faced with dwindling economic opportunities in a country that has undergone both a recession and a shift from a manufacturing economy (in which unskilled or semiskilled laborers are often needed) to a technological service economy (where only highly trained workers are essential).

In addition, the new Latinos face unprecedented ethnic prejudice from an Anglo community that views them as responsible for (a) contributing to the "welfare mess" of the economy and (b) threatening to alter the racial balance, language, and culture of America.

The border patrols of the Immigration and Naturalization Service are too few and too ill equipped to handle the flood tide of people fleeing their war-torn or drug-torn villages. "Coyotes," the traffickers who charge the immigrants hundreds of dollars to help them come to America, are too many and too well organized for La Migra to outsmart them all.

Few effective programs are in place to help the new immigrants, legal or illegal. Each month, thousands crowd the shelters of Los Angeles's El Rescate (one of a handful of social and legal service organizations set up to deal with new immigrants in California) and other makeshift shelters around the country. Thousands more migrate to Arizona and other states, hoping to find work harvesting hops, asparagus, strawberries, or anything they can find. It is not unusual for a county with only 60,000 farm jobs available to discover at least 150,000 Latino immigrant workers on its doorstep asking for work.

Government assistance grants geared to helping immigrants are scarce or nonexistent. The State Legislation Impact Assistance Grants (SLIAG), a result of the 1986 Immigration Reform Act, were supposed to provide $4 billion for states to aid newly legalized immigrants, but these grants have remained largely available only in theory. Because of the federal budget deficit, Congress transferred one full year of payment slated for SLIAG to funding for other programs. And although the Senate and House approved a fifth year to help new immigrants, it is doubtful that the money will actually become available.

On the other hand, new immigrants do find hundreds of jobs that many in the Anglo community would never take. New immigrants also help one another, and create small businesses that foster the growth of their own *barrios* and communities—as is the case for Dominicans in New York, Nicaraguans in Miami, and Ecuadorans and Salvadorans in California and Washington State.

Despite what many fearful or prejudiced people think, the new Latino immigrants actually contribute to the U.S. economy as a whole. They come to this country to work and make a better life for themselves and their families—the same reasons that compelled millions of Irish, Germans, Poles, and people of other nationalities to cross the Atlantic many decades ago.

According to **Julian Simon,** an economist and author of *The Economic Consequences of Immigration,* these new immigrants actually help America by lightening the Social Security load levied by the aging U.S. population. Typically, immigrants enter the country in the prime of their tax-paying, working lives, and make up the difference for retiring native workers on Social Security pensions. According to Simon, new immigrants use welfare services less than native families; only 5 percent of both legal and undocumented workers take advantage of free medical care, and only 1 percent use food stamps.

What Happened in the Dominican Republic?

The Dominican Republic occupies two thirds of the Caribbean island known as Hispaniola, which lies between Cuba and Puerto Rico. Haiti occupies the western third of the island. **Columbus** landed there in 1492 and established the first Spanish colony in the New World. In fact, the Admiral (as Dominicans refer to Columbus) made Hispaniola his home. Dominicans claim that his remains lie in the cathedral of Santo Domingo (the Spanish insist that his remains are in Seville).

At one point, Cuba and Mexico became more interesting to the Spanish crown, and Hispaniola was neglected. Slowly the French began to settle in the western end of Hispaniola, bringing with them thousands of African slaves. In 1795, the entire island of Hispaniola fell under French rule. But in 1804, African slaves under French rule revolted and declared this region an independent nation called Haiti. In 1822, the Haitians took over the eastern portion of the island. In 1844, the Spanish-speaking inhabitants of this eastern portion rebelled against the Haitians and proclaimed their own independence in their own separate nation—the Dominican Republic.

In 1905, the United States claimed partial control of the island to protect American investments there during a time of political and economic uncertainty. Mounting internal disorders and national debt to U.S. companies led to a U.S. invasion (Marines and all) in 1916. The United States occupied the island until 1924. In 1930, **Rafael Trujillo** came to power and established one of the longest-lasting dictatorships in Latin America (it endured until 1961, when he died). The following year, the first free elections in forty years brought to power a "leftist" populist reformer, President **Juan Bosch.** A military coup ousted him in 1963. When his supporters attempted to put Bosch back in power, civil war broke out and the U.S. Marines were sent in once again to restore the status quo. In 1966, **Joaquín Balaguer,** a right-wing president, was elected. Two other presidents followed **(Antonio Guzmán** and **Salvador Jorge Blanco),** but in 1992 Blanco was sentenced to thirty years in prison for corruption, and President Balaguer—by then elderly and blind—was put back into power by the narrowest possible margin. Counting the ballots took weeks. A narrow margin and a long wait before votes are counted usually mean only one thing in Latin America. In a close election, extra votes can always be found.

What Is the Columbus Lighthouse and Why Do Dominicans Call It the Wall of Shame?

The Columbus Lighthouse, built to commemorate the 500th anniversary in 1992 of the discovery of the Dominican Republic (and the New World) by **Cristobal Colón,** stands as a symbol of the inequities between the rich, governing elite and the millions of Dominicans who have yet to see their dreams of political and economic equality realized.

The lighthouse is actually an enormous cross, flat on the ground, facing the sky, bursting with lights, which cost hundreds of thousands of dollars to build, and which President **Joaquín Balaguer** dreamed up as a tourist attraction. But as it turns out, the lighthouse is situated right in the midst of a shantytown called Maquitería, where the real Santo Domingo lives by candlelight, without water or electricity, and where unpaved streets blow their dust into the sky and uncollected garbage mounts in heaps of stink and scuttling rats. The president's solution was to build a wall around the Maquitería so that those visiting the Columbus Lighthouse would not be exposed to the slum.

This wall surrounding the Maquitería has come to be known as "The Wall of Shame" by Dominicans who argue that their country needs jobs, industry, and basic services, such as electricity and buses, not expensive new monuments celebrating a man who, after all, would oppress all of them were he around today. About 80 percent of the Dominican people are mulatto—and in the poor *barrios,* that figure is closer to 100 percent.

Although the official pro-Columbus attitude that has existed for years in the Dominican Republic claims that Native Americans and African slaves were treated better in Hispaniola than elsewhere, the fact is that during the Spanish domination of Hispaniola, Taino Indians were systematically exterminated not just by European diseases they could not ward off, but also by mistreatment, enforced labor, and starvation. Digs undertaken in La Isabela, the first Spanish settlement in the New World, have uncovered horrifying instruments of torture used on African slaves, as well as "trophy" remnants of broken fingers, noses, and toes belonging to uncooperative slaves.

Still, throughout its long history of dictators, the Dominican Republic has held a kind of unofficial policy against "negritude," or people of African descent, and an official policy of affirmation of the island's Spanish roots. In part, this attitude dates to the war of independence against Haiti (an African-Caribbean country), and to the subsequent Haitian occupation of Santo Domingo in the early nineteenth century. In 1937, General **Rafael Trujillo** ordered the military to kill as many Haitians as it could find along the western frontier of the country. This maneuver resulted in the slaughter of at least twelve thousand people—although Trujillo's motives were never completely elucidated.

Why Do Dominicans Try to Pass as Puerto Ricans?

A treacherous little channel called the Mona Passage, an eighty-mile-wide expanse of water, separates the Dominican Republic and Puerto Rico. Here boats carrying thousands of undocumented Dominicans headed for Puerto Rico capsize every year. If the Dominicans make it through the eighty-foot swells and the turbulence from the colliding currents of the Atlantic Ocean and the Caribbean Sea, the U.S. border patrol may be waiting for them, rifles in hand, ready to turn them back.

They have been called the "new boat people." Many never make it, and although it's impossible to say precisely how many Dominicans lose their lives escaping their poverty-torn country, the toll is probably in the thousands. Amazingly, those who are caught and returned to the Dominican Republic often attempt the treacherous crossing again. For these Dominicans, it is preferable to pay the "coyote" the $150 he charges to land them on a Puerto Rican beach than the unimaginable $1,000 professional smugglers charge to bring them to New York by plane.

The ones who survive the trip and elude the patrol (an estimated twenty thousand do each year) find themselves free men and women, walking the streets of Aguadilla and then San Juan and eventually New York City or Providence, Rhode Island. How? Flights from Puerto Rico are considered domestic travel, and American citizens are not required to show passports before boarding airplanes bound from Puerto Rico to the mainland. To the unschooled eye, Dominicans look and sound like Puerto Ricans.

What's the Deal with the Panama Canal?

The Panama Canal, an artificial waterway across the Isthmus of Panama in Central America, connects the Atlantic and the Pacific oceans. It was completed in 1914 and at its opening was considered the greatest engineering accomplishment of modern times. By passing through this waterway, a ship shortens the trip from the Atlantic to the Pacific by 11,270 very strategic miles. For the United States, establishing the canal was a perfect way to commandeer both shores and accelerate commercial and military traffic from east to west and north to south.

Although the United States can take the credit for completing the Panama Canal, it was the French who started it, under the direction of **Ferdinand de Lesseps,** the same engineer who built the Suez Canal.

In 1902, the United States bought the rights to the completion of the canal from the French, who had bought them from the Colombian government (whose little piece of land the isthmus was). At the last minute, the Colombian government refused to give the United States all the rights it requested, so President **Theodore Roosevelt** quickly "supported" a rebellion in the Colombian region called Panama, where the waterway lay. Before all this started, though, Roosevelt had actually wanted to build a Nicaraguan canal, which, although it would prove a longer route, would be far easier to dig. The Senate, led by Senator **Mark Hanna,** argued in favor of the Panama Canal, and ultimately won.

By 1903, Roosevelt had recognized the new Republic of Panama, and within two weeks of its independence had secured a precious treaty—the Hay-Bunau-Varilla Treaty. This treaty called for the creation of the Panama Canal Zone under complete and absolute control of the United States in perpetuity. In exchange, the United States paid Panama $10 million and an annual rent of $250,000, which was increased slightly over the years—or, you might say, adjusted for inflation.

It took ten years, more than forty thousand workers, and more than $336 million to complete what became a lock canal rather than a sea-level waterway (as it was originally conceived). **George Washington Goethals** was the successful chief engineer of the canal, but it was also thanks to **Dr. William C. Gorgas,** who was able to rid the area of malaria and yellow fever, that Roosevelt's dream finally came to fruition during **Woodrow Wilson**'s administration.

Over the years, the Hay-Bunau-Varilla Treaty was amended, and in 1977 it was replaced by a new treaty which was deemed less "imperialistic" by the people of Panama.

President **Jimmy Carter** and Panamanian general **Omar Torrijos Herrera** negotiated the new Panama Canal Treaty, which stated that the canal would be a neutral zone by the year 2000. It stipulated that the United States would operate the canal with Panamanian participation until that year, when Panama would assume legal control. The Carter treaty became law in 1979, and the Panama Canal Zone (which covered about 648 square miles) was abolished. The United States returned 65 percent of the former Canal Zone to the Panamanian government, including eleven of the fourteen military bases, and the Panama City–Colón railway. In 1990, a Panamanian became head of the U.S.-Panamanian Panama Canal Commission, and by then more than 80 percent of all the canal's employees were Panamanian. In fact, by then the Panama Canal was the largest single employer of Panamanians.

Who Was Manuel Antonio Noriega and Did President George Bush Really Invade a Whole Country Just to Get Him?

General **Manuel Noriega** became commander of Panama's defense forces in 1983, and from that moment on he took charge of deposing or installing presidents as he saw fit. Noriega proved friendly to the United States by conducting CIA-backed operations in Latin America and safeguarding U.S. business interests in his country. However, Noriega was simultaneously defrauding the Bank of Panama by running an international drug syndicate and pocketing millions of dollars that had ben earmarked for jobs, public works, and social services. Aside from collecting rare wines, fast boats, and lavish real estate in Miami and elsewhere, Noriega is believed to have siphoned as much as $300 million out of Panama.

While posing as a U.S. ally, Noriega with his government backed several Latin American guerrilla groups, helped thousands of illegal immigrants enter the United States (charging each as much as $12,000 for a simple visa stamp on a passport), and provided drug shipments with safe passage to the United States through Panama's ports and airstrips. During the Iran-Contra episode under President **Ronald Reagan**'s administration, Noriega refused to join

U.S. efforts to isolate Nicaragua, and backed the Sandinistas in their efforts against U.S. troops—all this while he remained in power thanks to the protection and backing of the U.S. government.

For years, the United States, in an effort to keep Noriega friendly, had apparently turned a blind eye to the fact that he had his hand in the national till and was sending his cronies to the National Bank to cash government checks.

As the United States began to find Noriega's activities insupportable, Noriega allied himself with **Fidel Castro** and Libya's **Muamar Qadhafi,** who was sending him mass shipments of arms to defend himself against the United States. When the United States suggested that Noriega step down, he cried foul and accused Ronald Reagan, who had fiercely opposed President **Jimmy Carter**'s agreement to give up the Panama Canal, of simply looking for an excuse to rescind the treaty.

In 1988, Manuel Noriega was indicted by two U.S. grand juries for drug trafficking, racketeering, and money-laundering for the infamous Medellín Cartel, the drug empire run from Medellín, Colombia. The people of Panama wanted Noriega out, but the strongman was too strong and too well armed to oust. On December 20, 1989, President **George Bush** sent U.S. troops to Panama and eventually had Noriega captured and flown to Miami, to be tried before a U.S. court. In 1992, after a very complicated procedure involving classified U.S. military secrets, Noriega was convicted on eight of eleven counts and sentenced to forty years in prison. However, on December 8, 1992, a U.S. federal judge in Miami ruled that Noriega was a prisoner of war, and thus the terms and conditions of his jail sentence were subject to change.

SEVENTEEN LATINO FIRSTS

1. Linda Alvarado — First Latina owner of a baseball team; partner in the ownership group of the Colorado Rockies

2. Desi Arnaz — First Latino to star in his own television show

3. Jose A. Cabranes — First Latino federal judge in the continental United States

4. Franklin Chang-Diaz — Born in Costa Rica; first Latino astronaut

5. Dennis Chavez — First Latino senator; Democratic senator of New Mexico from 1935–62

6. Roberto Clemente — First Latino voted into the Baseball Hall of Fame

7. Emilio Estevez — First Latino to write, direct, and star in a major motion picture (*Wisdom*, 1986)

8. Elsa Gomez — First Latina to become president (in 1989) of a four-year liberal arts college in the United States (Kean College in New Jersey)

9. Henry B. Gonzalez — First Latino to head the House Banking Committee

10. Diego Hernandez — First Latino to command an aircraft carrier; as U.S. navy rear admiral, took command of the *John F. Kennedy*

11. Jackie Nespral	In 1992, first Latina anchor on a major network news program
12. Antonia Novello	First Latino U.S. surgeon general; also the first woman to fill the post
13. Ellen Ochoa	First Latina astronaut; on the space shuttle *Discovery* on its April 18, 1993, launch
14. Alex Rodriguez	First Latino to be the No. 1 pick in the major-league baseball draft, when the Seattle Mariners chose him in 1993
15. Margarita Rosa	First woman, youngest individual, and first Latino to serve as New York State's Commissioner of Human Rights
16. Ileana Ros-Lehtinen	First Latina elected to the U.S. Congress
17. Ritchie Valens	First Latino rock star to appear on a U.S. postage stamp and have his name in the Hollywood Walk of Fame

Who Rules Panama Today?

After Noriega's demise, Panama held democratic elections and its constitution was restored. **Guillermo Endara** was elected president in 1992.

During the building of the Panama Canal, English-speaking people of African descent from Jamaica and Barbados were brought in to help in the construction. This English-speaking group makes up about 10 percent of the

Panamanian population, which the last census put at 2.4 million.

Panamanians are about 62 percent *mestizo*, 14 percent of African descent, and 10 percent Caucasian. About 124,695 Panamanian-born people are known to live in the United States. The majority live in Florida. Second- and third-generation Panamanians are scattered throughout the United States.

IMPORTANT DATES	
August 15, 1914	The Panama Canal is opened for traffic.
1979	The United States turns over the Panama Canal Zone to Panama under the terms of two U.S.-Panamanian treaties. At the end of 1999, control of the canal will pass to Panama, with that nation guaranteeing neutral operation of the canal.
1983	General Manuel Noriega becomes commander of Panama's defense forces.
1988	General Noriega is indicted by two U.S. grand juries for drug trafficking.
December 24, 1992	George Bush issues a presidential pardon to all government operatives charged in the Iran-Contra investigation.

THE REST OF CENTRAL AMERICA

Which Countries Make Up Central America?

Seven small nations, once part of the Maya empire, constitute present-day Central America: Belize, Guatemala, El Salvador, Honduras, Nicaragua, Costa Rica, and Panama. There are Latinos in the United States with distant or recent roots buried in these beautiful countries whose jungles, volcanoes, and sparkling beaches have become a destination for eco-tourists around the globe. Unfortunately, many of these countries have also been the war-torn zones of conflicts between ideologues, idealists, democrats, tyrants, and superpowers.

What Happened in Nicaragua?

Nicaragua first became liberated from Spain in 1821. It was part of Mexico, and then part of the Central American Federation. In 1838, the federation collapsed, and a struggle for power between liberal and conservative forces ensued. In 1855, the liberals won and invited an American adventurer, **William Walker,** to come to Nicaragua. Walker made himself president, but was eventually overthrown by a joint Central American Army.

In 1909, the United States backed a revolution that overthrew the nationalist president, **José Santos Zelaya.** Then, in 1912, the United States sent in the Marines to put down political uprisings in Nicaragua. The Marines stayed until 1925 and then returned in 1926.

A military leader by the name of **Augusto César Sandino** opposed U.S. intervention and waged a guerrilla war that forced the United States to leave Nicaragua in 1933. Sandino was killed the following year by the National Guard, under the command of **Anastasio Somoza García.** Somoza, who received U.S. backing, seized power in 1936 and ruled until 1956, when he was assassinated. His two sons, **Luis** and **Anastasio Somoza Debayle,** took over for their father.

During the Somoza reign, bananas, coffee, and other agricultural goods were grown in vast quantities and exported to the United States via U.S.-owned corporations, such as the infamous United Fruit Company.

In 1978, an opposition leader named **Pedro Joaquín Chamorro** was assassinated. The people rose en masse to protest the killings and injustices perpetrated by the puppet Somoza regime. The result was the establishment of a new government by a Marxist-oriented party, the FSLN, known generally as the Sandinista party, and named after Nicaragua's old hero, **Augusto César Sandino**.

Soon the FSLN forged close ties with **Castro**'s Cuba and the Soviet bloc and began aiding the guerrillas in El Salvador. President **Ronald Reagan** supported the "Contras"—or anti-Sandinista guerrillas—who had a military base in neighboring Honduras.

In 1984, the FSLN leader, **Daniel Ortega Saavedra,** was elected president and instituted openly Marxist, anti-American policies, similar to those **Fidel Castro** had established in Cuba.

As the U.S. government's efforts to oust Ortega intensified and our government continued giving aid to the Contras, a Latin American group of nations known as the Contadora, comprised of Mexico, Colombia, Venezuela, and Panama, began negotiating a regional peace settlement between the Ortega government and the anti-Marxist guerrillas. In 1987, Ortega signed a regional peace pact and granted amnesty to some political prisoners, although restrictive measures, such as the banning of freedom of the press, continued. Finally, early in 1989, Ortega, abiding by the rules of the Central American accord, agreed to hold free elections in 1990. The Contras agreed to dismantle their military operations in Honduras.

Violeta Barrios Chamorro was elected president and took office April 25, 1990. She had previously owned a newspaper, which Ortega had closed down when her editorials opposed him. Amnesty was granted to all sides for the many crimes committed during the Nicaraguan civil war. Chamorro inherited a war-torn country with runaway inflation and a devastated agricultural economy. Her middle-of-the-road government was opposed by many right-wing elements who believed her tactics were too soft, but she received the full backing of the United States, which lifted the economic embargo and committed millions of dollars toward the normalization of the Nicaraguan economy. As a result of the devastating guerrilla war in Nicaragua, where hundreds of villages were torched and people were killed en masse, thousands of Nicaraguans fled their country and came to live in the United States.

What Did Iran Have to Do With Nicaragua?

The Iran-Contra scandals of the Reagan era served to make all Americans aware that the executive branch of the U.S. government had a long-standing tradition of intervention in the internal affairs of Central American governments. In November 1986, as civil war raged in Nicaragua, it came to light that the United States had been secretly selling arms to Iran. A few days after this was announced, Attorney General **Edwin Meese** discovered that part of the profit from the sale of arms to Iran had been diverted to aid the Nicaraguan Contra rebels. The whole matter became a terrific scandal. For one, President **Ronald Reagan** declared that the purpose of selling the arms to Iran was merely to improve relations with Iran, not to negotiate the release of U.S. hostages held in the Middle East under the auspices of the **Ayatollah Khomeini.** Later, the president acknowledged that the sale of arms had, in fact, become an arms-for-hostages swap. At the heart of the matter, though, was the fact that Congress had prohibited all aid to the Contras, and that these covert operations were positively illegal and, it appeared, sanctioned by the Reagan administration.

An independent special prosecutor, former federal judge **Lawrence E. Walsh,** was selected to investigate individuals involved in both the sale of arms to Iran and the diverting of moneys to the Contras. At his end, President Reagan appointed a review board on the matter, headed by former Republican senator **John Tower.** The Tower Commission Report in 1987 implicated the president by criticizing his laissez-faire management style. President Reagan accepted Tower's criticism and took responsibility for the actions conducted by people under his command.

As Walsh's investigation uncovered more facts, more members of President Reagan's administration were implicated. In 1988, **Robert McFarlane,** former national security adviser, pleaded guilty to criminal charges of withholding information from Congress on the matter of sending secret money to the Nicaraguan Contras. He was fined $20,000 and given two years' probation. In March 1988, a federal grand jury indicted Marine Lieutenant Colonel **Oliver North,** former national security adviser **John Poindexter,** and others on a variety of charges, including conspiracy to defraud the U.S. government. In May, North was convicted of three of the twelve criminal charges he had been tried on. However, the North convictions were eventually overturned by a federal appeals court, which uncovered defects in the trial's proceedings. In 1990, Poindexter was convicted on five counts of deceiving congressional investigators, and sentenced to six months in prison.

In July 1991, **Alan D. Fiers,** CIA chief of covert operations in Central America from 1984 to 1986, admitted that he had lied to Congress regarding CIA involvement in aid to the Contras. In 1992, former defense secretary **Caspar Weinberger** was indicted on five counts of lying to Congress. Then, on December 24, 1992, President **George Bush** gave all parties involved a Christmas present by issuing a presidential pardon to all the government operatives charged in the Iran-Contra investigations.

What Happened in El Salvador?

The Pipil people, whose culture was similar to that of the Aztec, lived in El Salvador before the Spanish came and ruled from 1524 to 1821. Like Nicaragua, El Salvador was originally part of the Central American Federation. And, because of its small size and strategic position, El Salvador was often under Guatemalan or Nicaraguan rule at different points in its history. Many Salvadorans also emigrated to Honduras, which led to border wars (the most recent of which was in 1969).

In 1977, General **Carlos Humberto Romero** became president, but he was deposed two years later by a right-wing military junta. In 1980, the "leftist" liberal Archbishop **Oscar Arnulfo Romero** was assassinated. This led to an uprising and much pressure from the United States on the military junta to put economic and human rights reforms in place. As a result, **José Napoleon Duarte,** a leader of the Christian Democratic Party, became president. However, civil war broke out between the right-wing elements, who executed peasants and workers who disagreed with them, and the two main leftist groups, the Farabundo Martí National Liberation Front (FMLN) and the Revolutionary Democratic Front (FDR), who, the government claimed, were being aided by Cuba, Nicaragua, and the Soviet Union. In June 1989, **Alfredo Cristiani** succeeded Duarte, who had become gravely ill, as president. By 1990, the civil war had claimed more than seventy-five thousand lives and El Salvador lay in shambles. On January 16, 1992, a cease-fire was reached thanks to a series of negotiations sponsored by the United Nations. Under the UN accord, Salvadoran forces were to return to civilian duties, an all-new national police force was to be created, and the long-awaited land reforms were to be put in place. In March 1993, a United Nations commission officially condemned senior military persons still in positions of power for the senseless killing of thousands of Salvadoran civilians.

Once again, as in Nicaragua, countless numbers were left homeless and without means of support or ways of cultivating the land. And, as had happened in other Central American countries, this plundered land saw its people flee to the north—namely to Los Angeles and other promised lands.

What About Guatemala?

Like Nicaragua and El Salvador, Guatemala has had its share of political and economic misery in recent times.

The Guatemalan people are of Maya ancestry, as their extraordinary ruins and other archaeological sites at Tikal and Uaxactún testify.

The Spaniard **Pedro Alvarado** conquered Guatemala in 1523, and the whole area remained under Spanish domination until 1821, when Guatemala won its independence and joined the Central American Federation.

Guatemala has a long history of rule by *caudillos,* or strongmen, who were sometimes from the left and sometimes from the right, but always totalitarian. In 1944, **Juan José Arevalo,** a university professor who had been in exile in Argentina, became president. He instituted democracy and a social security system and began to industrialize the highly agrarian country, whose main source of wealth was selling fruits and vegetables to the United States. In 1951, **Jacobo Arbenz Guzmán** succeeded Arevalo. Arbenz was a socialist (for whom **Ernesto "Che" Guevara** had worked), and he launched a massive agrarian reform.

In 1982, a Pentecostal Protestant political leader, **Efrain Ríos Montt,** took over the government in a military coup. Eventually he, in turn, was overthrown by Brigadier General

Oscar Humberto Mejia Victores, who promised universal suffrage and respect for human rights. Under his regime, an average of 100 political assassinations and more than forty political kidnappings took place per month.

In 1991, in the face of continuing strife and an increase in right-wing "death squads," another Evangelical Protestant, **Jorge Serrano Elias,** was elected president. Although violent political upheaval continued between the right- and left-wing elements in the country after his election, exacerbated by the peasants, who felt squeezed in the middle, the violent climate began to calm in Guatemala after the war in El Salvador began to lose its teeth and the United States adopted a new policy of nonsupport to right-wing groups in Central America.

Many new Guatemalans in the United States have blamed the policies of President **Ronald Reagan** in their country and in all of Central America for the devastation they have suffered. In 1983, a film called *El Norte,* which gained international attention, recorded the plight of Central American peasants finding their way up to the United States (*el norte,* or "the north") to escape the unspeakable inhumanity of a senseless civil war.

From the novel *How the Garcia Girls Lost Their Accents* by Dominican-American writer Julia Alvarez (1991)

The day the Garcias were one American year old, they had a celebration at dinner. Mami baked a nice flan and stuck a candle in the center. "Guess what day it is today?" She looked around the table at her daughters' baffled faces. "One year ago today," Papi was orating, "we came to the shores of this great country." When he was done misquoting the poem on the Statue of Liberty, the youngest, Fifi, asked if she could blow out the candle, and Mami said only after everyone had made a wish.

What do you wish for on the first celebration of the day you lost everything? Carla wondered. Everyone else around the table had their eyes closed as if they had no trouble deciding. Carla closed her eyes too. She should make an effort and not wish for what she always wished for in her homesickness. But just this last time, she would let herself. "Dear God," she began. She could not get used to this American wish-making without bringing God into it. "Let us please go back home, please," she half prayed and half wished. It seemed a less and less likely prospect. In fact her parents were sinking roots here.

SIETE

La Politica

Real power or paella in the sky: How much political clout do Latinos really have?

Are there any Latino watchdog organizations?

How much money do Latinos give to political organizations?

Is it true that most Latino contributions go to the Republican Party?

What do Latinos in Congress stand for?

Who are the Latinos in Congress?

What do Latinos in Congress think of the North American Free Trade Agreement?

What's all the fuss about redistricting and the Voting Rights Act?

Why is proportional representation such a hot tamale?

Does bilingual education mean we'll all be speaking Spanish soon?

Real Power or Paella in the Sky: How Much Political Clout Do Latinos Really Have?

If political power is measured by the number of elected representatives and federal and local governmental appointments, the answer to that question is *mucho*—at least as of the last elections—but not as much as the growing Latino population will undoubtedly wield by the year 2000.

An estimated 4.5 million Latinos voted in the last general elections (or one out of every 22 voters), putting more Latinos and more supporters of pro-Latino issues in office than ever before. In fact, while the national electorate increased by a mere 10 percent, Latino voters grew by more than 50 percent. The net results were 8 new Latinos in Congress (bringing the total to 17) and a 20 percent gain in Latino state legislators, upping the total to a record 157.

These gains, in addition to the appointment of one key cabinet member (**Henry Cisneros** as HUD secretary) and hundreds of other presidential appointees, seem to indicate that this is indeed the dawning of the age of Latinos.

According to the National Association of Latino Elected and Appointed Officials (NALEO), Latinos cast the swing vote in the 1992 presidential elections in several states. In Colorado, for example, **Bill Clinton** won by only 68,000 votes. A total of 170,000 Latinos voted in the Colorado elections, and 75 to 80 percent voted for Clinton. In Florida, where, according to Southwest Voter Research, the Cuban-American community votes 90 percent Republican in national elections, President **George Bush** beat Bill Clinton by fewer than 90,000 votes. Here, the 430,000 mostly Republican Latino voters made the difference.

However, according to several Latino leaders, Latino voters are still underrepresented in many key states in spite of the amendments to the 1965 Voting Rights Act that led to redistricting and the creation of Latino-dominated political seats. They cite as an example California, which has only four Latino members of Congress out of a total of fifty-two, in spite of the fact that one in four residents is Latino. They also point to the fact that no president has yet deemed it politically necessary to appoint a Latino to the Supreme Court.

Latinos hold less than 4 percent of the 435 House seats. Since the Latino population is 9 percent (22.4 million) of the present U.S. population, Latino leaders argue that more than 50 percent of all Latinos are represented by non-Latino members of Congress. They estimate that voter apathy and alienation, once regarded as the major reason for Latino underrepresentation in government, now runs second to the high cost of operating political campaigns and the lack of resources in the districts where most Latinos are running for office.

Another key factor in the political numbers game is the fact that a large number of Latino immigrants from Mexico, Colombia, the Dominican Republic, and Central America are not yet citizens and thus cannot vote. Also, since much of the Latino population was under eighteen years of age as of 1993, it will not affect the electoral machine until the next national election.

Many believe that the high numbers of Latino federal and local officials, from members of Congress to governors, mayors, and police commissioners, along with the promise of Puerto Rican statehood and the strengthening economic power base of the community on the whole (presently there are more than three hundred thousand Latino-owned businesses in the United States generating more than $20 billion per year), will help close the gaps in the not too distant future. In fact, since by all projections one in every three Americans will be Latino before the end of the new century, even the possibility of a Latino president does not look like paella in the sky anymore.

Are There Any Latino Watchdog Organizations?

There are many, representing both individual Latino groups (Mexican, Puerto Rican, and so on) and Latinos as a whole. Among the most active are the National Council of La Raza, the National Puerto Rican Coalition, the Cuban American National Council, the National Association of Hispanic Publications, the Aspira Association, the American GI Forum, the League of United Latin American Citizens (LULAC), and the Mexican American Legal Defense and Education Fund (MALDEF). Besides these groups, which carefully monitor the social and political arena, there is the Hispanic Association on Corporate Responsibility (HARC), whose principal directive is to monitor the private sector closely so that large corporations "do the right thing" and reinvest a portion of the money spent by Latino consumers into their communities, by way of higher-level jobs, franchise and dealership opportunities, and philanthropic donations.

How Much Money Do Latinos Give to Political Organizations?

The Federal Election Commission (FEC) began issuing comprehensive data on political contributions in the United States in 1979. Since then, political contributions have increased in general, but Latino political donations have grown twice as fast as others. For example, during the presidencies between 1970–80 and 1977–88, political giving increased 118 percent in the general electorate, while Latino contributions went up 286 percent. All told, it is estimated that individual Latinos and Latino businesses combined have given as much as $80 million to parties and candidates since 1979. The 1992 election coffers may have been the beneficiaries of as much as $8 million in Latino largesse.

Is It True That Most Latino Contributions Go to the Republican Party?

Ironically, yes, even if 65 percent of all Latinos consider themselves Democrats.

The reason is that Cuban-Americans, who constitute the most solvent Latino group and the one most active in mainstream politics, are 70 percent Republican and vote 90 percent Republican in national elections. This also explains why a disproportionate amount of Latino political contributions come from Florida, the home of more than half a million Cuban-Americans.

However, even Republican Cuban-Americans have made it a practice to contribute to both parties. It's called hedging your bets—and all powerful business institutions do it. During the last elections, **Bill Clinton,** too, benefited from Cuban-American giving, both from big business and small individual contributors. For example, just before the elections, after he clearly supported proposed legislation to tighten the

U.S. embargo on Cuba, Clinton raised $100,000 at a single political event in Miami's Little Havana.

The biggest individual Latino political contributor is **Jorge Mas Canosa,** CEO of Church & Tower, a Miami construction company whose clients include Southern Bell and all of Dade County itself. Mr. Mas Canosa, who many observers both in and out of the Cuban-American community believe may run for president of Cuba when (or if) **Fidel Castro**'s regime is toppled, has contributed in excess of $216,000 to national political candidates over twelve years—more than any other Latino individual in the United States. Mas Canosa is a true American success story. He arrived in Miami in 1960 at the age of twenty-one as a penniless refugee fleeing Castro's Cuba. He worked as a stevedore, a shoe salesman, and a milkman before buying a faltering construction company and building a personal fortune currently estimated at more than $9 million.

Mr. Mas Canosa was a previous chair of the Cuban American National Foundation (CANF), which he patterned after the successful pro-Israel lobby, the American Israel Public Affairs Committee. He has also been the leading light behind the Free Cuba PAC and is considered the most important individual lobbyist in the United States by most Washington insiders. The Free Cuba PAC contributed generously to forty-eight congressional campaigns in 1990, including that of New Jersey Democrat **Robert Torricelli,** who sponsored the Cuban Democracy Act signed into law by President **George Bush** in 1992. Since the Free Cuba PAC was founded, its directors and their political action committee have donated more than $7 million to presidential, Senate, and House candidates, and have helped to raise even more money through their sponsorship of fund-raising dinners. The PAC's agenda, as the name implies, is to oust Castro and establish a democratic government in Cuba.

One Free Cuba PAC president, **Domingo Moreira,** is ranked number four among U.S. Latinos in political contributions. Moreira is president of Ladex Corp., a wholesale seafood company in Miami.

Marife Hernández, a Puerto Rican and the former head of Cultural Communications, Inc., is the second largest individual political contributor and an active member of the Democratic party. **Alfonso Fanjul, Jr.,** a Cuban-American and the third largest individual contributor, is the head of the Flo-Sun Corporation of Palm Beach, America's largest sugar producer. Other political contributors include **Roberto G. Mendoza,** a Cuban-American, who serves as vice chairman of J. P. Morgan and Company Inc. in New York, the fifth largest U.S. bank; **Arturo Díaz,** a Puerto Rican businessman affiliated with various companies in Río Piedras and San Juan, Puerto Rico; **Earl Luna,** a Mexican-American and an attorney in Dallas; and **Roberto C. Goizueta,** a Cuban-American and CEO of the Coca-Cola Company.

What Do Latinos in Congress Stand For?

The overwhelming number of Latinos in Congress are Democrats. Their priorities vary according to the districts they represent, and they stand on many sides of the issues (from pro– to anti–North American Free Trade Treaty (NAFTA), to pro– and anti–women's reproductive rights). Most, however, are united under the banner of the Congressional Hispanic Caucus, a bipartisan group formed in 1976 by **Herman Badillo** and the four other Latino Democrats then in Congress. Their directive was to "voice and advance, through the legislative process, issues affecting Latino Americans."

Many of the ideals of the Congressional Hispanic Caucus have come out of the dozens of Mexican-American and Puerto Rican grass-roots organizations, such as LULAC, the GI Forum, and Aspira (a Puerto Rican group that has promoted education and ethnic advancement since the 1960s), La Raza Unida, and countless others, many of which began their struggle for political representation and fairness for Latino people as far back as the turn of the century.

Not all Latino representatives, however, belong to the Caucus. Thirty-year veteran **Henry B. Gonzalez** (Democrat of Texas), who began his third term as chairman of the House Banking, Finance, and Urban Affairs Committee in 1993, is not a member. However, his honorable and progressive legislative history on behalf of the disadvantaged has certainly embraced many of the principles of the Hispanic Caucus.

The Congressional Hispanic Caucus itself has undergone some recent transformations. It was originally formed to provide scholarships and training opportunities for Latinos, not necessarily to establish policies or introduce bills. In 1991, under the leadership of chairman **Solomon Ortiz** (Democrat of Texas), the caucus turned its attention to legislation. In 1992, under the new caucus chairman **José Serrano** (Democrat of New York), the group stepped up its efforts to deal with urban concerns, especially educational stimulus packages and health reform legislation.

After considerable lobbying, the caucus got passed the Voters Assistance Act of 1992 (known as the "bilingual voting bill"), which makes bilingual voting information easily available, thereby assuring that Spanish-speaking and other foreign-language-speaking minorities have ready access to the ballot. Another bill the caucus helped pass was the 1991 Hispanic Access to Higher Education Bill, which attempts to increase the number of Latino college graduates through a series of learning incentives and dropout prevention programs.

A third bill introduced by the caucus was the Birth Defects Registry Act of 1992. This legislation, which affects Chairman Ortiz's own South Texas district, where there is an alarmingly high rate of birth defects among Latinos, provides for the gathering and studying of statistical data on birth defects in racial and ethnic minorities.

As far as other, more universal issues that not only Latino representatives, but Latinos in general stand for, a deep commitment to the family (though not necessarily the nuclear family) is at the root of much of the Latino philosophy. Family commitment and the struggle to keep the family together have exemplified the way of millions of immigrants who cross the Rio Grande or fly over the Caribbean to support large groups of relatives, and sometimes whole villages, left behind.

A sense of duty when it comes to caring for children and the elderly runs through the Latino philosophy, as does an Amerindian cosmic vision that the world itself is a holy place. These traditions are also part of the issues Latino-elected representatives are expected to bring to the table when they move to Washington.

Who Are the Latinos in Congress?

The four Latino senior members of Congress of the last three decades are **Dennis Chavez** (Democrat of New Mexico), **Ed Roybal** (Democrat of California), **Eligio ("Kika") de La Garza** (Democrat of Texas), and **Henry B. Gonzalez** (Democrat of Texas). They loom like the giant figures on Mt. Rushmore before their Latino constituents. Dennis Chavez, who died in 1962, was the first Latino ever elected to the U.S. Senate.

In 1992, Ed Roybal retired after thirty years of service to the working-class voters of East Los Angeles. He had served as a member of the powerful House Appropriations Committee and was considered the most senior Latino representative. Latinos gained four new seats on Roybal's old committee. In one of those historical twists of fate that mark new beginnings, his daughter, **Lucille Roybal-Allard,** was elected to Congress the same year her father retired—although she represents a different district. Her interests include the Latino community, but she plans to concentrate much of her effort on fighting for women's civil rights.

In 1993, Henry B. Gonzalez began a third term as chairman of the House Banking, Finance, and Urban Affairs Committee, and this time he was joined by three Latino freshmen.

Kika de la Garza went back for another term as chairman of the House Agriculture Committee in 1993.

The 1992 general elections also marked other Latino firsts: **Nydia Velazquez** (Democrat of New York) won the Thirteenth District seat after redistricting, defeating **Stephen Solarz,** who had held a New York seat for years. Velazquez is the first Puerto Rican woman to serve in the House. She is serving on the Banking, Finance, and Urban Affairs Committee, and the Small Business Committee, both of which stand to benefit her inner-city district.

In 1989, **Claude Pepper,** the popular Democratic congressman from Florida, died after thirty years of service. A Republican Cuban-American, **Ileana Ros-Lehtinen,** was overwhelmingly elected to fill his seat. Among those who campaigned for her were President **George Bush** and his son **Jeb Bush,** who also served as her campaign chairman.

Cuban-born Republican **Lincoln Diaz-Balart** (who is related to **Fidel Castro**) ran unopposed in Miami's new Twenty-first District, which is 80 percent Cuban-American. He has secured a seat on the Foreign Affairs Committee, along with another Cuban-American, **Robert Menendez** (Democrat of New Jersey). But whereas Diaz-Balart is a conservative, with a clear anti-Castro mandate from his district and a clear opposition to NAFTA, Menendez represents Union City, New Jersey, a district which has a 12 percent unemployment rate, and his interests lie in creating enterprise zones and access to health care.

Another "first" was marked in congressional history as a result of the last election. For the first time in history, a Latino, **Bill Richardson** (Democrat of New Mexico), serves as chief deputy majority whip. The Democratic Steering and Policy Committee has three Latinos on board: Richardson,

Kika de la Garza, and **Ed Pastor** (Democrat of Arizona). And **Xavier Becerra** (Democrat of California), who was elected by many of Roybal's old constituents in the newly redrawn Thirtieth District, is one of three freshman whips assisting Speaker of the House **Tom Foley.**

Other Latinos to watch for on the Washington horizon include **Solomon Ortiz** (Democrat of Texas), ex-chairman of the Hispanic Caucus; **Frank Tejeda** (Democrat of Texas), who was elected without opposition in either the primary or the general election; **Luis Gutierrez** (Democrat of Illinois); and **José Serrano** (Democrat of New York), who will serve as chairman of the Congressional Hispanic Caucus through 1995, and who is popular not only among Latinos, but among gays and lesbians, and women and other minorities.

What Do Latinos in Congress Think of the North American Free Trade Agreement?

Like many Americans, Latinos were divided on NAFTA. In principle, the treaty, initiated by President **George Bush** and President of Mexico **Carlos Salinas de Gortari,** was designed to create a regional trading bloc of 370 million people producing $6 trillion worth of goods and services at free-market prices for all three countries involved—Mexico, the United States, and Canada. It is also aimed at making production more cost-effective for many U.S. industries.

Those who question the ultimate benefits of the treaty, such as Congressman **Ed Pastor** of Arizona and Congressman **Matthew Martinez** of California, point to the risk that too much capital investment from U.S. corporations will go south of the border, and that the large corporations and not small businesses will ultimately benefit. They contend that thousands of American workers will lose jobs, particularly in the automotive and garment industries. They worry that despite certain safeguards, Mexican workers themselves will be exploited, while their relatives north of the border will be unemployed. They argue for the creation of "safety nets" and a retooling of the American work force before the treaty is implemented. This view is strongly supported by the AFL-CIO and other workers' organizations. Pastor and Martinez added that there is a real need for environmental controls in Mexico. Although there are no conclusive tests, many observers have noted that Mexico's dumping of toxic wastes into the Rio Grande along the South Texas border may be responsible for the inordinate incidence of birth defects plaguing Mexican-American babies in that area.

Those in favor of the treaty, such as congressmen **Bill Richardson** (Democrat of New Mexico), and **Henry Bonilla** (Republican of Texas), believe that the treaty, which was ratified under President **Bill Clinton** in 1994, will help our hemisphere compete against the Far Eastern and European blocs, and that thousands of Latinos and other Americans will benefit from the free trade among all three countries. They also view NAFTA as a way to form closer ties with Mexico, the ancestral land of so many Latinos. Presently, Mexico is the United States' fastest growing export market, with more than 600,000 Americans employed in making and selling products to Mexico. Another argument in favor of NAFTA has been that the Mexican economy will rise and that the flow of undocumented workers into the United States will be stemmed.

What's All the Fuss About Redistricting and the Voting Rights Act?

The Voting Rights Act of 1965 was passed by Congress to correct discrimination against African-Americans, particularly in Southern states, which, despite laws on the books prohibiting discrimination (as a result of the broader Voting Rights Act of 1964), flagrantly denied African-Americans access to voting. The 1965 act, which gave the federal government the right to regulate elections in certain Southern states, was extremely effective. As a result of its enforcement, the number of African-American elected officials in the South went from a mere hundred in 1965 to almost five thousand by 1989. And the numbers of African-American voters increased in many Southern states by more than 50 percent within a couple of years.

NINE LATINO WOMEN WHO MADE A DIFFERENCE

1. Joan Baez

Born in 1941, this folk singer has been an activist for four decades; in 1965 founded the Center for Nonviolence; in 1979 founded Humanitas International; in 1985 participated in the Live AID concert in Philadelphia; has served on the national advisory board of Amnesty International

2. Fabiola Cabeza de Baca

Born in 1888, this early pioneer popularized native handicrafts of the Southwest worldwide; helped introduce modern food preparation systems to the people of New Mexico; was the first Latina to receive a U.S. Government Superior Service Award

3. Linda Chavez

In 1977 President Carter appointed her to the Office of Education; in 1983 President Reagan named her to the Civil Rights Commission, the first Latina to serve; in 1985 she was chosen to run the

---

	White House Office of Public Liaison and thus became the highest-ranking woman in the White House
4. Dolores Huerta	One of the greatest Chicana activists; as vice president of Cesar Chavez's United Farm Workers from 1970–73, helped win hundreds of victories
5. Virginia Musquiz	A top organizer of the Raza Unida Party who fought for the civil rights of farm workers
6. Antonia Novello	First Latino U.S. surgeon general and first woman selected for the post; became surgeon general in 1989 under President Bush
7. Helen Rodriguez	Doctor and activist who is a leading spokesperson on issues regarding women and medicine; was on the pediatrics faculty of Albert Einstein Medical School and an attending physician at Lincoln Hospital in the Bronx; served on committees addressing the development of children's health education
8. Josefina Sierro	Began an underground railroad in the 1930s, during the mass deportation of Mexican-Americans to Mexico, and brought back hundreds of citizens to the United States
9. Ema Tenayuca	Organized the first successful strike of pecan-shellers in San Antonio in the 1930s; her organization served as a model for César Chávez

The African-American civil rights movement has served as a model for many Latino political organizations. The Black Berets inspired the Brown Berets in the Latino community. The demand for African studies spurred the demand for Latino studies. And, most important, the legal models used by African-American leaders on both the national and local fronts served as a blueprint for Latino leaders eager to rectify social and political inequalities.

The first efforts toward making special legal provisions for Latinos occurred in New York in the early 1970s, when a Puerto Rican group brought a lawsuit against the state, alleging that English-only ballots were discriminatory, since Puerto Ricans, who are U.S. citizens by birth, speak Spanish. The case argued that expecting Puerto Ricans to read English was a discriminatory form of the English literacy test. The case was won; all election material immediately was made bilingual.

On the heels of the Puerto Rican victory, the Mexican American Legal Defense and Education Fund (MALDEF) began lobbying intensely for the passage of an amendment to the 1965 Voting Rights Act that would extend special considerations to Latinos.

There was much discussion and many congressional inquiries as to whether Latinos were systematically discriminated against at the polls—when, in fact, at the time of the hearings, two Mexican-Americans (**Jerry Apodaca** of New Mexico and **Raul Castro** of Arizona) were serving as governors, and there was one Mexican-American senator (**Joseph Montoya** of New Mexico) and five Latino members of Congress—**Henry B. Gonzalez, Kika de la Garza, Edward Roybal, Manuel Luján,** and **Herman Badillo.**

Although it was evident that voter discrimination against African-Americans had been much worse than against Latinos (after all, where were the African-American governors and other representatives in 1975?), MALDEF and other Latino groups proved that Mexican-Americans had been actively discriminated against in Texas, and that they were being generally and purposely underrepresented in Congress.

Finally, the 1975 Voting Rights Act amendments extended special provisions to Latinos and other minorities for seven years and then, in 1982, extended the rights for yet another ten years. The net result of the Voting Rights Act amendments was not only the emergence of a much larger Latino voter base thanks to bilingual materials at the polls, but the consequent redistricting—or the creation of special districts—in hundreds of municipalities all over the country where Latinos were in the majority.

These new apportionments, which were won region by region, with the federal government challenging local city councils (such as that of Los Angeles on two separate occasions), were made in order to ensure fair representation of Latinos in government by allowing them to elect their own candidates—Latino candidates, or candidates with proven sensitivity to the needs of the community.

Since the Voting Rights Act amendments remain in place, as the Latino population increases across the country, new "proportional representation" districts emerge. The last census resulted in the creation of new districts, which, in turn, brought a roster of new names to Congress.

Why Is Proportional Representation Such a Hot Tamale?

The question of "proportional representation" is actually hotter than a chile pepper. Presently, the tide is in favor of righting the wrongs of past underrepresentation by keeping the Voting Rights Act amendments on the books, and drawing geographical and political boundaries that give Latinos and other minorities majority power in neighborhoods where they are, in fact, a majority.

However, America has, until recently, subscribed to the "melting pot" theory, according to which character and ability supersede ethnicity at the polling booth, and the larger society beckons minorities to leave the ghetto and become integrated into the country as a whole. The idea behind the "melting pot" is that the Garcías should be able to live in the same district as the Solomons, the Cuomos, the O'Shaughnessys, and the Smiths, and not just next to the Gonzálezes; and that they should all, together, be able to elect Ms. Schroeder or Mr. Pérez to Congress, or whoever happens to be the best person for the job. That's the idea, anyway.

Many have questioned the wisdom of reapportionment. In her book *Out of the Barrio,* **Linda Chavez** argues that in order to maintain the political mandate that reapportionment has granted many Latinos, they are forced to stay in the *barrio*—and thus forced to remain the poor underclass, which political clout is supposed to save them from in the first place.

Congressman **Henry Hyde** of Illinois and others have questioned the wisdom of retaining bilingual provisions for people who have lived in the United States most of their lives if, after all, ours is an English-speaking nation. There are thousands of Latinos in the private sector who agree with Chavez and Hyde and believe that, if anything, reapportionment should be looked on as a transitory measure (which is how the Voting Rights Act was originally conceived) and not as a permanent legal fixture. Those who argue for reapportionment and representation along ethnic lines, such as Representative **Nydia Velazquez** of New York, believe that the "melting pot" concept may be good in principle, but that in the meantime it has deprived Latinos and other minorities of their constitutional rights to adequate housing, health care, social services, education, and economic opportunity. Like the revolutionaries of the Boston Tea Party, they argue on the side of "no taxation without representation," and believe that the rights of the Latino community will continue to be ignored until there are enough Latinos in government who can speak for them.

It is a continuing debate with more open-ended ramifications than you can shake a hot habanero chile at.

Does Bilingual Education Mean We'll All Be Speaking Spanish Soon?

In 1981, **Senator S. I. Hayakawa** of California introduced a joint Senate resolution to amend the U.S. Constitution to read, "The English language shall be the official language of the United States," but the bill went to sleep during the Ninety-seventh Congress.

What Hayakawa, as well as several grass-roots pro-English-only organizations, such as U.S. English, were reacting to, was probably that large *"Se Habla Español"* sign hanging up there somewhere in the U.S. sky. The large influx of new Spanish-speaking immigrants, together with native Spanish-speaking Latinos, and the strong currents of bicultural and bilingual ethnic pride running through the educational system from coast to coast, have created an undeniable Spanish-speaking climate in the country. They have also created a backlash in certain pockets of conservative populations.

Some states and municipalities have balked at the sound of "so much Spanish." In fact, since 1986, eighteen states have passed laws recognizing English as their official language. But forty others have either entirely ignored or dismissed the idea. In 1980, Dade County, Florida, passed a county-wide antibilingual referendum bill in reaction to the new wave of Cuban Marielitos. But by 1993, that law was unanimously voted off the books. You can see bumper stickers in Texas, Florida, California, and the Southwest that read "Monolingualism Is a Curable Disease."

Actually, bilingual, bicultural education had its official beginnings in Dade County. The first bilingual model began when hundreds of thousands of Cuban refugee children arrived in Miami in the 1960s and were enrolled in the public schools. Cuban educators, thinking that **Fidel Castro**'s dictatorship would end soon and that the children would return to their native land, devised a way to teach half a day in English and half a day in Spanish, so that the students would learn English while carrying on their education in their native language. Because these children were mostly middleclass and quite motivated, they scored high marks and did well in all subjects across the board. In fact, they did much better than other English-only students in Florida. This newfound success sparked an idea among politicians and teachers in the Southwest who wished to see their Latino students improve their performance.

Thus, at the behest of **Ralph Yarborough,** then a Texas senator, a bill was introduced in 1967 to provide federal aid for bilingual education for poor Mexican-American children in public schools. The idea was that these children, who were both linguistically and culturally disadvantaged, would learn more rapidly if taught in Spanish (while learning English) and would enjoy greater self-esteem. According to those who testified at the hearings, part of the reason these students faired poorly in school was a "damaged selfconcept"—i.e. a lack of cultural and ethnic identity because the schools failed to educate them about their own culture.

Thus, the Bilingual Education Amendment became Title VII of the Elementary and Secondary Education Act in 1968. The original funding for this program was $7.5 million.

That same year, with a growing awareness of their culture and a sense of outrage at having been denied access to their own cultural traditions, a group of Los Angeles high school students staged a massive walkout demanding compulsory bilingual and bicultural education for all Mexican-American students. The following year, the University of California at Berkeley started a Chicano studies program. Soon, other colleges and universities across the country began offering courses in Latino or Chicano studies and eventually devoted entire departments to the pursuit of Latino culture beyond what the traditional "Spanish departments" had presented.

These initiatives led the way to amplified bilingual and bicultural studies around the country in subsequent years, and to the eventual requirement by the Office for Civil Rights (OCR) of the Department of Health, Education, and Welfare that bilingual education be extended to all children coming from homes where English was not the first language. In 1973, Senator **Edward Kennedy** (Democrat of Massachusetts), Senator **Alan Cranston** (Democrat of California), and Senator **Edward Montoya** (Democrat of New Mexico) sponsored a bill requiring that bicultural education be added to native language classes. In 1978, further amendments to Title VII allowed for children who already spoke English (not merely those who were only Spanish-speaking) to be put in bilingual, bicultural programs.

Over the years, there has been considerable objection to the continuing expansion of bilingual programs, which, incidentally, also applies to other language minorities, although it affects Latinos most. Many of the objections have issued from within the Latino community itself; some have come from well-known novelist and journalist **Richard Rodriguez,** author of *Days of Obligation: An Argument with My Mexican Father.*

Many Latino intellectuals believe that when Latino students are put into "segregated" classes, they are held back and their English proficiency suffers. They argue that a program that was supposed to enhance their children's education has become a stumbling block and that, if given the choice, the children would prefer to be in "nonspecific" or mainstream classes. Some have even argued that bilingual programs, in which students with Spanish surnames are made to take regular academic courses in Spanish, are a form of subtle and insidious discrimination, by which, under the guise of liberalism, Latino students wind up in separate classes from the Anglos and, eventually, in different worlds.

Those who object point to the New York State Department of Education formula as an example of a good idea gone overboard. There, students whose first language is not English are tested in their own language and are held to a lower standard on tests of competency in English. Opponents argue that this regulation puts all students in the New York public schools in jeopardy, since potential employers may decide that the students' diplomas are not on a par with those from other schools because students with lower or questionable proficiency in English are allowed to graduate.

Another New York Department of Education policy encourages all students in the state "to become fully bilingual and knowledgeable about and sensitive to other cultures." This has been interpreted by many as a desire on the part of the regents to make everyone Spanish-speaking. Others see it as the dawning of a new, anti-isolationist, multicultural age in the United States, where Americans will eventually become proficient in two languages, much as many Europeans speak two or more languages, and just as people all over the world, from Argentina to Tokyo, learn to speak English.

Today, as a result of the early bicultural and bilingual efforts on behalf of Latino students, high schools and universities across the land are expanding their curriculums to include courses in non-European cultures, and turning biculturalism and bilingualism into an educational imperative. Since 1990, all students at the University of California at Berkeley must enroll in a course called "American Cultures," in which Latino and other cultures are taught and the emphasis is away from Eurocentric education. At the University of Maryland, all students must take at least one "cultural diversity" course. At San Diego State, students at the College of Arts and Sciences are required to take at least one "cross-cultural" class. At Pennsylvania State, students are expected to take one "diversity" class or four "culturally enhanced" classes; 25 percent of each course is devoted to a particular minority group—Latinos, African-Americans, Native Americans, Asians, women, or gays and lesbians. At Harvard, where the Harvard Foundation was formed in 1981 for the purpose of presenting diverse cultures—from Latino artists to African-American philosophers—to students in all departments, there is a policy in place to educate all students about ethnic minorities, including Latino culture.

This effort to integrate Latino and other cultures into the large curriculum has become a paragon for high schools, colleges, and universities, large and small, all across the country. Ethnic studies departments, Chicano studies departments, Puerto Rican studies departments, and whole courses of study devoted to Latino culture have been organized in colleges, universities, and even some progressive high schools.

This shift in American education has also resulted in countless numbers of corporate grants and special fellowships for Latino students, and in a federal program of contributions to bilingual and bicultural education that exceeds $750 million a year—a far cry from its meager beginnings almost thirty years ago.

Whether bilingual education means that we'll all be speaking Spanish soon is far from certain. What is certain is that those *"Se Habla Español"* signs will be hanging on more store windows in the years to come.

OCHO

Famous Latinos

RITMO LATINO

What is Latin rhythm all about?

Was Desi Arnaz responsible for bringing Latin rhythm to the U.S.A.?

Where can you find the best Latino music in the United States?

Is the tango considered Latin rhythm?

FRONT AND CENTER

Who were the first Latino actors and what roles did they play?

Why do Latinos hate Tonto?

Who are some famous Latino actors?

Is Plácido Domingo the only Latino classical-music star?

ARTISTS AND WRITERS

Who's writing the books?

Who's painting the pictures?

TAKE ME OUT TO THE BALL GAME ... BOXING RING ... TENNIS COURT ...

Is soccer numero uno*?*

Who are the great Latino baseball players and why is Roberto Clemente the father of them all?

Who are some Latinos in other sports?

RITMO LATINO

What Is Latin Rhythm All About?

Mambo, salsa, conga, son, son montuno, guaracha, merengue, bugalu, danzón, bolero, Afro-Cuban Latin jazz, and even the cha-cha (called *cha cha cha* in Spanish) are all part of that singular Latino beat at the heart of so much American and international popular music. Like the Latino amalgam itself, Latin rhythm is a combination of the sounds and musical instruments of many nations—from Cuba to Puerto Rico and the Dominican Republic, down to Bogotá, Colombia, and Mexico's Yucatán Peninsula—although Cuba is where it all got started. Its roots are African, since the tambour, the conga, and the bongo drums, brought over by African slaves, are the heart and soul of that contagious Latino beat.

To the African drums were added the Spanish guitar, accordion, fiddle, trumpet, saxophone, and a variety of native African and Amerindian instruments, such as the marimba (xylophone), the maraca and other rattles, bells, the *güiro* (a serrated gourd that is played by scraping it with a stick), and the *claves,* the wooden sticks that keep the beat. The result: a distinctively Spanish Caribbean beat that defies even the tin-eared to sit still.

Latin jazz, the Latino rhythm expression from Nueva York that has become the hit of the 1990s, is a mélange of the African-Cuban music of the 1940s and 1950s, with overtones of the kind of jazz **Dizzy Gillespie** made famous, peppered with Jamaican reggae, calypso, Puerto Rican salsa, and Brazilian bossa nova. It is a true celebration of the happy meeting of many nations.

Latin music has found its way to fans all around the world. Salsa, conga, guaracha, merengue, and Latin jazz bands play to full houses in Amsterdam, London, Montevideo, New York, Miami, and Little Rock. Broadway musicals and Radio City Music Hall extravaganzas feature Latin sounds, and in Japan, an all-Japanese salsa band called Orquesta de la Luz has recently transformed Latino rhythm into its own brand of musical *wasabi*. In the United States, where Latino musicians thrive, hardly a nightclub, a ballroom, a disco, a television show, a television commercial, an ice-skating rink, or a dance company has not felt the influence of that irrepressible sound called Latin rhythm.

Was Desi Arnaz Responsible for Bringing Latin Rhythm to the U.S.A.?

"I Love Lucy's" **Desi Arnaz,** a Cuban-born actor and musician (known to his parents as **Desiderio Alberto Arnaz y de Acha**), was certainly responsible for introducing mainstream television-watching America to the sounds of the African-Cuban drums with his famous song "Babaloo," which, incidentally, is a song to the Yoruba deity **Babalú,** a much beloved *santo* of the *santería* religion.

But even before Desi played and sang with his band in the 1950s and 1960s, **Xavier Cugat,** a Spanish orchestra leader who lived in Cuba and Mexico, had introduced African-Cuban music to Hollywood. Cugat and his band starred in many popular movies in the 1930s and 1940s, and he worked his Latin magic behind the scenes for several of **Charlie Chaplin**'s silent movies.

For years, even though a Latin beat was incorporated into many big-band performances, the two worlds remained separate. In one part of town, Latino musicians played "undiluted" Latin rhythms; in another part, Anglo musicians incorporated the Latin beat into their jigs, but toned it down considerably. Each group played to different audiences and recorded on different labels. One exception was **Damaso Perez Prado,** who managed to make a huge splash in every major American city with the introduction of his mambo tunes in the 1950s. In the 1960s, **Joe Cuba**'s "Bang Bang," a *bugalu* tune, crossed over from the Latino charts to the big Anglo charts, becoming an overnight hit. At the same time, **Fats Domino, Bo Diddley,** and many other African-American musicians began incorporating pure Latin compositions into their repertoire. By then, Latin jazz had become an art form in its own right; Mexican-American **Trini Lopez** was climbing the charts; Puerto Rican crooner **José Feliciano** had already wooed audiences with his suggestive "Light My Fire," and Mexican-American **Carlos Santana** had hypnotized millions with his "Oye Como Va." Also, **Ritchie Valens,** the 1950s rocker whose short career ended tragically in a plane accident, had begun making waves with mainstream audiences.

In the late 1980s, Valens became known to a new generation of fans when the movie based on his life, *La Bamba,* became an overnight success, and the traditional Mexican song he had popularized was on everyone's lips. Even those who couldn't say *"para bailar la Bamba se necesita . . ."* would hum *"La la la la la Bamba la la la la la . . ."*

By the early 1960s, the great Puerto Rican bongo player, orchestra leader, and composer **Tito Puente,** known as "the king of Latin music," had begun to gain recognition among the Anglo public.

Improvisational singer and composer **Celia Cruz** came from Cuba in the 1960s. Shortly after her arrival, she performed live with Tito Puente and made several records with him. Cruz became the instant idol of Latinos all over the United States, but her strong, metallic, very African rhythms did not catch on in the Anglo community until much later. Thirty years after arriving from Cuba, Celia Cruz appeared on *The Tonight Show* with her old friend Puente—a true sign of having finally "made it" in the crossover game from *barrio* to mainstream.

Congero (conga player) **Mongo Santamaría;** flutist **Dave Valentin;** pianist **Hilton Ruiz;** saxophonist **Paquito D'Rivera;** bassist **Andy González;** and performers and bandleaders

Eddie Palmieri, Machito, José Curbelo, Pupi Campo, Miguelito Valdéz, Marcelino Guerra, and **Frank Marti** were all among the many greats of the last three decades who helped establish the Latin sound in the United States and open the doors for the new generations of Latino musicians.

Tito Puente is in his sixties and still going strong, performing with his *timbales* (drums) year-round all over the world. His performance in the film *The Mambo Kings* brought him Hollywood fame and broad recognition that led to more and more concert appearances, music videos, and, of course, albums. Puente has recorded more than a hundred albums and has many more in the works. He has also established a scholarship fund to help young musicians continue the Latin music tradition.

Where Can You Find the Best Latino Music in the United States?

Possibly in your living room, where El Paso trumpeter **Sal Marquez,** a star on the successful record label GRP, appears courtesy of *The Tonight Show* every night with **Branford Marsalis**'s band. Also in your living room, singer and composer **Gloria Estefan** appears with her Miami Sound Machine on MTV, VHS, and dozens of entertainment shows.

Estefan is credited with being the performer who clearly marked the moment when Latin music went mainstream in a big way (she topped a *Billboard* magazine pop chart and then proceeded to sell millions of records with her popular song *"Si Voy a Perderte"*), and when a new generation of bilingual music was born. Because Estefan is comfortable both in English and Spanish, her compositions celebrate both languages. Her words may be in English more often than not, but her soul is purely Latin, and this combination has inspired a whole new crop of Latino musicians. She warned her audience in her contagious tune that "the rhythm is gonna get you"—and it did.

Estefan's popularity is so tremendous among Latinos that some years ago, when she was hurt in a bus accident while traveling with her band and her manager and husband, **Emilio,** the people of Miami held a candlelight prayer vigil for her all night in Calle Ocho, Eighth Street, the heart of Little Havana. Later, when she made a miraculous recovery, she performed to cheering, sold-out crowds all over the world and was interviewed by **Barbara Walters** on her ABC show, *20/20,* among dozens of other shows.

Other top contemporary Latino pop music artists who perform in your living room, around the country, and around the world, and whose CDs and music videos have recently topped the charts, include **Jon Secada,** a singer and composer who used to belong to Estefan's band; the Mexican folk group **Los Lobos;** the hard-hitting Puerto Rican group **Barrio Boyzz** and the teenage group **Menudo;** streetwise humorist, singer, and composer **Rubén Blades;** bilingual performers **The Cover Girls, The Triplets, Lisa Lisa,** and **India;** Southwest artists **Little Joe Hernández** and **Flaco Jiménez;** brassmen **Charlie Sepulveda** and **Humberto Ramírez;** Cuban bandleader **Israel "Cachao" López;** romantic Spanish crooner **Julio Iglesias;** and **Linda Ronstadt,** whom everyone thought of as strictly Anglo until she crossed over (or crossed back) to her Mexican roots and recorded an album in Spanish.

Among more mainstream performers, rocker **Mariah Carey** belongs to a new group of Latino performers who sing in English and whose sounds are mainly rock. Singer **Judy Torres** created a special niche for herself with her 1993 album, *My Soul,* which tells of battered women taking back their lives and opened the way for feminist, political music among popular Latino performers. More than twenty years ago, **Vikki Carr,** winner of a 1991 Grammy for her album

Cosas del Amor, established a scholarship to help Latino students go to college.

Thanks to these and other artists too numerous to name, Columbia House, the country's largest direct-marketing operation for recorded music, spawned Club Musica Latina, and TCI, the large cable franchise, offers two channels that broadcast Latino music twenty-four hours a day. Latino radio stations send their Latin sounds over the airwaves to every major U.S. city with a Latino population, and two major Spanish-language television networks beam out variety shows on which Latin music is the only music to local stations across the United States.

Billboard, the leading music-industry weekly, tracks and rates the sales and success of all Latin-style recordings—from merengue to salsa—and runs an important column on Latino music. *Latin Jazz U.S.A.,* a yearly concert and awards show that started in a Latino *barrio* in New Jersey in 1988, has become so popular that it went to Carnegie Hall and finally found a home at Avery Fisher Hall in New York's Lincoln Center, where it could accommodate its sellout crowds of Anglos and Latinos alike.

Is the Tango Considered Latin Rhythm?

No. But it *is* a Latin dance that became popular in Buenos Aires at the beginning of the twentieth century, and twenty years later it spread to Latin America, Hollywood, and Europe. The tango is derived from the *milonga,* a sexy and suggestive Argentinean dance, and the *habanera,* a graceful and flowing dance that originated in Cuba during the Spanish colonial period. (There's a *habanera* song in Bizet's opera *Carmen.*) By the 1920s, the tango had become an elegant, stylized dance with specific backward and forward steps, accompanied by extremely melancholic music and songs. Singer **Carlos Gardel** popularized tango songs around World

War I, and put Argentina on the musical map. **Evita Perón** (of *Evita* fame) was said to be a very big tango *aficionada*.

FRONT AND CENTER

Who Were the First Latino Actors and What Roles Did They Play?

Ever since **Ramon Navarro,** the heartthrob of a whole generation, seduced audiences of the silent screen and talkies with his artful expressions and dashing good looks; and **Cesar Romero** played both foreign villains and leading men in the 1940s and 1950s; and a handsome redheaded woman performing under the name of **Rita Hayworth** (but born **Rita Cansino),** sang, danced, and acted with the likes of **Gary Cooper** and **Glenn Ford,** Latino actors have been romancing the silver screen.

In fact, early Hollywood pictures are filled with the mystery and myth of the Latin lover—the belief that somehow Latinos are more sensual, sultry, and captivating than Anglos. Of course, Hollywood also promoted the flip side of that myth, portraying Mexicans as dirty, devious, or stupid in plenty of legendary cowboy films, and attributing slickness and dishonesty to "foreign" characters who spoke with Spanish accents and came from places like "Southamerica," Spain, and Buenos Aires.

Sometimes Latino actors and actresses were cast in those roles (and, like most actors, they were happy to get the jobs), but often these parts went to non-Latino actors, whose hair was died shoe-polish black and whose pencil-thin mustaches were made to look particularly suspect.

Although this typecasting has diminished, Hollywood and Broadway continue to pigeonhole Latino artists. Actress

Julie Carmen, for instance, who starred in the film *The Milagro Beanfield War,* says that she's no longer just offered what she called "Chiquita-banana roles," but **Elizabeth Peña,** who played the role of **Ritchie Valens**'s sister-in-law in the 1987 movie *La Bamba,* said in an interview with *The Los Angeles Times,* "I'm usually offered the roles of the prostitute, the mother with seventeen children, or the screaming wife getting beaten up." Until **Joseph Papp** opened the classical stage to actors who belonged to ethnic minorities with his New York Shakespeare Festival productions in Central Park and his classical plays at the Public Theater, very few audiences had ever seen a Latino like **Raul Julia** playing "serious" dramatic parts, let alone one as monumental as Hamlet.

Why Do Latinos Hate Tonto?

The Lone Ranger's sidekick, Tonto, was supposed to be kind of dumb. In fact, his name in Spanish means "dopey" or "slow-witted." To add insult to injury, this (we assume) Pueblo Indian (of mixed Native American and Mexican heritage?) calls his boss *kimasabe,* which is a corruption of the Spanish phrase *quien más sabe,* literally "he who knows best." This movie and comic-book duo has come to symbolize the prejudice and insensitivity that Latino groups have been laboring to change for years, both in and out of the movies.

Who Are Some Famous Latino Actors?

Let's start with **Rita Moreno,** the Puerto Rican star of the movie version of *West Side Story.* Moreno has received all four of the most coveted awards in entertainment: the Oscar, the Tony, the Grammy, and the Emmy.

Another Puerto Rican actress, **Chita Rivera,** whose long theatrical career includes the 1993 Broadway hit *Kiss of the Spider Woman,* was also responsible for creating the part of

Rose in *Bye Bye Birdie,* and was a regular on *The New Dick Van Dyke Show,* playing his next-door neighbor.

Actor, writer, and director **Anthony Quinn,** born **Anthony Rudolph Oaxaca Quinn** in Mexico, has had a long and distinguished stage and Hollywood career that includes not only dozens of "bad guy" and Mexican Indian parts in his early career, when he worked for **Cecil B. De Mille** (and married his daughter), but memorable roles in movies like *Viva Zapata!, La Strada, Lust for Life,* in which he plays artist Paul Gauguin, and *Lawrence of Arabia,* and his unforgettable performance in the classic *Zorba the Greek.*

José Ferrer, who created both the stage and movie role of Cyrano de Bergerac (in 1946 and 1950, respectively) was a much revered stage, movie, and television star, remembered for his performances in **Shakespeare**'s *Richard III* and *Othello,* in the **Maxwell Anderson** play *Key Largo,* and in **Woody Allen**'s *A Midsummer Night's Sex Comedy,* as well as for his many appearances in the television series *Columbo.*

Mexican-American **Ricardo Montalban,** star of the television series *Fantasy Island,* as well as of hundreds of movies and television shows, is also credited with being among the first Latinos to appear in national television commercials without typecasting (remember his Chrysler commercials and his "Corinthian leather" lines?).

Raquel Welch (born **Raquel Welch Tejada),** whose career goes back to movies with **Orson Welles** (*Casino Royale)* and **Elvis Presley** (*Roustabout)*, is the star of dozens of movies and television shows, and a consummate singer, dancer, and entertainer. In recent years, her exercise videos, in which her legendary beauty and agility are remarkably in evidence, have led her down new and diverse entrepreneurial paths.

Raul Julia (born **Raul Rafael Carlos Julia**) is one of the most prolific actors in stage, film, and television. His success in *The Threepenny Opera* in 1977 catapulted him to fame. After that came *The Eyes of Laura Mars* with Faye Dunaway, *Kiss* *of the Spider Woman,* and hundreds of stage and television roles.

Cuban-born **Andy Garcia,** who is remembered for his parts in *The Godfather Part III* and *The Untouchables,* spans both the "serious actor" and "heartthrob" categories. He has also directed his interests toward producing movies with Latino roots. One of his latest projects, *The Lost City,* was written by novelist **Guillermo Cabrera Infante** and deals with pre-**Castro** Cuba.

Edward James Olmos, whose tough-cop role in the popular television series *Miami Vice* made him an instant success, is one of the busiest actors on both coasts, often filming movies and taping television shows simultaneously. Actor **Martin Sheen** (born **Ramon Estevez),** who is by now a Hollywood legend with a stellar thirty-year movie career, has spawned a new generation of Latino actors—his own sons, **Charlie Sheen** and **Emilio Estevez,** both of whom are top box-office draws and critically acclaimed actors and directors in their own right.

Among the hundreds of other Latino stage and television stars are **Miriam Colón,** actress, director, and founder of the Puerto Rican Traveling Theater, a bilingual group famous around the world for more than twenty-five years; **Josie de Guzman,** whose performance in the role of Sarah, the missionary sergeant, in the 1993 hit revival of *Guys and Dolls* on Broadway won her a Tony Award nomination; and **John Leguizamo,** the actor, writer, and director whose one-man show *Spic-O-Rama* earned him an Obie and an Outer Critics Circle Award. His success in the 1993 movies *Super Mario Brothers* and **Brian De Palma**'s *Carlito's Way,* and his 1993 book, *Mambo Mouth—The Book,* have made Leguizamo a household word. **Irene Cara,** is known for dancing, commercials, singing, and voice-overs, including movie animations, and had a starring role in the 1980 movie *Fame.* **Rosie Perez** is an actress and choreographer whose roles in *Untamed Heart, Do the Right Thing,* and *White Men Can't Jump* catapulted her to fame in the early 1990s. She won an Academy Award nomination in 1994 for her role in the movie *Fearless*. **Ofelia Gonzalez** won an Obie for her work in the Spanish-language New York theater company Repertorio Español. This septuagenarian, born in Cuba, had received several Best Actress awards for her stage, film, and television work before coming to the United States in 1971. **Olga Meredith,** an actress and singer who appeared in Broadway's *Les Misérables* and *The Human Comedy,* and recently finished the film *White Lies,* has been widely acclaimed by *New York* magazine critic **John Simon,** among many.

In television, **Geraldo Rivera** and **Sally Jessy Raphaël,** hosts of their own national TV shows, and **Jackie Nespral,** the host of the weekend edition of *The Today Show,* stand out—but dozens of Latino newscasters and commentators work at local English-speaking television stations from coast to coast.

Is Plácido Domingo the Only Latino Classical-Music Star?

Plácido Domingo, born in Spain, raised in Mexico, and living in New York City, is certainly *the* Latino superstar of opera. But there are hundreds of Latinos in the worlds of classical music and dance. Among the musicians: Metropolitan Opera mezzo-soprano **Dulce Reyes, Ruth Fernandez,** and basso **Justino Diaz;** tenor **Cesar Hernandez;** cellist **Andres Diaz;** orchestra maestro **Jorge Mester;** and flutist **Viviana Guzman,** who has worked with Plácido Domingo and **Mikhail Baryshnikov,** among many others. Among the dancers: the Joffrey Ballet's **Beatriz Rodriguez, Nicole Marie Duffy,** and **Lissette Salgado;** the Alvin Ailey Repertory Ensemble's **Cristina Gonzalez;** the American Ballet Theater's **Paloma Herrera;** and Ballet Latino's **Pedro Ruiz, Tina Ramirez,** and **José Costas.** All of these follow in the tradition of two great classical Latino masters who had their own dance companies: **José Greco** and **José Limón.**

José Quintero, a theater director of Panamanian descent, is considered a pillar of the Broadway and Off Broadway stages. His presentations of **Eugene O'Neill**'s plays, including *Long Day's Journey into Night* and *A Moon for the Misbegotten,* are considered among the great productions of all time.

Two other Latino "classics" of a different sort are fashion designers **Oscar de la Renta,** who was born in the Dominican Republic, and **Adolfo,** who was born in Cuba. Both designers have received numerous Coty Awards (the fashion world's Oscar equivalent) and have created international billion-dollar businesses that run the gamut from couture dressing to ready-to-wear, ties, and fragrances.

Antonia Novello, U.S. surgeon general under President **George Bush,** and **Anthony Cavazos,** secretary of education under President **Ronald Reagan,** are two more Latinos considered "classics" in their fields.

ARTISTS AND WRITERS

Who's Writing the Books?

Carlos Castaneda, the Peruvian-born Californian anthropologist, author of such magical and magnificent best-sellers as *The Teachings of Don Juan, A Yaqui Way of Knowledge, A Separate Reality,* and *The Eagle's Gift,* is perhaps the most successful Latino writer of the 1970s and 1980s.

Oscar Hijuelos, the author of *The Mambo Kings Play Songs of Love* and *The Fourteen Sisters of Emilio Montez,* launched a whole new era of recognition and popularity for Latino writers in the United States, especially when his first novel, about New York pop culture in the 1950s, became the movie *The Mambo Kings.* That era was preceded by the sudden acceptance in the past decade of works by Latin American writers, such as **Gabriel García Márquez**'s *One Hundred Years of Solitude,* written in a surrealistic style labeled "magic realism." This style had been established years before in Latin America by my father, **Lino Novas Calvo,** author of *El Negrero,* a novel about the African slave trade in the Americas, among others.

After García Márquez's success, other Latin American writers, such as **Mario Vargas Llosa, Isabel Allende,** and **Carlos Fuentes,** found a receptive audience for their works. Once acquainted with the Latino spirit, the Anglo reading public was ready for more—and this time, the works of Latinos in the United States, writing in English, but thinking Latino.

TWENTY IMPORTANT BOOKS WRITTEN BY LATINOS

1. John Rechy, *City of Night* (1963)

2. Piri Thomas, *Down These Mean Streets* (1967)

3. Jose Antonio Villarreal, *Pocho* (1970)

4. Rudolfo Anaya, *Bless Me, Ultima* (1972)

5. Carlos Castaneda, *Journey to Ixtlan: The Lessons of Don Juan* (1972)

6. Juan Soto, *Spiks* (1973)

7. Miguel Piñero, *Short Eyes* (1975)

8. Gloria Anzaldúa and Cherríe Moraga, eds., *This Bridge Called My Back: Writings by Radical Women of Color* (1981)

9. Edward Rivera, *Family Installments: Memories of Growing Up Hispanic* (1982)

10. Cherríe Moraga, *Loving in the War Years* (1983)

11. Helena Maria Viramontes, *The Moths and Other Stories* (1985)

12. Acosta, Oscar "Zeta," *The Autobiography of a Brown Buffalo* (1972)

13. Ana Castillo, *The Mixquiahuala Letters* (1986)

14. Tomás Rivera, *And the Earth Did Not Devour Him* (1987)

15. Oscar Hijuelos, *The Mambo Kings Play Songs of Love* (1989)

16. Julia Alvarez, *How the Garcia Girls Lost Their Accents* (1991)

17. Sandra Cisneros, *Woman Hollering Creek and Other Stories* (1991)

18. Victor Villaseñor, *Rain of Gold* (1991)

19. Laura Esquivel, *Like Water for Chocolate* (1992)

20. Richard Rodriguez, *Days of Obligation: An Argument with My Mexican Father* (1992)

Today, aside from Oscar Hijuelos, a host of works by Latino writers can be found at the bookstore. Although their themes are often related to the Latino experience, their humanity and universality appeal to an ever-increasing variety of readers. Among them: **Sandra Cisneros,** author of *The House on Mango Street* and *Woman Hollering Creek and Other Stories;* **Guy Garcia,** author of *Skin Deep* and *Obsidian Sky;* **Ernesto Galarza,** author of *Barrio Boy;* **Ed Vega,** author of *I Don't Care How Much You Promise to Cook or Pay the Rent You Blew It Cause Bill Bailey Ain't Never Coming Home Again;* **Cristina Garcia,** author of *Dreaming in Cuban,* chosen as one of 1992's best novels by *The New York Times;* **Judith Ortiz Cofer,** author of *The Line of the Sun;* **Alejandro Morales,** author of *The Brick People;* **Jaime Manrique,** author of *Latin Moon in Manhattan;* **Ana Castillo,** author of *So Far from God, The Mixquiahuala Letters,* and *Sapogonia;* **Victor Villaseñor,** author of *Rain of Gold;* **Julia Alvarez,** author of *How the Garcia Girls Lost Their Accents;* **Laura Esquivel,** whose novel *Like Water for Chocolate* became a critically acclaimed movie in 1993; **Floyd Salas,** author of *Buffalo Nickel;* **Patricia Preciado Martin,** author of *Images and Conversations: Mexican-Americans Recall a Southwestern Past;* poet **Cherríe Moraga,** who writes on feminist and lesbian themes; **Gloria Anzaldúa,** editor of a number of anthologies, including *This Bridge Called My Back: Writings by Radical Women of Color;* **Alma Villanueva,** author of *Bloodroot;* **Helena Maria Viramontes,** author of *The Moths and Other Stories;* **Antonio Villareal,** author of *Poncho;* activist **Rodolfo "Rudy" Acuña,** author of *Occupied America: A History of Chicanos;* author, journalist, and TV essayist (on *The MacNeil/Lehrer Newshour*) **Richard Rodriguez,** known for his novels *Hunger of Memory* and, more recently, *Days of Obligation: An Argument with My Mexican Father;* **Tomás Rivera,** author of *And the Earth Did Not Part;* **Rudolfo Anaya,** author of *Bless Me, Ultima;* **Oscar "Zeta" Acosta,** known for his *The Autobiography of a Brown Buffalo;* and, although his work is seldom included in lists of "ethnic" literature, **John Rechy,** author of *City of Night* and *Numbers,* among many others.

Who's Painting the Pictures?

In Spain and Latin America, the tradition of the plastic arts is as near and dear to the man and woman in the street as their songs, dances, and culinary traditions. Today Latino artists, imbued with the traditions of their past, are painting and exhibiting their works in galleries and museums and at street and church fairs in every large metropolis of the United States. **Pablo Picasso, Joan Miró, Salvador Dalí, Diego Rivera, Alfonso Osorio,** and **Rufino Tamayo** are only a handful of the hundreds of twentieth-century artists whose energy and tradition they draw upon. The Venezuelan-born sculptor **Marisol (Marisol Escobar),** who attained great notoriety in the 1970s as a friend and kindred spirit of **Andy Warhol,** and whose work has hung at the Museum of Modern Art in New York and many other museums around the world, has also served as an inspiration to the new crop of Latino artists working in the United States today.

Among the Latino artists who have recently received recognition at top New York and Los Angeles galleries, as well as at the Museo del Barrio and other Latino museums: **Juan Sanchez,** through whose mixed-media works the theme of Puerto Rican independence runs; **Arturo Cuenca,** who before his defection to the United States was considered one of Cuba's most prominent young artists; **Pepon Osorio,** whose multimedia installations dealing with Latino culture have been shown in the Whitney Museum's Biennial Exhibition; **German Perez,** a Dominican-American artist whose canvases vibrate with primary colors and the flavor of the Caribbean in New York; Peruvian-born **Alberto Insua,** whose works evoke those of **Salvador Dalí;** Argentine-American **Susana Jaime Mena,** whose work combines painting and sculpture; **Jorge Tacla,** a Chilean-born artist whose landscape paintings sell for up to $50,000, and whose recent commissions include a mural for a Bronx courthouse commissioned by the

City of New York; Mexican-American **Jaime Palacios,** whose androgynous, disjointed, and compelling figures have made him a popular New York artist; and **Kukuli Velarde,** originally from Peru, who works in clay.

TAKE ME OUT TO THE BALL GAME ...
BOXING RING ... TENNIS COURT ...

Latinos love sports. Doesn't everyone? you may ask. According to American Sports Data, Inc., Latinos surpass the U.S. average for participation in sports. Aerobics, basketball, bicycling, hiking, racquetball, running, skiing, soccer, softball, swimming, tennis, and weight training are Latino pastimes. Twelve percent of Latinos play tennis, long considered an Anglo sport, which puts them ahead of whites (9 percent) and African-Americans (7 percent). And more Latinos (26 percent) watch tennis on television than any other group.

Is Soccer Numero Uno?

Among games, baseball is the Latino favorite. But soccer runs a close second. Last year, 3.5 million adults played soccer in the United States. And one billion people around the world watched the World Cup on television in 1993. There are about eight hundred soccer teams in various U.S. cities, whose players are mostly Latinos.

Who Are the Great Latino Baseball Players and Why Is Roberto Clemente the Father of Them All?

The real fathers and mothers of baseball for all Latinos could actually be said to be the native Taino and Siboney Indians who lived in the Caribbean, where **Columbus** first "discovered" them. They played a game with a wooden stick and ball similar to baseball, which both the Spanish and the African people of the Caribbean adopted. In the United States, the game of baseball as we know it today was derived from the British games cricket and rounders, and was popularized in the Northeast around the 1800s.

For Latinos, both **Orlando Manuel Cepeda,** a leading batter and Most Valuable Player (1967) with the St. Louis Cardinals, and **Roberto Walker Clemente** are considered the true fathers of modern-day Latino players. Latinos also have a large place in their hearts for African-American **Jackie Robinson,** the first baseball player to break the color barrier in the modern era.

Roberto Clemente, born in Carolina, Puerto Rico, in 1934, was the first Latino ever named to the Baseball Hall of Fame, and the only player for whom baseball writers waived the obligatory five-year wait so that he could be inducted immediately. He is considered one of history's greatest baseball players, and remembered as a great humanitarian who lost his life in a dangerously overloaded plane filled with food and medicines he had personally collected for the victims of the 1972 Nicaragua earthquake.

Clemente joined the Pittsburgh Pirates in 1955 and spent his major-league career with the team. In the 1960s, he became baseball's best all-around outfielder, and won National League batting titles in 1961, 1964, 1965, and 1967. In 2,433 games, he batted .317 with 440 doubles, 166 triples, and 240 home runs. He was proud to be a Puerto Rican of African and Spanish descent, and often spoke out against the discrimination he perceived against African and Latino people in all sports. He once told a reporter: "The Latin player doesn't get the recognition he deserves, and neither does the Negro, unless he does something really spectacular." Clemente's spectacular career inspired hundreds of Little League and major-league Latino baseball players in the field today.

Much has changed in the world of sports since Roberto Clemente's day—at least in the world of baseball, where 12.5

percent of baseball players are Latinos. In 1993, New York Mets outfielder **Bobby Bonilla** was the most highly paid player in all of baseball, clearing a path of success for all Latinos in and out of the sport.

Four Latinos are listed among the twenty-eight most highly paid baseball players today: **Roberto Alomar,** second baseman for the Toronto Blue Jays; **Bobby Bonilla,** New York Mets outfielder; **José Canseco,** Texas Rangers outfielder (1988 Most Valuable Player), and **Ruben Sierra** of the Oakland Athletics.

Among other Latino winners of Most Valuable Player awards are **Joe Torre** (1971, St. Louis) and **Willie Hernandez** (1984, Detroit), who also won the 1984 Cy Young Award, as did **Fernando Valenzuela** (Los Angeles) in 1981. There are also two Latino team managers: **Felipe Alou** of the Montreal Expos and **Tony Perez** of the Cincinnati Reds. Perez made history when a retiring **Lou Piniella** recommended him for his job on October 30, 1992. Perez is the fifth Latin American–born baseball manager in major-league history, and the fourth from Cuba. During his twenty-three-year career, he played first and third base with Cincinnati, Montreal, Boston, and Philadelphia. He appeared in seven All-Star games and was named Most Valuable Player in the 1967 game after hitting the winning home run. His total of 1,652 RBIs puts him fifteenth on the all-time list. Alou came originally from the Dominican Republic. His major-league career began in San Francisco in 1958 and ended in 1974 in Milwaukee. He distinguished himself as a first baseman and outfielder and made history in 1963, when he appeared in the same outfield with his younger brothers, **Jesus** and **Matty.**

Although there are still no women in professional baseball, at least one Latina, **Linda Alvarado,** recently became part owner of the Colorado Rockies. And there are dozens of rising Latino stars, such as **Danny Tartabull** of the New York Yankees and **Francisco Cabrera,** who knocked in the winning run in the final game of the 1992 playoffs and won the pennant for the Atlanta Braves.

Who Are Some Latinos in Other Sports?

Mention the name **Lee Trevino** and golfing *aficionados* smile. That response from fans across America has secured for Trevino valuable sponsorship contracts with Cadillac, Motorola, and R. J. Reynolds, to name a few. Trevino turned pro back in the 1960s, when the only other Latino on the professional golfing greens was **Juan "Chi Chi" Rodriguez.** Both men made history not only as players extraordinaire, but as Latinos who had mastered a sport usually reserved for Anglos. Later, **Nancy Lopez** followed in their footsteps and opened doors for Latinas through her many victories, as well as through her dedication to women and Latinos in sports. All three continue to play, teach, and serve as role models. However, the golfing greens are not nearly as replete with Latinos as are the baseball fields—and neither are the tennis courts. Many Latinos in sports believe that this disparity is related to the lack of access and encouragement that Latino youngsters often encounter growing up.

TWENTY-TWO FAMOUS ATHLETES	
1. Lyle Alzado	One of the few Latinos in football; played for the Broncos, the Browns, and the Raiders; All-Pro lineman for the Raiders
2. Bobby Bonilla	Outfielder and slugger for the New York Mets; in 1993 the highest-paid player in

	all of baseball; named to the National League All-Star Team in 1988 and 1989
3. José Canseco	Outfielder with the Texas Rangers; the 1988 American League's Most Valuable Player; one of the twenty-eight highest-paid baseball players today
4. Rosemary Casals	Tennis star whose parents came from El Salvador; winner of more than ninety tournaments, including five Wimbledon doubles titles with partner Billie Jean King
5. Roberto Clemente	One of history's greatest baseball players; played with the Pittsburgh Pirates from 1955–72 and earned twelve Gold Glove awards as a right–fielder; a great humanitarian
6. Oscar de la Hoya	Boxer who won the only gold for the United States in boxing at the 1992 Olympics in Barcelona
7. Trent Dimas	Gymnast who won a gold medal at the 1992 Olympics in Barcelona
8. Mary Joe Fernandez	Top-seeded tennis player who appeared at Wimbledon at age fourteen in 1986; won a gold medal in doubles with Gigi Fernandez at the 1992 Olympics in Barcelona
9. Gigi Fernandez	Top-seeded tennis player; winner of many Grand Slam women's doubles titles including the U.S. Open in 1988,

	1990, 1992; took the gold medal in doubles at the 1992 Olympics in Barcelona
10. Tom Flores	Football player who quarterbacked the Raiders through six seasons; ranks among the most successful NFL coaches, winning NFL Coach of the Year in 1982
11. Marty Garcia	Golden Glove champion
12. Pancho Gonzales	Tennis star who won the U.S. National championships and the U.S. Clay Court Championships in 1948 and 1949
13. Nancy Lopez	Golfer who was the 1978 Player of the Year; inducted into the LPGA Hall of Fame in 1987; opened the door for Latinas in golf and has devoted much energy to women and Latinos in sports
14. Pablo Morales	Swimmer who won gold twice at the 1992 Olympics in Barcelona
15. Rafael Palmeiro	Superstar of the Texas Rangers; played on the All-Star team in 1988
16. Lou Piniella	Baseball player who was Rookie of the Year in 1969; managed the Yankees after retiring in 1984; since 1989, has managed the Cincinnati Reds
17. "Chi Chi" Rodriguez	One of the first Latino golfers; real success began at age fifty; career earnings have passed $3 million

18. Gabriela Sabatini	Top-seeded tennis player who won the U.S. Open singles title in 1990
19. Pancho Segura	Tennis legend, originally from Ecuador, who won the U.S. Pro Championships singles in 1950–52 and the doubles in 1954 and 1958; in 1974, coached Jimmy Connors to his first Wimbledon title
20. Lee Trevino	One of the first Latino golfers; has earned almost $6.5 million in prize money; in 1971 was the International Sports Personality of the Year
21. Fernando Valenzuela	Baseball player with the Los Angeles Dodgers; first rookie to win the Cy Young Award; on the All-Star team from 1981–1986
22. Tony Zendejas	One of five members of the Zendejas family to play in the National Football League as a kicker; currently with the Rams

In tennis, three Latinas have stood out as Wimbledon, French Open, and U.S. Open superstars in the late 1980s and early 1990s: **Gabriela Sabatini,** who was born in Argentina but moved to the United States and lives in Florida; **Mary Joe Fernandez,** who was born in the Dominican Republic to Cuban and Spanish parents; and Puerto Rican **Gigi Fernandez.** Another darling of the singles and doubles circuit, **Arantxa Sánchez Vicario,** is Spanish and makes her home in Spain. **Pancho Gonzalez** and **Pancho Segura,** two tennis greats who continued coaching winning players long after they retired, elevated the sport of tennis to the great crowd-pleaser it has recently become.

Football, the great American sport, has not attracted many Latinos. Many Latinos are smaller and slighter than the average football player. Still, there have been notable exceptions. **Tom Flores,** who has been in football for almost thirty years, is certainly one. Flores won the Super Bowl as a player with the Kansas City Chiefs (in 1967) and as assistant coach of the Oakland Raiders (1981) and head coach with the Los Angeles Raiders (1984). He is president and head coach of the Seattle Hawks and has been such a leading light to football players of several generations that his autobiography, *Fire in the Iceman,* is considered a classic for football enthusiasts.

Lyle Alzado was another exception, with scores of victories and fans from every corner of the globe. The former All-Pro lineman for the Los Angeles Raiders, who died of brain cancer at age forty-three in 1992, also played for the Denver Broncos and the Cleveland Browns during his extraordinary career.

And then there was the **Zendejas** family, who launched a whole dynasty of pro kickers in the 1980s, when five members played in the National Football League. Among the most famous are **Tony Zendejas,** currently a kicker for the Rams. His brother **Marty** and his cousins **Luis, Max,** and **Joaquín** also achieved professional success before retiring.

Boxing has attracted many Latinos to the ring. Univisión, the Spanish-language television network, runs a boxing show once a month that is rated among the favorites, reaching 531,000 households nationwide.

Carlos Ortiz ranks among the early greats. **Marty Garcia** was another Golden Glove champion. Today, **Oscar de la Hoya,** gold medalist at the 1992 Barcelona Olympics, is the role model for many young Latinos all across America hoping to box their way to fame.

The Barcelona Olympics proved fertile ground for Latinos. **Pedro Morales** won a gold medal in swimming; **Mary Joe Fernandez** took a gold in tennis; Oscar de la Hoya won gold in boxing; and **Trent Dimas** won a gold medal for gymnastics. It was a proud moment when Americans of Spanish descent won those medals right in the heart of Spain.

Selected
Readings

General Works

ABALOS, DAVID T. *Latinos in the United States: The Sacred and the Political.* Notre Dame, IN: University of Notre Dame Press, 1986.

ACOSTA-BELEN, EDNA, AND BARBARA R. SJOSTROM, EDS. *The Hispanic Experience in the United States: Contemporary Issues and Perspectives.* New York: Praeger, 1988.

ALARCON, NORMA, AND SYLVIA KOSSNAR. *Bibliography of Hispanic Women Writers.* Bloomington, IN: Chicano-Riqueno Studies, 1980.

ANDERSON, ROBERT ROLAND. *Spanish American Modernism: A Selected Bibliography.* Tucson: University of Arizona Press, 1970.

AUGENBRAUM, HAROLD, AND ILAN STAVANS, EDS. *Growing Up Latino: Memoirs and Stories.* New York: Houghton Mifflin, 1993.

BERRIAN, BRENDA F., AND AART BROEK. *Bibliography of Women Writers from the Caribbean (1831–1986).* Washington, DC: Three Continents, 1989.

BODNAR, JOHN E. *The Transplanted: A History of Immigrants in Urban America.* Bloomington: Indiana University Press, 1985.

BOGAN, MARCOS M. *La emigración laboral centroamericana hacia los Estados Unidos: experiencias y prognósticos.* Heredia, Costa Rica: Universidad Nacional, 1982.

BORJAS, GEORGE J. *Friends or Strangers: The Impact of Immigrants on the U.S. Economy.* New York: Basic Books, 1990.

CAFFERTY, PASTORA SAN JUAN, BARRY R. CHISWICK, ANDREW M. GREELEY, AND TERESA A. SULLIVAN. *The Dilemma of American Immigration: Beyond the Golden Door.* New Brunswick, NJ: Transaction Books, 1983.

CANTO, LEANDRO. *Todos fuimos a Miami.* Caracas: SEDECO, 1986.

CHAVEZ, LINDA. *Out of the Barrio: Toward a New Politics of Hispanic Assimilation.* New York: Basic Books, 1991.

CHRISTENSEN, THOMAS, AND CAROL CHRISTENSEN, EDS. *The Discovery of America and Other Myths: A New World Reader.* San Francisco: Chronicle Books, 1992.

COLLIER, SIMON, HAROLD BLAKEMORE, AND THOMAS E. SKIDMORE. *The Cambridge Encyclopedia of Latin America and the Caribbean.* New York: Cambridge University Press, 1992.

CONTRERAS, CARLOS ALBERTO, AND JAMES W. WILKIE, EDS. *Statistical Abstract of Latin America.* Los Angeles: UCLA Latin American Center Publications, University of California, 1991.

CORTINA, LYNN ELLEN RICE. *Spanish-American Women Writers: A Bibliographical Research Checklist.* New York: Garland, 1983.

CRAWFORD, JAMES. *Bilingual Education: History, Politics, Theory, and Practice.* Trenton, NJ: Crane, 1989.

DEFREITAS, GREGORY. *Inequality at Work: Hispanics in the U.S. Labor Force.* New York: Oxford University Press, 1991.

DINNERSTEIN, LEONARD, AND DAVID M. REIMERS. *Ethnic Americans: A History of Immigration.* New York: Harper & Row, 1988.

FERNANDEZ-SHAW, CARLOS M. *Presencia española en los Estados Unidos.* Madrid: Instituto de Cooperacion Iberoamericana, Ediciones Cultura Hispanica, 1987.

FONER, NANCY, ED. *New Immigrants in New York.* New York: Columbia University Press, 1987.

GANN, LEWIS H. *The Hispanics in the United States: A History.* Boulder, CO: Westview Press, 1986.

GLAZER, NATHAN, ED. *Clamor at the Gates: The New American Immigration.* San Francisco: ICS Press, 1985.

GONZALEZ, RAY, ED. *After Aztlán: Latino Poets of the Nineties.* Boston: D. R. Godine, 1992.

GONZALEZ-WIPPLER, MIGENE. *The Santería Experience.* Englewood Cliffs, NJ: Prentice-Hall, 1982.

HADLEY-GARCIA, GEORGE. *Hispanic Hollywood: The Latins in Motion Pictures.* New York: Carol, 1990.

HAGUE, ELEANOR. *Latin American Music: Past and Present.* Detroit: B. Etheridge, 1982.

HANDLIN, OSCAR. *A Pictorial History of Immigration.* New York: Crown, 1972.

HENDERSON, JAMES D., AND LINDA RODDY HENDERSON. *Ten Notable Women of Latin America.* Chicago: Nelson-Hall, 1978.

HERNANDEZ-CHAVEZ, EDUARDO. "Language Maintenance, Bilingual Education, and Philosophies of Bilingualism in the United States," in James A. Alatis, ed., *International Dimensions of Bilingual Education.* Washington, DC: Georgetown University Press, 1978.

HIGHAM, JOHN. *Strangers in the Land: Patterns of American Nativism, 1860–1925.* New Brunswick, NJ: Rutgers University Press, 1988.

Hispanic. Washington, DC: Hispanic Publishing Corp., April 1990–June 1993.

Hispanic Business. Santa Barbara, CA: Hispanic Business Publications, February 1990–June 1993.

Anuario hispano = Hispanic Yearbook, 1993. McLean, VA: T.I.Y.M., 1993.

JACKSON, RICHARD L. *The Afro-Spanish American Author: An Annotated Bibliography of Criticism.* New York: Garland, 1980.

LACHAGA, JOSÉ MARIA DE. *El pueblo hispano en USA: minorias etnicas y la Iglesia Catolica.* Bilbao: Desclee de Brouwer, 1982.

LAMM, RICHARD D., AND GARY IMHOFF. *The Immigration Time Bomb: The Fragmenting of America.* New York: Truman Talley Books, 1986.

Los hispanos: problemas y oportunidades. New York: Ford Foundation, 1984.

MARTING, DIANE E., ED. *Spanish American Women Writers: A Bio-Bibliographical Source Book.* New York: Greenwood Press, 1990.

MONCADA, ALBERTO. *La americanización de los hispanos.* Barcelona: Plaza & Janes, 1986.

MOORE, JOAN W., AND HARRY PACHON. *Hispanics in the United States.* Englewood Cliffs, NJ: Prentice-Hall, 1985.

MORENO FRAGINALS, MANUEL, FRANK MOYA PONS, AND STANLEY L. ENGERMAN, EDS. *Between Slavery and Free Labor: The Spanish-Speaking Caribbean in the Nineteenth Century.* Baltimore: Johns Hopkins University Press, 1985.

MULLER, THOMAS, AND THOMAS J. ESPENSHADE. *The Fourth Wave: California's Newest Immigrants.* Washington, D.C.: Urban Institute Press, 1985.

NATELLA, ARTHUR A. *The Spanish in America, 1513–1974: A Chronology and Fact Book.* Dobbs Ferry, NY: Oceana, 1975.

ORTEZ, ELISABETH LAMBERT. *The Book of Latin American Cooking.* New York: Vintage Books, 1979.

O'SHAUGHNESSY, HUGH. *Latin Americans.* London: BBC Books, 1988.

POEY, DELIA, AND VIRGIL SUAREZ, EDS. *Iguana Dreams: New Latino Fiction.* New York: Harper Perennial, 1992.

PORTER, ROSALIE PEDALINO. *Forked Tongue: The Politics of Bilingual Education.* New York: Basic Books, 1990.

RATLIFF, WILLIAM E. *Castroism and Communism in Latin America, 1959–1976: The Varieties of Marxist-Leninist Experience.* Washington, DC: American Enterprise Institute for Public Policy Research, 1976.

RAVITCH, DIANE. *The Troubled Crusade: American Education, 1945–1980.* New York: Basic Books, 1983.

REIMERS, DAVID M. *Still the Golden Door: The Third World Comes to America.* New York: Columbia University Press, 1992.

RICHARD, ALFRED CHARLES. *The Hispanic Image on the Silver Screen: An Interpretive Filmography from Silents into Sound, 1898–1935.* New York: Greenwood Press, 1992.

ROBERTS, JOHN S. *The Latin Tinge: The Impact of Latin American Music on the United States.* New York: Oxford University Press, 1979.

ROUT, LESLIE B., JR. "History of the Black Peoples of Spanish America." In *World Encyclopedia of Black Peoples.* Vol. 1, edited by Harry Waldman. Michigan: Scholarly Press, 1981.

SANDOVAL, MOISES. *On the Move: A History of the Hispanic Church in the United States.* Maryknoll, NY: Orbis Books, 1990.

SANTOLI, AL. *New Americans: An Oral History.* New York: Viking, 1988.

SHORRIS, EARL. *Latinos: A Biography of the People.* New York: W. W. Norton, 1992.

SIMON, JULIAN LINCOLN. *The Economic Consequences of Immigration.* Cambridge: B. Blackwell, 1989.

SOTOMAYOR, MARTA, ED. *Empowering Hispanic Families: A Critical Issue for the '90s.* Milwaukee: Family Service America, 1991.

SUTTON, CONSTANCE R., AND ELSA M. CHANEY, EDS. *Caribbean Life in New York City: Sociocultural Dimensions.* New York: Center for Migration Studies of New York, Inc., 1987.

TRASK, DAVID F., MICHAEL C. MEYER, AND ROGER R. TRASK, EDS. *A Bibliography of United States–Latin American Relations Since 1810.* Lincoln: University of Nebraska Press, 1979.

VIGIL, MAURILIO E. *Hispanics in American Politics: The Search for Political Power.* Lanham, MD: University Press of America, 1987.

VILLARREAL, ROBERTO E., AND NORMA G. HERNANDEZ, EDS. *Latinos and Political Coalitions: Political Empowerment for the 1990s.* New York: Greenwood Press, 1991.

WEYR, THOMAS. *Hispanic U.S.A.: Breaking the Melting Pot.* New York: Harper & Row, 1988.

WILLIAMSON, EDWIN. *The Penguin History of Latin America.* London: Penguin, 1992.

ZUCKER, NORMAN L., AND NAOMI F. ZUCKER. *The Guarded Gate: The Reality of American Refugee Policy.* San Diego: Harcourt, Brace, Jovanovich, 1987.

The Spanish Conquest

BERNALDEZ, A. *Historia de los reyes catolicos don Fernando y doña Isabel.* Grenada, 1856. English translation: *Selected Documents Illustrating the Four Voyages of Columbus.* Vol. 1. London: Hakluyt Society, 1930.

CABEZA DE VACA, A. N. *Naufragios y comentarios.* Madrid: Taurus, 1969. English translation: *Adventures in the Unknown Interior of America.* New York: Collier Books, 1961.

CASAS, BARTOLOME DE LAS. *Opusculos, cartas y memoriales.* Vol. 110. Madrid: Biblioteca de Autores Españoles, 1958. English translation: *The Devastation of the Indies.* New York: Seabury Press, 1974.

COLÓN, C. *Raccolta colombiana.* I, Vols. 1 and 2, Rome, 1892–94. English translation: *Journals and Other Documents.* New York: Heritage Press, 1963.

CUNEO, M. DE. "Lettre a Annari," 28.10.1495. In *Raccolta colombiana*. III, Vol. 2, pp. 95–107.

DÍAZ DE CASTILLO, B. *Historia verdadera de la conquista de la Nueva España*. 2 vols. Mexico: Porrua, 1955. English translation: *The True History of the Conquest of New Spain*. 5 vols. London: Hakluyt Society, 1908–16.

DURÁN, DIEGO. *Historia de las Indias de Nueva España e Islas de la Tierra Firme*. 2 vols. Mexico: Porrua, 1967. English translation: *Book of the Gods and Rites and the Ancient Calendar*. Norman: University of Oklahoma Press, 1971.

FERDINAND, ISABELA. "Carta . . . a D. C. Colón." In M. Fernández de Navarrette, *Colección de los viajes y descumbrimientos*. Vol. 2. Madrid, 1825, pp. 21–22.

GODOY, DIEGO. "Relación a H. Cortés." In *Historiadores primitivos de Indias*. Vol 1. Madrid: Biblioteca de Autores Españoles, 1877, pp. 465–70. French translation: Henri Ternaux-Compans. *Recueil de pièces relatives à la conquete du Mexique*. Paris, 1838.

SOLANO Y OTROS, FRANCISCO DE. *Proceso historico al Conquistador*. Madrid: Alianza Editorial, 1988.

TODOROV, TZVETAN. *The Conquest of America: The Question of The Other*. New York: Harper & Row, 1984.

Mexicans

BAYLESS, RICK, AND DEANN GROEN BAYLESS. *Authentic Mexican: Regional Cooking from the Heart of Mexico*. New York: William Morrow, 1987.

BINDER, WOLFGANG, ED. *Partial Autobiographies: Interviews with Twenty Chicano Poets*. Erlangen: Palm & Enke, 1985.

BLEA, IRENE I. *La Chicana and the Intersection of Race, Class, and Gender*. New York: Praeger, 1992.

BRUCE-NOVOA. *RetroSpace: Collected Essays on Chicano Literature, Theory, and History*. Houston: Arte Publico Press, 1990.

CALDERON, HECTOR, AND JOSE DAVID SALDIVAR, EDS. *Criticism in the Borderlands: Studies in Chicano Literature, Culture, and Ideology. Durham: Duke University Press, 1991.

Commission on Civil Rights. The Excluded Student: Educational Practices Affecting Mexican-Americans in the Southwest. Washington, DC: Government Printing Office, 1972.

ELIZONDO, VIRGILIO P. The Future Is Mestizo: Life Where Cultures Meet. Oak Park, IL: Meyer-Stone Books, 1988.

FOSTER, DAVID WILLIAM. Mexican Literature: A Bibliography of Secondary Sources. Metuchen, NJ: Scarecrow, 1981.

GALARZA, ERNESTO. Barrio Boy. Notre Dame, IN: University of Notre Dame Press, 1971.

GLAZER, MARK. A Dictionary of Mexican American Proverbs. New York: Greenwood Press, 1987.

GRAHAM, JOE S., ED. Hecho en Tejas: Texas-Mexican Folk Arts and Crafts. Denton: University of North Texas Press, 1991.

HERRERA-SOBEK, MARIA. The Bracero Experience: Elitelore Versus Folklore. Los Angeles: UCLA Latin American Center Publications, University of California, 1979.

IGLESIAS PRIETO, NORMA. Medios de communicación en la Frontera Norte. Mexico: Fundación Manuel Buendia; Programa Cultural de las Fronteras, 1990.

JUSSAWALLA, FEROZA F., AND REED WAY DASENBROCK, EDS. Interviews with Writers of the Post-Colonial World. Jackson: University Press of Mississippi, 1992.

LANGLEY, LESTER D. MexAmerica: Two Countries, One Future. New York: Crown, 1988.

LATTIN, VERNON E., ED. Contemporary Chicano Fiction: A Critical Survey. Binghamton, NY: Bilingual Press/Editorial Bilingue, 1986.

LIMÓN, JOSÉ EDUARDO. Mexican Ballads, Chicano Poems: History and Influence in Mexican-American Social Poetry. Berkeley: University of California Press, 1992.

LONG, HANIEL. The Marvelous Adventure of Cabeza de Vaca. Clearlake, CA: Dawn Horse Press, 1992.

LÓPEZ DE GOMARA, FRANCISCO. Historia de la conquista de Mexico. Mexico: P. Robredo, 1943. English translation:

Cortés: The Life of the Conqueror by His Secretary. Berkeley: University of California Press, 1964.

MAYBERRY, JODINE. *Mexicans.* New York: Franklin Watts, 1990.

MCWILLIAMS, CAREY. *North from Mexico: The Spanish-Speaking People of the United States.* New York: Greenwood Press, 1990.

MEIER, MATT S., AND FELICIANO RIVERA. *The Chicanos: A History of Mexican Americans.* New York: Hill and Wang, 1972.

MILLER, TOM. *On the Border: Portraits of America's Southwestern Frontier.* Tucson: University of Arizona Press, 1985.

MOQUIN, WAYNE, WITH CHARLES VAN DOREN, EDS. *A Documentary History of the Mexican Americans.* New York: Praeger, 1971.

PAZ, OCTAVIO. *The Labyrinth of Solitude.* New York: Grove Press, 1985.

PENUELAS, MARCELINO C. *Cultura hispanica en Estados Unidos: los chicanos.* Madrid: Ediciones Cultura Hispanica del Centro Iberoamericano de Cooperación, 1978.

PETTIT, ARTHUR G. *Images of the Mexican-American in Fiction and Film.* College Station: Texas A&M University Press, 1980.

PIERRI, ETTORE. *Chicanos, el poder mestizo.* Mexico: Editores Mexicanos Unidos, 1979.

SAMORA, JULIAN, AND PATRICIA VANDEL SIMON. *A History of the Mexican-American People.* Notre Dame, IN: University of Notre Dame Press, 1977.

SEWELL, DORITA. *Knowing People: A Mexican-American Community's Concept of a Person.* New York: AMS Press, 1989.

TAFOLLA, CARMEN. *To Split a Human: mitos, machos, y la mujer chicana.* San Antonio, TX: Mexican American Cultural Center, 1985.

TATUM, CHARLES M., ED. *New Chicana/Chicano Writing.* Tucson: University of Arizona Press, 1992.

TIME-LIFE BOOKS, EDS. *Mexico.* Alexandria, VA: Time-Life Books, 1986.

TRUJILLO, CARLA, ED. *Chicana Lesbians: The Girls Our Mothers Warned Us About.* Berkeley: Third Woman Press, 1991.

WEIGLE, MARTA, AND PETER WHITE. *The Lore of New Mexico.* Albuquerque: University of New Mexico Press, 1988.

WEIGLE, MARTA, ED. *Two Guadalupes: Hispanic Legends and Magic Tales from Northern New Mexico.* Santa Fe: Ancient City Press, 1987.

WEST, JOHN O., ED. *Mexican-American Folklore: Legends, Songs, Festivals, Proverbs, Crafts, Tales of Saints, of Revolutionaries, and More.* Little Rock: August House, 1988.

Dominicans

BOGEN, ELIZABETH, *Caribbean Immigrants in New York City: A Demographic Summary.* New York: Department of City Planning/Office of Immigrant Affairs and Population Analysis Division, 1988.

GRASMUCK, SHERRI, AND PATRICIA R. PESSAR. *Between Two Islands: Dominican International Migration.* Berkeley: University of California Press: 1991.

HAGGERTY, RICHARD A., ED. *Dominican Republic and Haiti: Country Studies.* Washington, DC: Federal Research Division, Library of Congress, 1991.

HENDRICKS, GLENN. *The Dominican Diaspora: The Case of Immigrants from the Dominican Republic in New York City.* Doctoral Thesis, Columbia University, 1972.

Puerto Ricans

ALIOTTA, JEROME J. *The Puerto Ricans.* New York: Chelsea House, 1991.

BOTHWELL GONZALEZ, REECE B. *La ciudadania en Puerto Rico.* Rio Piedras: Editorial Universitaria, Universidad de Puerto Rico, 1980.

CARR, RAYMOND. *Puerto Rico: A Colonial Experiment.* New York: New York University Press, 1984.

CARRION, ARTURO MORALES, ED. *Puerto Rico: A Political and Cultural History.* New York: W. W. Norton & Company, 1984.

COLL Y TOSTE, CAYETANO. *Puertoriquenos ilustres.* Rio Piedras, PR: Editorial Cultural, Inc., 1971.

DIETZ, JAMES L. *Economic History of Puerto Rico: Institutional Change and Capitalist Development.* Princeton, NJ: Princeton University Press, 1986.

FITZPATRICK, JOSEPH P. *Puerto Rican Americans: The Meaning of Migration to the Mainland.* Englewood Cliffs, NJ: Prentice-Hall, 1987.

FOSTER, DAVID WILLIAM. *Puerto Rican Literature: A Bibliography of Secondary Sources.* Westport, CT: Greenwood Press, 1982.

HAUBERG, CLIFFORD A. *Puerto Rico and the Puerto Ricans.* New York: Twayne Publishers, 1975.

HAUPTLY, DENIS J. *Puerto Rico: An Unfinished Story.* New York: Atheneum, 1991.

LARSEN, RONALD J. *The Puerto Ricans in America.* Minneapolis: Lerner Publications Company, 1989.

LOPEZ, ADALBERTO, AND JAMES F. PETRAS, EDS. *Puerto Rico and the Puerto Ricans: Studies in History and Society.* Cambridge, MA: Schenkman Publishing, 1974.

MELENDEZ, EDWIN, AND EDGARDO MELENDEZ, EDS. *Colonial Dilemma: Critical Perspectives on Contemporary Puerto Rico.* Boston: South End Press, 1993.

MOHR, EUGENE V. *The Nuyorican Experience: Literature of the Puerto Rican Minority.* Westport, CT: Greenwood Press, 1982.

PEREZ Y MENA, ANDRES ISIDORO. *Speaking with the Dead: Development of Afro-Latin Religion Among Puerto Ricans in the United States: A Study into the Interpenetration of Civilizations in the New World.* New York: AMS Press, 1991.

SAMOILOFF, LOUISE CRIPPS. *A Portrait of Puerto Rico.* New York: Cornwall Books. 1984.

SANCHEZ KORROL, VIRGINIA. *From Colonia to Community: The*

History of Puerto Ricans in New York City, 1917–1948. Westport, CT: Greenwood Press, 1983.

Cubans

BLIGHT, JAMES G. *The Shattered Crystal Ball: Fear and Learning in the Cuban Missile Crisis.* Savage, MD: Rowman and Littlefield, 1990.

BONACHEA, RAMON L., AND MARTA SAN MARTIN. *The Cuban Insurrection, 1952–1959.* New Brunswick, NJ: Transaction Books, 1974.

BOSWELL, THOMAS D., AND JAMES R. CURTIS. *The Cuban-American Experience: Culture, Images, and Perspectives.* Totowa, NJ: Rowman and Allanheld, 1984.

CORTES, CARLOS E., ED. *The Cuban Experience in the United States.* New York: Arno Press, 1980.

DEL AGUILA, JUAN M. *Cuba: Dilemmas of a Revolution.* Boulder, CO: Westview Press, 1988.

DUNCAN, WALTER RAYMOND. *The Soviet Union and Cuba: Interests and Influence.* New York: Praeger, 1985.

GEYER, GEORGIE ANNE. *Guerrilla Prince: The Untold Story of Fidel Castro.* Boston: Little, Brown, 1991.

GONZALEZ, EDWARD, ED. *José Martí and the Cuban Revolution Retraced.* Los Angeles: UCLA Latin American Center Publications, University of California, 1986.

GRUPO AREITO. *Contra viento y marea.* La Habana: Casa de las Americas, 1978.

KIPLE, KENNETH F. *Blacks in Colonial Cuba, 1774–1899.* Gainesville: University Presses of Florida, 1976.

LLANES, JOSE. *Cuban Americans: Masters of Survival.* Cambridge, MA: Abt Books, 1982.

MEDINA, PABLO. *Exiled Memories: A Cuban Childhood.* Austin: University of Texas Press, 1990.

MESA-LAGO, CARMELO. *The Economy of Socialist Cuba: A Two-Decade Appraisal.* Albuquerque, NM: University of New Mexico, 1981.

PADILLA, HERBERTO. *Self-Portrait of the Other: A Memoir.* New York: Farrar, Straus, & Giroux, 1990.

PEREZ, LOUIS A., JR. *Cuba: Between Reform and Revolution.* New York: Oxford University Press, 1988.

ROGG, ELEANOR R. *The Assimilation of Cuban Exiles: The Role of Community and Class.* New York: Aberdeen Press, 1974.

SCOTT, REBECCA J. *Slave Emancipation in Cuba: The Transition to Free Labor, 1860-1899.* Princeton, NJ: Princeton University Press, 1985.

SUCHLICKI, JAIME. *Cuba: From Columbus to Castro.* Washington, DC: Pergamon-Brassey's, 1986.

TIMERMAN, JACOBO. *Cuba: A Journey.* New York: Alfred A. Knopf, 1990.

Central and South Americans

ANDERSON, THOMAS P. *Politics in Central America: Guatemala, El Salvador, Honduras, and Nicaragua.* New York: Praeger, 1982.

BARRY, TOM. *Roots of Rebellion: Land and Hunger in Central America.* Boston: South End Press, 1987.

BLACK, GEORGE. *The Good Neighbor: How the United States Wrote the History of Central America and the Caribbean.* New York: Pantheon Books, 1988.

BUCKLEY, KEVIN. *Panama: The Whole Story.* New York: Simon & Schuster, 1991.

BUCKLEY, TOM. *Violent Neighbors: El Salvador, Central America, and the United States.* New York: Times Books, 1984.

CHILD, JACK, ED. *Conflict in Central America: Approaches to Peace and Security.* London: C. Hurst & Co., 1986.

CRAWLEY, EDUARDO. *Nicaragua in Perspective.* New York: St. Martin's Press, 1984.

DIDION, JOAN. *Salvador.* New York: Simon & Schuster, 1983.

FOSTER, DAVID WILLIAM. *Argentine Literature: A Research Guide.* New York: Garland, 1982.

FOSTER, DAVID WILLIAM. *Chilean Literature: A Working Bibliography of Secondary Sources.* Boston: G. K. Hall, 1978.

HAMILTON, NORA, JEFFRY A. FRIEDEN, LINDA FULLER, AND MANUELA PASTOR, JR., EDS. *Crisis in Central America: Regional Dynamics and U.S. Policy in the 1980s.* Boulder, CO: Westview Press, 1988.

KRAUSS, CLIFFORD. *Inside Central America: Its People, Politics, and History.* New York: Summit Books, 1991.

MCNEIL, FRANK. *War and Peace in Central America.* New York: Scribner's, 1988.

PAINTER, JAMES. *Guatemala: False Hope, False Freedom: The Rich, the Poor, and the Christian Democrats.* London: Catholic Institute for International Relations, 1989.

SIMON, JEAN-MARIE. *Guatemala: Eternal Spring, Eternal Tyranny.* New York: W. W. Norton, 1987.

WILLIAMS, ROBERT G. *Export Agriculture and the Crisis in Central America.* Chapel Hill: University of North Carolina Press, 1986.

WOODWARD, RALPH LEE. *Central America: A Nation Divided.* New York: Oxford University Press, 1985.

Index

FSLN, 249
Fuentes, Carlos, 293

Gadsden, James, 85
Gadsden Treaty, 85–86
Galarza, Ernesto, 295
Garcia, Andy, xii, 179, 290
García, Calixto, 202
Garcia, Cristina, 295
Garcia, Guy, 295
Garcia, Marty, 302, 304
García Marquez, Gabriel, 293
Gardel, Carlos, 286–87
Garza, Carmen, 130
Gentleman's Agreement Act, 101
Giancana, Sam, 220
Gillespie, Archibald, 87
Gillespie, Dizzy, 281
Goethals, George Washington, 242
Goizueta, Roberto C., xii, 204, 206, 263
Gold, 29–30, 33, 58, 63, 146, 147, 189
  California Gold Rush, 88–91
Goldberg, Arthur, 110
Gomez, Elsa, 245
Gómez, Máximo, 194, 202
Gonzales, Pancho, 302
González, Andy, 283
Gonzalez, Cristina, 180, 291
Gonzalez, Henry B., xii, 97–98, 245, 264, 265, 266, 271
Gonzalez, Ofelia, 291
Gonzalez, Pancho, 303–304
González, Rodolfo "Corky," 121, 122, 129
Gore, Robert, 166
Gorgas, Dr. William C., 242
Granada, 42
Grant, Ulysses S., 82
Greco, José, 292
Gringo, 56
Grito de Dolores, 71, 127
Grito de Lares, El, 154
Grito de Yara, 199
Guadalete, Battle of, 37
Guam, 159, 204
"Guantanamera," 202
Guantánamo Bay, naval base at, 208, 209

Guatemala, 152, 219, 235, 248, 253–54
Guerra, Marcelino, 284
Guevara, Ernesto "Che," 124, 214, 216, 219, 253
Gusanos, 217–18
Gutiérrez, José Angel, 122
Gutierrez, Luis, 267
Guzmán, Antonio, 238
Guzman, Josie de, 290
Guzman, Viviana, 291

Haiti, 18, 43, 152, 237, 238, 240
Haitians, 209
Ha-Levi, Judah, 39
Hanna, Mark, 242
Havana, Cuba, 191, 192, 193, 211, 212
  Florida exchanged with the English for, 190–91, 195
Hay, John, 159, 209
Hayakawa, S. I., 274
Hay-Bunau-Varilla Treaty, 242
Hayworth, Rita, 180, 287
Head of household, women as, 6
  Puerto Rican, 171
Healers *(curanderas),* 126
Hearst, William Randolph, 158
Hernandez, Cesar, 291
Hernandez, Diego, 245
Hernández, Little Joe, 285
Hernández, Marife, 263
Hernandez, Willie, 299
Herrera, Paloma, 291
Hidalgo y Costillo, Father Miguel, 71–72
Hijuelos, Oscar, 292–93, 294
Hispanic Access to Higher Education Bill, 264
Hispanic Association on Corporate Responsibility (HARC), 260
Hispanics:
  defined, 4–5
  persons included in classification of, 2–4
  see also Latinos
Hispaniola, 18, 43, 189, 237–38, 239–40
Hispanos, 7–8
Historia de las Indias de la Nueva

cowboys, 92–93
cuisine, 131–35
desperados, 93–94
fiestas, 137–39
foods, 131–35
migration to U.S., 98–102
mojados, see Mojados ("wetbacks")
mural painting, 123–24
population statistics, 7, 98–99, 102
as railroad workers, 102, 103
repatriation of, 104–107
women, 125–31
see also Mexico
Mexican-American War, 75, 81–83
Mexican-American Women's
  National Association
  (MANA), 130
Mexican-American Youth
  Organization, 122
Mexican Revolution of 1910, 95–98,
  127
"Mexican stand-off," 81–82
Mexico, 219
  conquest by the Spanish, 56–62
  conquistadors, see Conquistadors
  first meeting of Anglos and
    Mexicans, 72–73
  Gadsden Treaty and, 85–86
  Mexican-American War, 75, 81–83
  naming of, 25
  revolt against Spain, 68–69, 70–72,
    127, 152
  Revolution of 1910, 95–98, 127
  Texas' independence from, 76–80
  Treaty of Guadalupe Hidalgo and,
    7, 83–85, 86, 88
  see also Mexican-Americans
Mexico City (Tenochtitlán), 17, 23,
  25, 57, 122
Miami, Florida, Cuban-Americans in,
  186, 225–28, 230
  Little Havana, 225–26, 227
  Little Managua, 227–28
Migrant workers, 99
  see also Undocumented workers
Milton, José, 205
Mining:
  in California, Latinos' role in
    success of, 89–90
  see also Gold; Silver

Miró, Juan, 35, 296
Missionaries, conversion of Native
  Americans by, 20, 24, 42, 58,
  65–66
Missions, Franciscans, 68
Mojados ("wetbacks"), 8, 9, 110,
  112–13
  "drying out" program, 113–14
Mole poblano sauce, 132, 133–34
Monroe, James, 156
Monroe Doctrine, 96, 156–57
Montalban, Ricardo, 180, 289
Montezuma II, 23–24, 56, 61, 65, 131
  halls of, 23, 24
Montoya, Edward, 276
Montoya, Joseph, 271
Moors, 37–42
Moraga, Cherríe, xiv, 131, 294, 295
Morales, Alejandro, 295
Morales, Pablo, 302, 305
Moreira, Domingo, 262–63
Morelos y Pavón, Father José María,
  72
Moreno, Rita, 288
Moriscos, 41
Mountain men, 73
Movimiento Estudiantil Chicano de
  Aztlán (MECHA), 120
Mulattoes, 68, 239
Muñoz Marín, Luis, 163, 165,
  166–68, 174
Muñoz Rivera, Luis, 155, 163, 165
Mural painting, 123–24
Murieta, Joaquín, 93–94
Museo del Barrio, 27, 130
Museum of Contemporary Hispanic
  Art, 130
Music, Latin, 281–87
Musquiz, Virginia, 129, 270
Mystics, 64

NAFTA, 267–68
Names, last, 34
Napoleon III, 156
National Association of Hispanic
  Publications, 260
National Association of Latino
  Elected and Appointed
  Officials (NALEO), 259

National Catholic Welfare Council, 110

National Council of Churches of Christ, 110

National Council of La Raza, 260

National Farmers Union, 110

National Puerto Rican Coalition, 260

Naufragios (Shipwrecks) (Cabeza de Vaca), 64

Navarro, Ramon, 180, 287

Nebraska, Spanish settlement of, 62, 65

Negro/negra to Puerto Ricans, 148

Nespral, Jackie, 180, 246, 291

Nevada, 82, 83

New Mexico, 82, 83

Spanish settlement of, 62, 65

Newspapers, Spanish-language, 107

New York City:

Latino-owned businesses in, 7

Puerto Ricans in, 8, 169, 170, 171–73

New York State Department of Education, 277

Nicaragua, 152, 235, 244, 248–52

Iran-Contra scandals, 247, 250–52

Nicaraguans, 237, 248, 250

Niles, Nelson A., 159

Niza, Fray Marcos de, 63

Noriega, Manuel Antonio, 243–44, 247

North, Oliver, 251

North Atlantic Free Trade Agreement (NAFTA), 267–68

Northwest Passage, 64–65

Novas Calvo, Lino, 293

Novello, Antonia, xii, 246, 270, 292

Ochoa, Ellen, 246

O'Higgins, Bernardo, 152

Oklahoma, Spanish settlement of, 62, 65

Olé, 37–38

Olmec culture, 20, 21

Olmos, Edward James, 290

Oregon, 75

O'Reilly, Alejandro, 151

Organization of American States (OAS), 157

Oroña, Margo, 130

Orozco, José Clemente, 123

Ortega Saavedra, Daniel, 249, 250

Ortiz, Carlos, 304

Ortiz, Solomon, 264, 267

Ortiz Cofer, Judith, 295

Ortiz de Dominguez, Doña Josefa, 127

Ortiz Muriada, Thelma, 130

Osorio, Alfonso, 296

Osorio, Pepon, 296

Ostend Manifesto, 197

Our Country (Strong), 163–64

Out of the Barrio (Chavez), 273

Pahry, 177

Palacios, Jaime, 296–97

Palmieri, Eddie, 284

Palmiero, Rafael, 302

Panama, 160, 241–44, 246–47, 248

Panama Canal, 241–43, 246–47

Panamanians, 235

Papp, Joseph, 288

Paraguay, 152

Paredes y Arillaga, General Mariano, 81

Parteras, 126–27

Pastor, Ed, 267, 268

Pena, Albert, 117

Peña, Elizabeth, 288

Pennsylvania State University, 278

Pepper, Claude, 266

Perez, German, 296

Perez, Rosie, 180, 290–91

Perez, Tony, 299

Perez Prado, Damaso, 282–83

Perón, Evita, 287

Perón, Juan, 219

Pershing, John J., 95

Peru, 152

Peruvians, 234, 235

Peyton, John, 73

Philip II, King of Spain, 70

Philippines, 101, 159, 160, 204

Picasso, Pablo, 35, 124, 296

Pierce, Franklin, 197

Pike, Captain Zebulon, 73

Piñata party, 135–36

Piñero, Jesús T., 164

Pinero, Miguel, 293

Piniella, Lou, 299, 302

Reformist Party (Cuba), 197–98
Religion, 6
 of Aztecs, 28
 Catholicism, *see* Catholicism and
  Catholics
 of Inca, 29–30
 Jews of Spain, 34, 38–42
 Santería, 7, 178, 230–31, 282
Remesas (remittances), 115
Remington, Frederic, 158
Republican Party, *see* Politics and
  Latino politicians, party
  affiliation
Revolutionary Democratic Front
  (FDR), 252
Reyes, Dulce, 291
Rhythm, Latin, 281–87
Richardson, Bill, 266, 268
Ríos Montt, Efrain, 253
Rivera, Carlos, 173
Rivera, Chita, 180, 288–89
Rivera, Dennis, 173
Rivera, Diego, 123, 130, 296
Rivera, Edward, 294
Rivera, Geraldo, 291
Rivera, Tomás, 131, 294, 295
Robinson, Jackie, 298
Rodriguez, Alex, 246
Rodriguez, Beatrice, 291
Rodriguez, Doña Chapita, 128
Rodriguez, Helen, 270
Rodriguez, Juan "Chi Chi," 302
Rodriguez, Richard, xi, 131, 138–39,
  276, 294, 295
Rok, Natan R., 205
Romero, Cesar, 181, 287
Romero, Frank, 123
Romero Barcelo, Carlos, 175
Ronstadt, Linda, 181, 285
Roosevelt, Eleanor, 105, 165–66
Roosevelt, Franklin D., 104, 165, 166
Roosevelt, Theodore, 96, 157, 158,
  160
 Rough Riders and, 159
Roosevelt, Theodore, Jr., 164, 242
Roosevelt Corollary, 157
Root, Elihu, 207
Roots, 11–42
Rosa, Margarita, 246
Roselli, John, 220

Roselló, Pedro, 174
Ros-Lehtinen, Ileana, 246, 266
Rough Riders, 159
Rowe, James A., Jr., 174
Roybal, Edward R., 117, 265, 271
Roybal-Allard, Lucille, 265
Ruiz, Hilton, 283
Ruiz Tomas, Pedro, 291
Ruiz Belvis, Segundo, 161

Sabatini, Gabriela, 181, 303
Salas, Floyd, 295
Salgado, Lissette, 291
Salinas de Gortari, Carlos, 267
Salvadorans, 237
Sanchez, Juan, 296
Sánchez Vicario, Arantxa, 303
Sandanistas, 244, 249
San Diego State University, 277–78
Sandino, Augusto César, 248, 249
San Juan, Puerto Rico, 146
San Martin, José Francisco de, 152,
  197, 198, 210
San Salvador, 17
Santa Anna, Antonio López de, 72,
  74–75, 77, 78–79, 85, 151, 152
Santa Fe, New Mexico, 57, 65
Santa Fe Trail, 73, 74, 75
Santamaría, Mongo, 283
Santana, Carlos, 283
Santas, Miriam, xii
Santería, 7, 178, 230–31, 282
Santo, 178
Secada, Jon, 181, 285
Segovia, Josefa, 128
Segura, Pancho, 303–304
Seminole Indians, 19
Sephardim, 40
Sepulveda, Charlie, 285
Serra, Junípero, 67, 68
Serrano, José, 172–73, 264, 267
Serrano Elias, Jorge, 254
Seven Years' War, 190
Sexism, 59–60
Sheen, Charlie, 181, 290
Sheen, Martin (né Estevez), xii, 290
Shoob, Marvin, 225
Siboney, 19, 20, 187–88, 189, 297–98
Sierra, Father Junípero, 68
Sierra, Ruben, 299